Fodor's

Maui and Lāna'i

"When it comes to information on regional history, what to see and do, and shopping, these guides are exhaustive."

—*USAir Magazine*

"Usable, sophisticated restaurant coverage, with an emphasis on good value."

—Andy Birsh, *Gourmet Magazine* columnist

"Valuable because of their comprehensiveness."

—*Minneapolis Star-Tribune*

"Fodor's always delivers high quality...thoughtfully presented...thorough."

—*Houston Post*

"An excellent choice for those who want everything under one cover."

—*Washington Post*

D0034217

Portions of this book appear in *Fodor's Hawai'i*

Fodor's Travel Publications, Inc.
New York • Toronto • London • Sydney • Auckland
http://www.fodors.com/

Fodor's Maui and Lāna'i

Editor: Rebecca Miller

Editorial Contributors: Robert Andrews, Bob Blake, David Brown, Steve Crohn, Audra Epstein, Donnë Florence, Laura M. Kidder, Heidi Sarna, Helayne Schiff, Mary Ellen Schultz, M. T. Schwartzman (Gold Guide editor), Dinah Spritzer, Marty Wentzel.

Cartographer: David Lindroth

Creative Director: Fabrizio La Rocca

Cover Photograph: Harald Sund/Image Bank

Design: Between the Covers

Copyright © 1996 by Fodor's Travel Publications, Inc.

Seventh Edition

ISBN 0–679–03248–7

Grateful acknowledgment is made to Richard J. Pietschmann for permission to reprint "Heavenly Hana" and "Highway to Hana" from *Travel & Leisure,* April 1989. Copyright © 1989 by Richard J. Pietschmann.

Special Sales

CONTENTS

ON THE ROAD WITH FODOR'S

WE'RE ALWAYS THRILLED to get letters from readers, especially one like this:

It took us an hour to decide what book to buy and we now know we picked the best one. Your book was wonderful, easy to follow, very accurate, and good on pointing out eating places, informal as well as formal. When we saw other people using your book, we would look at each other and smile.

Our editors and writers are deeply committed to making every Fodor's guide "the best one"—not only accurate but always charming, brimming with sound recommendations and solid ideas, right on the mark in describing restaurants and hotels, and full of fascinating facts that make you view what you've traveled to see in a rich new light.

About Our Writers

Our success in achieving our goals—and in helping to make your trip the best of all possible vacations—is a credit to the hard work of our extraordinary writers and editors.

Linda Kephart, who originally wrote most of this guide, has written articles for *Hawai'i Business, Aloha, RSVP, Modern Bride,* and *Pleasant Hawai'i.* She is a former editor of *Discover Hawai'i.*

Donnë Florence, who updated *Fodor's Maui and Lāna'i,* ran away from New York City to Honolulu in 1991. In addition to writing about the Islands, she writes about mass media, computer networks, higher education, and anything else she can get paid for.

We'd also like to thank the Hawai'i Visitors Bureau on Maui for assistance in the preparation of this guidebook.

New This Year

This year we've reformatted our guides to make them easier to use. *Fodor's Maui and Lāna'i,* has brand-new walking and driving tours and a timing section that tells you exactly how long to allot for each tour—and what time of day, day of the week, or season of the year is optimal. You may also notice our fresh graphics, new in 1996. More readable and more helpful than ever? We think so—and we hope you do, too.

You'll also find a new chapter on Lāna'i. Many Maui visitors take jaunts over to this neighboring island, so we've included all the information you need for a day trip or an overnight stay.

Also check out Fodor's Web site (http://www. fodors.com/), where you'll find travel information on major destinations around the world and an ever-changing array of travel-savvy interactive features.

Let Us Do Your Booking

Our writers have scoured Maui to come up with a well-balanced list of the best B&Bs, inns, resorts, rental condos, and hotels, both small and large, new and old. But you don't have to beat the bushes for a reservation. Now that we've teamed up with an established hotel-booking service, reserving a room at the property of your choice is easy. It's fast and free, and confirmation is guaranteed. If your first choice is booked, the operators can recommend others. Call 1–800/FODORS–1 or 1–800/363–6771 (0800–89–1030 in Great Britain; 0014–800–12–8271 in Australia; 1–800/55–9101 in Ireland).

How to Use This Book

Organization

Up front is the **Gold Guide.** Its first section, **Important Contacts A to Z,** gives addresses and telephone numbers of organizations and companies that offer destination-related services and detailed information and publications. **Smart Travel Tips A to Z,** the Gold Guide's second section, gives specific information on how to accomplish what you need to in Maui as well as tips on savvy traveling. Both sections are in alphabetical order by topic.

The Exploring chapter is subdivided into four geographical regions; each subsection recommends a walking or driving tour in the area and lists sights alphabetically. Off the Beaten Path sights appear after the places from which they are most easily accessible. The remaining chapters are arranged in alphabetical order by subject (dining, lodging, nightlife and the arts, outdoor activities and sports, and side trips).

At the end of the book you'll find Portraits, wonderful essays about Hāna and Haleakalā, followed by suggestions for pre-trip reading, both fiction and nonfiction, and movies on tape with Hawai'i as a backdrop.

Icons and Symbols

★   Our special recommendations
✕   Restaurant
🏨   Lodging establishment
✕🏨   Lodging establishment whose restaurant warrants a detour
☼   Rubber duckie (good for kids)
☞   Sends you to another section of the guide for more information
✉   Address
☎   Telephone number
☉   Opening and closing times
🎟   Admission prices (those we give apply only to adults; substantially reduced fees are almost always available for children, students, and senior citizens)

Numbers in white and black circles—② and ❷, for example—that appear on the maps, in the margins, and within the tours correspond to one another.

Restaurant Reservations and Dress Codes

Reservations are always a good idea; we note only when they're essential or when they are not accepted. Book as far ahead as you can, and reconfirm when you get to town. Unless otherwise noted, the restaurants listed are open daily for lunch and dinner. We mention dress only when men are required to wear a jacket or a jacket and tie.

Credit Cards

The following abbreviations are used: **AE,** American Express; **D,** Discover; **DC,** Diners Club; **MC,** MasterCard; and **V,** Visa.

Don't Forget to Write

You can use this book in the confidence that all prices and opening times are based on information supplied to us at press time; Fodor's cannot accept responsibility for any errors. Time inevitably brings changes, so always confirm information when it matters—especially if you're making a detour to visit a specific place. In addition, when making reservations be sure to mention if you have a disability or are traveling with children, if you prefer a private bath or a certain type of bed, or if you have specific dietary needs or any other concerns.

Were the restaurants we recommended as described? Did our hotel picks exceed your expectations? Did you find a museum we recommended a waste of time? If you have complaints, we'll look into them and revise our entries when the facts warrant it. If you've discovered a special place that we haven't included, we'll pass the information along to our correspondents and have them check it out. So send your feedback, positive *and* negative, to the Maui editor at 201 East 50th Street, New York, New York 10022—and have a wonderful trip!

Karen Cure

Karen Cure
Editorial Director

Maui

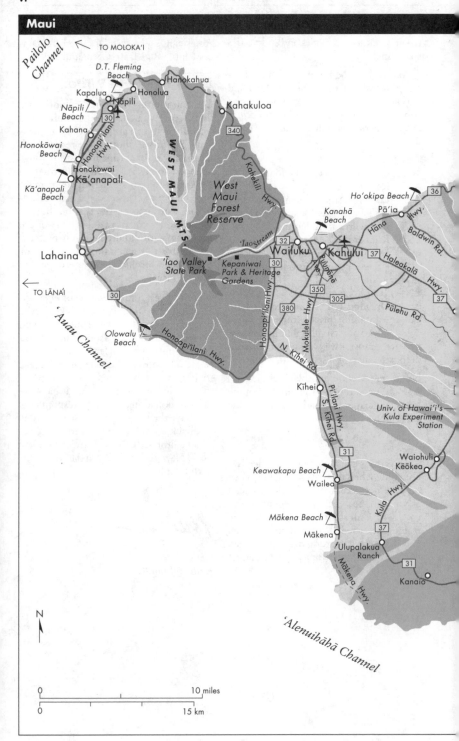

TO MOLOKA'I

D.T. Fleming Beach

Kapalua

Nāpili Beach

Honolua

Hanokahua

Nāpili

Kahakuloa

30

Kahana

340

Honokōwai Beach

Honokowai

Kā'anapali

Kā'anapali Beach

WEST MAUI MTS.

West Maui Forest Reserve

Kahekili Hwy.

Ho'okipa Beach

36

Kanahā Beach

Pā'ia

Hāna Hwy.

Baldwin Rd.

'Iaostream

Wailuku

Kahului

37

Haleakalā Hwy.

Lahaina

30

'Ĩao Valley State Park

Kepaniwai Park & Heritage Gardens

32

30

'Iao Valley State Park

350

305

37

Pūlehu Rd.

TO LĀNA'I

'Auau Channel

Olowalu Beach

Honoapi'ilani Hwy.

Honoapi'ilani Hwy.

380

N. Kīhei Rd.

Mokulele Hwy.

Kīhei

S. Kīhei Rd.

Pi'ilani Hwy.

Univ. of Hawai'i's Kula Experiment Station

31

Waiohuli

Kēōkea

Keawakapu Beach

Wailea

Kula Hwy.

Mākena Beach

Mākena

37

Ulupalakua Ranch

31

Kanaio

Mākena Hwy.

'Alenuihāhā Channel

N

0   10 miles

0   15 km

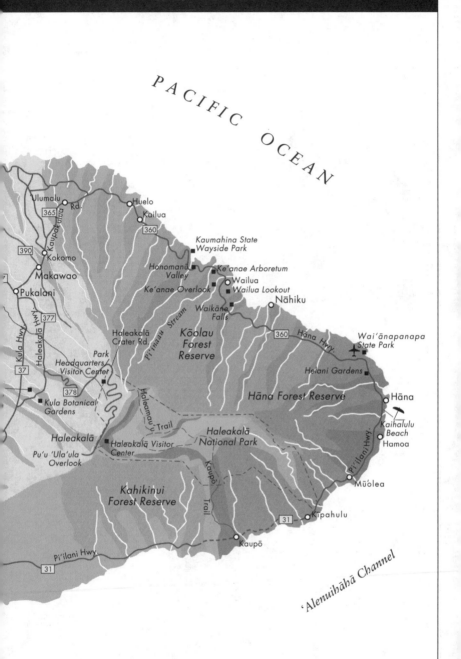

PACIFIC OCEAN

Ulumalu
365
Kaupakulua Rd.
Huelo
Kailua
360
Kaumahina State
Wayside Park
390
Kokomo
Honomanū
Valley
Keʻanae Arboretum
Makawao
Keʻanae Overlook
Wailua
Pukalani
Wailua Lookout
Nāhiku
377
Waikāne
Falls
Kula Hwy
Haleakalā
Crater Rd.
Kōolau
Forest
Reserve
360
Hāna Hwy.
Waiʻānapanapa
State Park
37
Haleakalā Hwy.
Park
Headquarters
Visitor Center
Piʻinaʻau Stream
Helani Gardens
378
Halemauʻu Trail
Hāna Forest Reserve
Hāna
Kula Botanical
Gardens
Haleakalā Visitor
Center
Haleakalā
National Park
Kaihalulu
Beach
Haleakalā
Hamoa
Puʻu ʻUlaʻula
Overlook
Kaupō Trail
Mūolea
Kahikinui
Forest
Reserve
Piʻilani Hwy.
Kīpahulu
31
Piʻilani Hwy.
Kaupō
31
ʻAlenuihāhā Channel

TO HAWAIʻI

The Hawaiian Islands

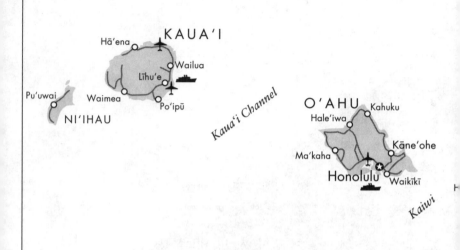

KAUA'I

Hā'ena

Wailua

Līhu'e

Waimea

Po'ipū

Pu'uwai

NI'IHAU

Kaua'i Channel

O'AHU

Kahuku

Hale'iwa

Kāne'ohe

Ma'kaha

Honolulu

Waikīkī

Kaiwi

PACIFIC OCEAN

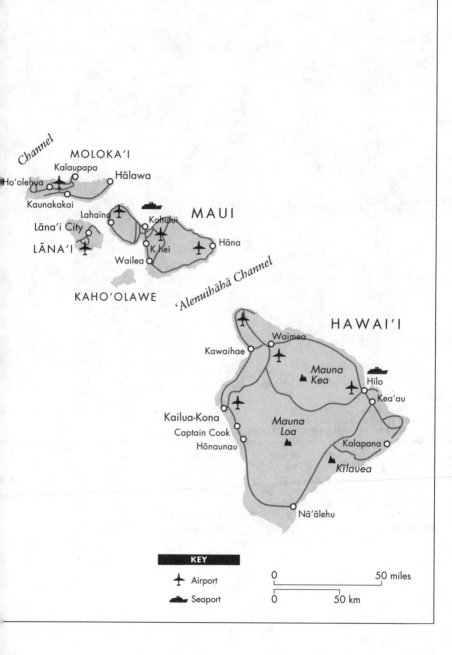

N

Channel

MOLOKA'I

Kalaupapa

Ho'olehua

Hālawa

Kaunakakai

Lahaina

MAUI

Kahului

Lāna'i City

K hei

Hāna

LĀNA'I

Wailea

KAHO'OLAWE

'Alenuihāhā Channel

HAWAI'I

Waimea

Kawaihae

Mauna
Kea

Hilo

Kea'au

Kailua-Kona

Mauna
Loa

Captain Cook

Hōnaunau

Kalapana

Kīlauea

Nā'ālehu

KEY

✈ Airport

⚓ Seaport

0		50 miles

0		50 km

x

World Time Zones

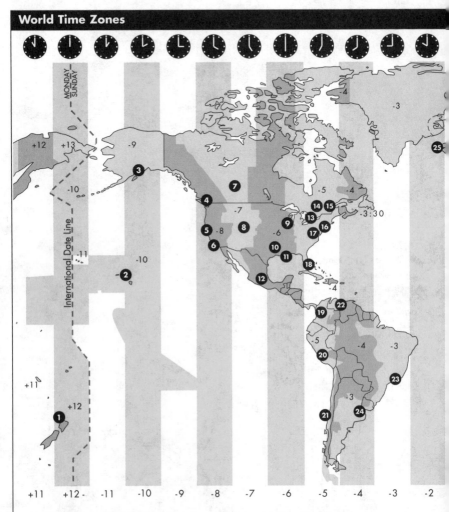

Numbers below vertical bands relate each zone to Greenwich Mean Time (0 hrs.).
Local times frequently differ from these general indications,
as indicated by light-face numbers on map.

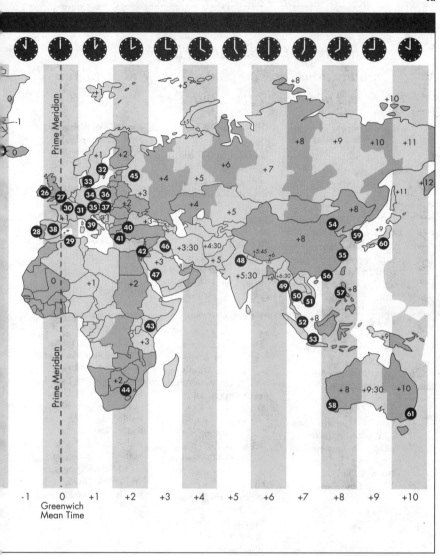

IMPORTANT CONTACTS A TO Z

An Alphabetical Listing of Publications, Organizations, & Companies That Will Help You Before, During, & After Your Trip

THE GOLD GUIDE / IMPORTANT CONTACTS

A

AIR TRAVEL

Maui has two airports: **Kahului Airport** (☎ 808/872–3803), in the island's central town of Kahului, and **Kapalua-West Maui Airport,** which is the easiest arrival point for visitors to West Maui (it saves about an hour's drive from the Kahului airport). The tiny town of **Hāna** in east Maui also has an airstrip (☎ 808/248–8208), but it is only serviced by one commuter and one charter airline.

CARRIERS

Carriers from the mainland with flights to Maui include **American** (☎ 800/433–7300), **Delta** (☎ 800/221–1212), **Hawaiian** (☎ 800/367–5320), and **United** (☎ 800/241–6522).

COMPLAINTS

To register complaints about charter and scheduled airlines, contact the U.S. Department of Transportation's **Aviation Consumer Protection Division** (✉ C-75, Washington, DC 20590, ☎ 202/366–2220). Complaints about lost baggage or ticketing problems and safety concerns may also be logged with the **Federal Aviation Administration (FAA) Consumer Hotline** (☎ 800/322–7873).

CONSOLIDATORS

For the names of reputable air-ticket consolidators, contact the **United States Air Consolidators Association** (✉ 925 L St., Suite 220, Sacramento, CA 95814, ☎ 916/441–4166, FAX 916/441–3520). For services that will help you find the lowest airfares, ☞ Discounts, *below.*

PUBLICATIONS

For general information about charter carriers, ask for the Department of Transportation's free brochure **"Plane Talk: Public Charter Flights"** (✉ Aviation Consumer Protection Division, C-75, Washington, DC 20590, ☎ 202/366–2220). The Department of Transportation also publishes a 58-page booklet, **"Fly Rights,"** available from the Consumer Information Center (✉ Supt. of Documents, Dept. 133B, Pueblo, CO 81009; $1.75).

For tips and hints about traveling, consult the Consumers Union's monthly **"Consumer Reports Travel Letter"** (✉ Box 53629, Boulder, CO 80322, ☎ 800/234–1970; $39 1st year) and the newsletter **"Travel Smart"** (✉ 40 Beechdale Rd., Dobbs Ferry, NY 10522, ☎ 800/327–3633; $37 per year).

Some worthwhile publications on air travel are **The Official Frequent Flyer Guidebook,** by Randy Petersen (✉ Airpress, 4715-C Town Center Dr., Colorado Springs, CO 80916, ☎ 719/597–8899 or 800/487–8893; $14.99 plus $3 shipping); **Airfare Secrets Exposed,** by Sharon Tyler and Matthew Wunder (✉ Studio 4 Productions, Box 280400, Northridge, CA 91328, ☎ 818/700–2522 or 800/408–7369; $16.95 plus $2.50 shipping); **202 Tips Even the Best Business Travelers May Not Know,** by Christopher McGinnis (✉ Irwin Professional Publishing, 1333 Burr Ridge Pkway., Burr Ridge, IL 60521, ☎ 800/634–3966; $11 plus $3.25 shipping); and **Travel Rights,** by Charles Leocha (✉ World Leisure Corporation, 177 Paris St., Boston, MA 02128, ☎ 800/444–2524; $7.95 plus $3.95 shipping).

For information on how to avoid jet lag, try one of these two publications: **Jet Lag, A Pocket Guide to Modern Treatment** (✉ MedEd Publishers, 1421 W. 3rd Ave., Columbus, OH 43212, ☎ 800/875–8489; $5.95) and **How to Beat Jet Lag** (✉ Henry Holt, 115 W. 18th St., New York, NY 10011, ☎ 800/288-2131; $14.95).

Travelers who experience motion sickness or ear problems in flight should get the brochures **"Ears, Altitude, and Airplane Travel"** and **"What You Can Do for Dizziness & Motion Sickness"** from the American Academy of Otolaryngology (✉ 1 Prince St., Alexandria, VA 22314, ☎ 703/836–4444, FAX 703/683–5100, TTY 703/519–1585).

LEI GREETING

For some visitors it's a rude awakening to get off a plane in Hawai'i with no lei to greet them. Some arrangement needs to be made in advance should you want such a welcome. If you've purchased a package tour, lei greetings are sometimes included; if friends are meeting you at the airport, they'll also know the island custom. If you're traveling independently, however, you can still receive a lei upon arrival by making arrangements with one of several companies. **Greeters of Hawai'i** (✉ Box 29638, Honolulu 96820, ☎ 800/366–8559) operates statewide. **Airport Flower & Fruit** (✉ 460 Dairy Rd., Kahului 96732, ☎ 800/922–9352), based on Maui, also does a good job.

AIRPORT TRANSFERS

The **Kahului Airport** (☎ 808/877–6431) is the only airport on Maui that has direct service from the mainland. Its chief disadvantage is its distance from the major resort destinations in West Maui and Wailea.

It will take you about an hour, with traffic in your favor, to get to a hotel in West Maui and about 20 to 30 minutes to go to Wailea.

BY BUS/SHUTTLE

The **TransHawaiian Airporter Shuttle** (☎ 808/877–7308) leaves Kahului Airport on the hour 7 AM–6 PM, bound for Kapalua, with stops in Lahaina and Kā'anapali; one-way fare is $14.

BY TAXI

You could also opt for a taxi. Maui has nearly two dozen taxi companies, and they make frequent passes through the airport. If you don't see a cab, you can call **Yellow Cab** (☎ 808/877–7000) or **La Bella Taxi** (☎ 808/242–8011) for islandwide service from the airport, or **Kīhei Taxi** (☎ 808/879–3000) if you're staying in the Kīhei, Wailea, or Mākena area. Charges from Kahului Airport to Kā'anapali run about $49; to Wailea, about $31; and to Lahaina, about $42.

BY CAR

The best way to get from the airport to your destination is in your own rental car. You're going to need it for the rest of the trip, so you may as well get it right away. Most major car-rental companies have conveniently located desks at each airport (☞ Car Rentals, *below*).

B

BETTER BUSINESS BUREAU

Contact the BBB in Honolulu at ✉ 1600

Kapi'olani Blvd., Ste. 201, Honolulu, HI 96814, ☎ 808/941–5222.

BUS TRAVEL

Although Maui has no public transit system, a private company, **Akina Express** (☎ 808/661–4567), operates 30-seat buses on routes in West Maui (between Kapalua Bay and Whalers Village in Lahaina) and South Maui (between Kīhei and Wailea). The low fare ($1) makes this a worthwhile alternative to renting a car if you plan to spend nearly all your time at a full-service resort in Kapalua, Kā'anapali, or Wailea and only need occasional transportation to the towns of Lahaina or Kīhei. Akina Express also runs the West Maui–South Maui Link, connecting Lahaina Harbor and the resorts and beaches of South Maui (cost: $8 per person; reservations required).

TransHawaiian Services (☎ 808/877–0380) operates a Maui Shopping Express, providing service between the island hubs of Wailea, Kahului, and Kapalua Mon.–Sat. 9:30 AM–7:30 PM and Sun. 9:30 AM–5 PM. One-way, round-trip, and all-day passes are available.

The **Kā'anapali–Lahaina Shuttle** runs daily from the Royal Lahaina Resort in Kā'anapali to the Wharf Cinema Center in Lahaina every half hour between 8 AM and 10:25 PM, with stops at all Kā'anapali hotels. The cost is $1.50. The **Kā'anapali Shuttle** runs within the resort between 7 AM

THE GOLD GUIDE / IMPORTANT CONTACTS

and 11 PM and stops automatically at all hotels and at condos when requested. It also goes to and from Lahaina at 55-minute intervals. It's free. All Kā'anapali hotels have copies of schedules, or you can call the Kā'anapali Beach Operators Association (☎ 808/661–3271). The free **Aston Hotels Shuttle** in the Kā'anapali area runs from 8 PM to 6 PM for guests who want to go to the Whalers Village Shopping Center and Lahaina. You can get schedules at Aston hotel desks. The **Wailea Shuttle** and the **Kapalua Shuttle** run within their respective resorts and are free; schedules are available throughout each resort.

C

CAR RENTAL

Budget (☎ 800/527–0700 or, in Canada, ☎ 800/268–8900), Dollar (in the U.S. and Canada, ☎ 800/800–4000), and **National** (☎ 800/227–7368) have courtesy phones at the Kapalua–West Maui Airport, while **Hertz** (☎ 800/654–3131 or, in Canada, ☎ 800/263–0600) and **Alamo** (☎ 800/327–9633) are nearby. All the above, plus **Avis** (☎ 800/331–1212 or, in Canada, 800/879–2847), have desks at or near Maui's major airport in Kahului. **Roberts Tours** (☎ 808/523–9323) offers car rentals through package tours. In addition, quite a few locally owned companies rent cars on Maui, including **Rent-A-Jeep** (☎ 808/877–6626),

which will pick you up at Kahului Airport. If you fly into the Hāna Airport, you can call **Dollar Rent A Car** to pick you up (☎ 808/248–8237) or if you have reserved a car from another company, the agent will usually know your arrival time and meet you. Rates in Maui begin at about $28 a day and $170 a week for an economy car with unlimited mileage, but special packages offered by hotels and interisland airlines may lower your cost. This does not include tax on car rentals, which is 4.16%. There is a $2 daily surcharge on all rental cars in Hawai'i.

RENTAL WHOLESALERS

Contact **Auto Europe** (☎ 207/828–2525 or 800/223–5555).

CHILDREN & TRAVEL

FLYING

Look into **"Flying with Baby"** (⊠ Third Street Press, Box 261250, Littleton, CO 80163, ☎ 303/595–5959; $4.95 includes shipping), cowritten by a flight attendant. **"Kids and Teens in Flight,"** free from the U.S. Department of Transportation's Aviation Consumer Protection Division (⊠ C-75, Washington, DC 20590, ☎ 202/366–2220), offers tips on children flying alone. Every two years the February issue of *Family Travel Times* (☞ Know-How, *below*) details children's services on three dozen

airlines. **"Flying Alone, Handy Advice for Kids Traveling Solo"** is available free from the American Automobile Association (AAA) (send stamped, self-addressed, legal-size envelope: ⊠ Flying Alone, Mail Stop 800, 1000 AAA Dr., Heathrow, FL 32746).

GAMES

Milton Bradley has games to help keep little (and not so little) children from fidgeting while in planes, trains, and automobiles. Try packing the Travel Battleship sea-battle game ($7); Travel Connect Four, a vertical strategy game ($8); the Travel Yahtzee dice game ($6), the Travel Trouble dice and board game ($7), and the Travel Guess Who mystery game ($8). Parker Brothers has travel versions of Clue!, Sorry, and Monopoly.

KNOW-HOW

Family Travel Times, published quarterly by Travel with Your Children (⊠ TWYCH, 40 5th Ave., New York, NY 10011, ☎ 212/477–5524; $40 per year), covers destinations, types of vacations, and modes of travel.

The *Family Travel Guides* catalog (⊠ Carousel Press, Box 6061, Albany, CA 94706, ☎ 510/527–5849; $1 postage) lists about 200 books and articles on traveling with children. Also check *Take Your Baby and Go! A Guide for Traveling with Babies, Toddlers and Young*

Children, by Sheri Andrews, Judy Bordeaux, and Vivian Vasquez (⊠ Bear Creek Publications, 2507 Minor Ave. E, Seattle, WA 98102, ☎ 206/322–7604 or 800/326–6566; $5.95 plus $1.50 shipping). The Globe Pequot Press (⊠ Box 833, 6 Business Park Rd., Old Saybrook, CT 06475, ☎ 203/395–0440) publishes *100 Best Family Resorts in North America,* by Jane Wilson with Janet Tice ($14.95), and eastern and western editions of *50 Great Family Vacations in North America* ($18.95 plus $3 shipping).

TOUR OPERATORS

Contact **Grandtravel** (⊠ 6900 Wisconsin Ave., Suite 706, Chevy Chase, MD 20815, ☎ 301/986–0790 or 800/247–7651), which has tours for people traveling with grandchildren ages 7–17; or **Rascals in Paradise** (⊠ 650 5th St., Suite 505, San Francisco, CA 94107, ☎ 415/978–9800 or 800/872–7225).

If you're outdoorsy, look into the family adventure tours, ranches, and lodges of **American Wilderness Experience** (⊠ Box 1486, Boulder, CO 80306, ☎ 303/444–2622 or 800/444–0099).

CRUISING

Approaching the Valley Isle from the deck of a ship is a great orientation. If a cruise is an option that appeals to you, you can book passage through

American Hawai'i Cruises (⊠ 2 North Riverside Plaza, Chicago 60606, ☎ 312/466–6000 or 800/765–7000), which offers seven-day interisland cruises departing from Honolulu on the SS *Constitution* and the SS *Independence.* Ask about the company's seven-day cruise-resort combination packages.

CUSTOMS & DUTIES

IN MAUI

For full details on regulations concerning animals entering and leaving Hawai'i, write to the **Animal Quarantine Station, Department of Agriculture,** ⊠ State of Hawai'i, 99–951 Hālawa Valley Rd., 'Aiea, O'ahu, HI 96701, ☎ 808/483–7171). (☞ Customs & Duties *in* Smart Travel Tips A to Z).

IN CANADA

Contact **Revenue Canada** (⊠ 2265 St. Laurent Blvd. S, Ottawa, Ontario K1G 4K3, ☎ 613/993–0534) for a copy of the free brochure **"I Declare/Je Déclare"** and for details on duty-free limits. For recorded information (within Canada only), call 800/461–9999.

IN THE U.K.

HM Customs and Excise (⊠ Dorset House, Stamford St., London SE1 9NG, ☎ 0171/202–4227) can answer questions about U.K. customs regulations and publishes a free pamphlet, **"A Guide for Travellers,"** detailing standard procedures and import rules.

CAR RENTALS

Those who prefer to do their own driving may rent hand-controlled cars from **Avis** (☎ 800/331–1212), which suggests a one-month advance reservation. **Hertz** (☎ 800/654–3131) also rents left- or right-hand controlled cars at no additional charge. A three-day notice is required, and an additional $25 deposit is required from customers renting on a cash basis. You can use the windshield card from your own state to park in spaces reserved for people with disabilities.

COMPLAINTS

To register complaints under the provisions of the Americans with Disabilities Act, contact the U.S. Department of Justice's **Disability Rights Section** (⊠ Box 66738, Washington, DC 20035, ☎ 202/514–0301 or 800/514–0301, FAX 202/307–1198, TTY 202/514–0383 or 800/514–0383). For airline-related problems, contact the U.S. Department of Transportation's **Aviation Consumer Protection Division** (☞ Air Travel, *above*). For complaints about surface transportation, contact the Department of Transportation's **Civil Rights Office** (☎ 202/366–4648).

LOCAL INFO

The Commission on Persons with Disabilities (⊠ 5 Waterfront Plaza, Suite 210, 500 Ala Moana Blvd., Honolulu

THE GOLD GUIDE / IMPORTANT CONTACTS

96813) has information concerning accessibility on the Islands; it also publishes helpful travelers' guides that list support services on the Islands for disabled visitors.

ORGANIZATIONS

TRAVELERS WITH HEARING IMPAIRMENTS➤ The **American Academy of Otolaryngology** (✉ 1 Prince St., Alexandria, VA 22314, ☎ 703/836–4444, FAX 703/683–5100, TTY 703/519–1585) publishes a brochure, "Travel Tips for Hearing Impaired People."

TRAVELERS WITH MOBILITY PROBLEMS➤ Contact the **Information Center for Individuals with Disabilities** (✉ Box 256, Boston, MA 02117, ☎ 617/450–9888; in MA, 800/462–5015; TTY 617/424–6855); **Mobility International USA** (✉ Box 10767, Eugene, OR 97440, ☎ and TTY 503/343–1284, FAX 503/343–6812), the U.S. branch of a Belgium-based organization (☞ *below*) with affiliates in 30 countries; **MossRehab Hospital Travel Information Service** (☎ 215/456–9600, TTY 215/456–9602), a telephone information resource for travelers with physical disabilities; the **Society for the Advancement of Travel for the Handicapped** (✉ 347 5th Ave., Suite 610, New York, NY 10016, ☎ 212/447–7284, FAX 212/725–8253; membership $45); and **Travelin' Talk** (✉ Box 3534, Clarksville, TN 37043, ☎ 615/552–6670, FAX 615/552–1182) which provides

local contacts worldwide for travelers with disabilities.

TRAVELERS WITH VISION IMPAIRMENTS➤ Contact the **American Council of the Blind** (✉ 1155 15th St. NW, Suite 720, Washington, DC 20005, ☎ 202/467–5081, FAX 202/467–5085) for a list of travelers' resources or the **American Foundation for the Blind** (✉ 11 Penn Plaza, Suite 300, New York, NY 10001, ☎ 212/502–7600 or 800/232–5463, TTY 212/502–7662), which provides general advice and publishes "Access to Art" ($19.95), a directory of museums that accommodate travelers with vision impairments.

IN THE U.K.

Contact the **Royal Association for Disability and Rehabilitation** (✉ RADAR, 12 City Forum, 250 City Rd., London EC1V 8AF, ☎ 0171/250–3222) or **Mobility International** (✉ rue de Manchester 25, B-1080 Brussels, Belgium, ☎ 00–322–410–6297, FAX 00–322–410–6874), an international travel-information clearinghouse for people with disabilities.

PUBLICATIONS

Several publications for travelers with disabilities are available from the **Consumer Information Center** (✉ Box 100, Pueblo, CO 81009, ☎ 719/948–3334). Call or write for its free catalog of current titles. The Society for the Advancement of Travel for the Handicapped (☞ Organizations,

above) publishes the quarterly magazine *"Access to Travel"* ($13 for 1-year subscription).

The 500-page *Travelin' Talk Directory* (✉ Box 3534, Clarksville, TN 37043, ☎ 615/552–6670, FAX 615/552–1182; $35) lists people and organizations who help travelers with disabilities. For travel agents worldwide, consult the *Directory of Travel Agencies for the Disabled* (✉ Twin Peaks Press, Box 129, Vancouver, WA 98666, ☎ 360/694–2462 or 800/637–2256, FAX 360/696–3210; $19.95 plus $3 shipping). The Sierra Club publishes *Easy Access to National Parks* (✉ Sierra Club Store, 730 Polk St., San Francisco, CA 94109, ☎ 415/776–2211 or 800/935–1056; $16 plus $3 shipping).

TRAVEL AGENCIES & TOUR OPERATORS

The Americans with Disabilities Act requires that all travel firms serve the needs of all travelers. That said, you should note that some agencies and operators specialize in making travel arrangements for individuals and groups with disabilities, among them **Access Adventures** (✉ 206 Chestnut Ridge Rd., Rochester, NY 14624, ☎ 716/889–9096), run by a former physical-rehab counselor.

TRAVELERS WITH MOBILITY PROBLEMS➤ Contact **Accessible Journeys** (✉ 35 W. Sellers Ave., Ridley Park, PA 19078, ☎ 610/521–0339 or 800/846–4537, FAX 610/521–6959), a registered nursing service that arranges vacations; **Hinsdale Travel Service** (⊠ 201 E. Ogden Ave., Suite 100, Hinsdale, IL 60521, ☎ 708/325–1335 or 800/303–5521), a travel agency that benefits from the advice of wheelchair traveler Janice Perkins; **Over the Rainbow** (⊠ 186 Mehani Circle, Kihei, HI 96753, ☎ 808/879–5521); and **Wheelchair Journeys** (⊠ 16979 Redmond Way, Redmond, WA 98052, ☎ 206/885–2210 or 800/313–4751), which can handle arrangements worldwide.

TRAVELERS WITH DEVELOPMENTAL DISABILITIES➤ Contact the nonprofit **New Directions** (⊠ 5276 Hollister Ave., Suite 207, Santa Barbara, CA 93111, ☎ 805/967–2841) and **Sprout** (⊠ 893 Amsterdam Ave., New York, NY 10025, ☎ 212/222–9575), which specializes in custom-designed itineraries for groups but also books vacations for individual travelers.

TRAVEL GEAR

The **Magellan's** catalog (☎ 800/962–4943, FAX 805/568–5406), includes a range of products designed for travelers with disabilities.

DISCOUNTS & DEALS

AIRFARES

For the lowest airfares to Maui, call 800/FLY–4–LESS. Also try 800/FLY–ASAP.

STUDENTS

Members of Hostelling International–American

Youth Hostels (☞ Students, *below*) are eligible for discounts on car rentals, admissions to attractions, and other selected travel expenses.

PUBLICATIONS

Consult *The Frugal Globetrotter,* by Bruce Northam (⊠ Fulcrum Publishing, 350 Indiana St., Suite 350, Golden, CO 80401, ☎ 800/992–2908; $15.95). For publications that tell how to find the lowest prices on plane tickets, *see* Air Travel, *above.*

TRAVEL CLUBS

Contact **Entertainment Travel Editions** (⊠ Box 1068, Trumbull, CT 06611, ☎ 800/445–4137; $28–$53, depending on destination), **Great American Traveler** (⊠ Box 27965, Salt Lake City, UT 84127, ☎ 800/548–2812; $49.95 per year), **Moment's Notice Discount Travel Club** (⊠ 163 Amsterdam Ave., Suite 137, New York, NY 10023, ☎ 212/486–0500; $25 per year, single or family), **Privilege Card** (⊠ 3391 Peachtree Rd. NE, Suite 110, Atlanta, GA 30326, ☎ 404/262–0222 or 800/236–9732; $74.95 per year), **Travelers Advantage** (⊠ CUC Travel Service, 49 Music Sq. W, Nashville, TN 37203, ☎ 800/548–1116 or 800/648–4037; $49 per year, single or family), or **Worldwide Discount Travel Club** (⊠ 1674 Meridian Ave., Miami Beach, FL 33139, ☎ 305/534–2082; $50 per year for family, $40 single).

DRIVING

AUTO CLUBS

On Maui, the one **AAA** garage that offers 24-hour islandwide service is **Sunset Towing** (⊠ Bldg. 30, Halawai Rd., Kāʻanapali, ☎ 808/667–7048). It specializes in serving West Maui and Kahului but will travel anywhere on Maui with a tow truck.

E
EMERGENCIES

Police, fire, or **ambulance,** ☎ 911.

DOCTORS

Doctors on Call (⊠ Hyatt Regency Maui-Nāpili Tower, Suite 100, Kāʻanapali, ☎ 808/667–7676) serves patients in West Maui. A walk-in clinic at Whalers Village, **West Maui Healthcare Center** (⊠ 2435 Kāʻanapali Pkwy., Suite H-7, Kāʻanapali, ☎ 808/667–9721) also serves West Maui. The clinic is open daily 8 AM–10 PM. **Kīhei Clinic** (⊠ 2349 S. Kīhei Rd., Suite D, Kīhei, ☎ 808/879–1440) serves walk-in clients in Central Maui, Kīhei, and Wailea. All of the above groups are geared toward working with visitors.

HOSPITALS

Hāna Medical Center (⊠ Hāna Hwy., Hāna, ☎ 808/248–8294).

Kula Hospital (⊠ 204 Kula Hwy., Kula, ☎ 808/878–1221).

Maui Memorial Hospital (⊠ 221 Mahalani, Wailuku, ☎ 808/244–9056).

THE GOLD GUIDE / IMPORTANT CONTACTS

PHARMACIES

Maui doesn't have any 24-hour pharmacies, but there are several where you can get prescriptions filled during daylight hours. The least expensive are the island's two **Longs Drug Stores** (⊠ Maui Mall, 70 Ka'ahumanu Ave., Kahului, ☎ 808/877–0068; ⊠ Lahaina Cannery Shopping Center, Honoapi'ilani Hwy., ☎ 808/667–4390; both open daily, 8:30 AM–9 PM). **Kīhei Drug** is in the Kīhei Town Center (⊠ 1881 S. Kīhei Rd., Kīhei, ☎ 808/879–1915; ⊘ weekdays 8:30–7, Saturday 8:30–5:30, Sunday 10–3).

OTHERS

Coast Guard Rescue Center (☎ 808/244–5256).

Suicide and Crisis Center Help Line (☎ 808/244–7407).

G
GAY & LESBIAN TRAVEL

ORGANIZATIONS

The **International Gay Travel Association** (⊠ Box 4974, Key West, FL 33041, ☎ 800/448–8550, FAX 305/296–6633), a consortium of more than 1,000 travel companies, can supply names of gay-friendly travel agents, tour operators, and accommodations.

PUBLICATIONS

The premier international travel magazine for gays and lesbians is **Our World** (⊠ 1104 N. Nova Rd., Suite 251, Daytona Beach, FL 32117, ☎ 904/441–

5367, FAX 904/441–5604; $35 for 10 issues). The 16-page monthly **"Out & About"** (☎ 212/645–6922 or 800/929–2268, FAX 800/929–2215; $49 for 10 issues and quarterly calendar) covers gay-friendly resorts, hotels, cruise lines, and airlines.

TOUR OPERATORS

Toto Tours (⊠ 1326 W. Albion St., Suite 3W, Chicago, IL 60626, ☎ 312/274–8686 or 800/565–1241) offers group tours to worldwide destinations.

TRAVEL AGENCIES

The largest agencies serving gay travelers are **Advance Travel** (⊠ 10700 Northwest Fwy., Suite 160, Houston, TX 77092, ☎ 713/682–2002 or 800/695–0880), **Islanders/Kennedy Travel** (⊠ 183 W. 10th St., New York, NY 10014, ☎ 212/242–3222 or 800/988–1181), **Now Voyager** (⊠ 4406 18th St., San Francisco, CA 94114, ☎ 415/626–1169 or 800/255–6951), and **Yellowbrick Road** (⊠ 1500 W. Balmoral Ave., Chicago, IL 60640, ☎ 312/561–1800 or 800/642–2488). **Skylink Women's Travel** (⊠ 3577 Moorland Ave., Santa Rosa, CA 95407, ☎ 707/588–9961 or 800/225–5759) serves lesbian travelers.

GROCERS

Three major supermarkets are open 24 hours a day. **Safeway,** at the Lahaina Cannery Shopping Center (⊠ Honoapi'ilani Hwy., Lahaina, ☎ 808/667–4392), serves West

Maui, while **Foodland,** in the Kīhei Town Center (⊠ 1881 S. Kīhei Rd., Kīhei, ☎ 808/879–9350), and **Safeway** (⊠ 170 E. Kamehameha Ave., Kahului, ☎ 808/877–3377) serve Kīhei and Wailea.

I
INSURANCE

IN THE U.S.

Travel insurance covering baggage, health, and trip cancellation or interruptions is available from **Access America** (⊠ Box 90315, Richmond, VA 23286, ☎ 804/285–3300 or 800/284–8300), **Carefree Travel Insurance** (⊠ Box 9366, 100 Garden City Plaza, Garden City, NY 11530, ☎ 516/294–0220 or 800/323–3149), **Near Travel Services** (⊠ Box 1339, Calumet City, IL 60409, ☎ 708/868–6700 or 800/654–6700), **Tele-Trip** (⊠ Mutual of Omaha Plaza, Box 31716, Omaha, NE 68131, ☎ 800/228–9792), **Travel Guard International** (⊠ 1145 Clark St., Stevens Point, WI 54481, ☎ 715/345–0505 or 800/826–1300), **Travel Insured International** (⊠ Box 280568, East Hartford, CT 06128, ☎ 203/528–7663 or 800/243–3174), and **Wallach & Company** (⊠ 107 W. Federal St., Box 480, Middleburg, VA 22117, ☎ 703/687–3166 or 800/237–6615).

IN CANADA

Contact **Mutual of Omaha** (⊠ Travel Division, 500 University Ave., Toronto, Ontario M5G 1V8, ☎ 800/268–8825 or 416/598-4321).

IN THE U.K.

The **Association of British Insurers** (✉ 51 Gresham St., London EC2V 7HQ, ☎ 0171/ 600–3333) gives advice by phone and publishes the free pamphlet **"Holiday Insurance,"** which sets out typical policy provisions and costs.

L
LIMOUSINES

Arthur's Limousine Service (✉ Box 11865, Lahaina 96761, ☎ 800/345–4667) provides a chauffeured superstretch Lincoln complete with bar, two TVs, and two sunroofs for $85 per hour. Arthur's fleet also includes less grandiose Lincoln Town Cars, for $65 per hour with a two-hour minimum.

LODGING

APARTMENT, HOUSE & VILLA RENTAL

Among the companies to contact are **Europa-Let** (✉ 92 N. Main St., Ashland, OR 97520, ☎ 541/482–5806 or 800/462–4486, ℻ 541/482–0660), **Property Rentals International** (✉ 1008 Mansfield Crossing Rd., Richmond, VA 23236, ☎ 804/378–6054 or 800/220–3332, ℻ 804/379–2073), **Rental Directories International** (✉ 2044 Rittenhouse Sq., Philadelphia, PA 19103, ☎ 215/985–4001, ℻ 215/985–0323), **Rent-a-Home International** (✉ 7200 34th Ave.

NW, Seattle, WA 98117, ☎ 206/789–9377 or 800/488–7368, ℻ 206/789–9379, hmaria@ol.com), **Vacation Home Rentals Worldwide** (✉ 235 Kensington Ave., Norwood, NJ 07648, ☎ 201/767–9393 or 800/633–3284, ℻ 201/767–5510). Members of the travel club **Hideaways International** (✉ 767 Islington St., Portsmouth, NH 03801, ☎ 603/430–4433 or 800/843–4433, ℻ 603/430–4444, info@hideaways.com; $99 per year) receive two annual guides plus quarterly newsletters and arrange rentals among themselves.

By writing to the following management companies in Hawai'i, you can get more information on specific houses, including brochures with photographs and details of the types of properties. Try: **Premier Connections of Hawai'i** (✉ 1993 S. Kīhei Rd., Suite 209, Kīhei, Maui 96753, ☎ 808/329–6284); **Villas of Hawai'i** (✉ 4218 Wai'alae Ave., Suite 203, Honolulu 96816, ☎ 800/522–3030); **Windsurfing West Ltd.** (✉ Box 330104, Kahului, Maui 96733, ☎ 800/782–6105).

BED & BREAKFASTS

Bed & Breakfast Honolulu (✉ 3242 Kā'ohinani Dr., Honolulu 96817, ☎ 800/595–7533 or 800/288–4666) has statewide listings, with about 50 B&Bs on Maui. **Bed & Breakfast Maui-Style** (✉ Box 98, Kīhei

96784, ☎ 808/879–7865 or 800/848–5567) has listings for about 25 B&Bs on Maui. **Island Bed & Breakfast** (✉ Box 449, Kapa'a, Kaua'i 96746, ☎ 808/822–7771 or 800/733–1632) is headquartered on Kaua'i and has listings throughout the state. It handles about 35 B&Bs on Maui; a directory is available for $12.95.

CONDOMINIUM RENTAL AGENTS

Multi-property agents include: **Ameri Resort Management, Inc.** (✉ 5500 Honoapi'ilani Rd., Kapalua, Maui 96761, ☎ 808/669–5635 or 800/786–7387); **Aston Hotels & Resorts** (✉ 2255 Kūhiō Ave., 18th Floor, Honolulu 96815, ☎ 800/342–1551); **Condofree Resorts Hawai'i** (✉ 2155 Kalākaua Ave., Suite 706, Honolulu 96815, ☎ 800/535–0085); **Destination Resorts** (✉ 3750 Wailea Alanui Dr., Wailea, Maui 96753, ☎ 800/367–5246); **Hawaiian Apartment Leasing Enterprises** (✉ 479 Ocean Ave., #B, Laguna Beach, CA 92651, ☎ 714/497–4253 or 800/854–8843); **Hawaiian Resorts, Inc.** (✉ 1270 Ala Moana Blvd., Honolulu 96814, ☎ 800/367–7040 or, in Canada, ☎ 800/877–7331); and **Vacation Locations–Hawai'i** (Box 1689, Kīhei, Maui 96753, ☎ 808/874–0077 or 800/522–2757).

HOME EXCHANGE

Some of the principal clearinghouses are **HomeLink International/Vacation**

Exchange Club (⊠ Box 650, Key West, FL 33041, ☎ 305/294–1448 or 800/638–3841, FAX 305/294–1148; $70 per year), which sends members three annual directories, with a listing in one, plus updates; and Intervac International (⊠ Box 590504, San Francisco, CA 94159, ☎ 415/435–3497, FAX 415/435–7440; $65 per year), which publishes four annual directories.

M
MONEY MATTERS

ATMS

For specific Cirrus locations in the United States and Canada, call 800/424–7787. For U.S. Plus locations, call 800/843–7587 and enter the area code and first three digits of the number from which you're calling (or of the calling area in which you want to locate an ATM).

WIRING FUNDS

Funds can be wired via MoneyGram℠ (for locations and information in the U.S. and Canada, ☎ 800/926–9400) or Western Union (for agent locations or to send money using MasterCard or Visa, ☎ 800/325–6000; in Canada, ☎ 800/321–2923; in the U.K., ☎ 0800/833833; or visit the Western Union office at the nearest major post office).

MOPEDS/
MOTORCYCLES

Mopeds from A&B Moped Rental (⊠ 3481 Lower Honoapi'ilani Hwy., Lahaina, ☎ 808/669–0027) go for about $10/day, and are for local on-road use only. Be especially careful navigating the roads on Maui, since there are no designated bicycle or moped lanes.

N
NATIONAL PARKS

A variety of passes is available for senior citizens, travelers with disabilities, and frequent visitors. The passes can be purchased at any park that charges admission or obtained by mail from the National Park Service (⊠ Dept. of the Interior, Washington, DC 20240).

P
PACKING

For strategies on packing light, get a copy of The Packing Book, by Judith Gilford (⊠ Ten Speed Press, Box 7123, Berkeley, CA 94707, ☎ 510/559–1600 or 800/841–2665, FAX 510/524–4588; $7.95).

PASSPORTS &
VISAS

U.K. CITIZENS

For fees, documentation requirements, and to request an emergency passport, call the London Passport Office (☎ 0990/210–410). For U.S. visa information, call the U.S. Embassy Visa Information Line (☎ 01891/200–290; calls cost 49p per minute or 39p per minute cheap rate) or send a self-addressed, stamped envelope to the U.S. Embassy Visa Branch (⊠ 5 Upper Grosvenor St., London W1A 2JB).

If you live in Northern Ireland, write to the U.S. Consulate General (⊠ Queen's House, Queen St., Belfast BTI 6EO).

PHOTO HELP

The Kodak Information Center (☎ 800/242–2424) answers consumer questions about film and photography. The Kodak Guide to Shooting Great Travel Pictures (available in bookstores; or contact Fodor's Travel Publications, ☎ 800/533–6478; $16.50) explains how to take expert travel photographs.

S
SAFETY

"Trouble-Free Travel," from the AAA, is a booklet of tips for protecting yourself and your belongings when away from home. Send a stamped, self-addressed, legal-size envelope to Flying Alone (⊠ Mail Stop 75, 1000 AAA Dr., Heathrow, FL 32746).

SENIOR CITIZENS

EDUCATIONAL TRAVEL

The nonprofit Elderhostel (⊠ 75 Federal St., 3rd Floor, Boston, MA 02110, ☎ 617/426–7788), for people 60 and older, has offered inexpensive study programs since 1975. Courses cover everything from marine science to Greek mythology and cowboy poetry. Fees for programs in the United States and Canada, which usually last one week, run about $300, not including transportation.

ORGANIZATIONS

Contact the **American Association of Retired Persons** (✉ AARP, 601 E St. NW, Washington, DC 20049, ☎ 202/434–2277; annual dues $8 per person or couple). Its Purchase Privilege Program secures discounts for members on lodging, car rentals, and sightseeing, and the AARP Motoring Plan (☎ 800/334–3300) furnishes domestic trip-routing information and emergency road-service aid for an annual fee of $39.95 ($59.95 for a premium version). Senior citizen travelers can also join the AAA for emergency road service and other travel benefits (☞ Driving, *above, and* Discounts & Deals *in* Smart Travel Tips A to Z).

Additional sources for discounts on lodgings, car rentals, and other travel expenses, as well as helpful magazines and newsletters, are the **National Council of Senior Citizens** (✉ 1331 F St. NW, Washington, DC 20004, ☎ 202/347–8800; annual membership $12) and Sears's **Mature Outlook** (✉ Box 10448, Des Moines, IA 50306, ☎ 800/336–6330; annual membership $9.95).

PUBLICATIONS

The 50+ Traveler's Guidebook: Where to Go, Where to Stay, What to Do, by Anita Williams and Merrimac Dillon (✉ St. Martin's Press, 175 5th Ave., New York, NY 10010, ☎ 212/674–5151 or 800/288–2131; $13.95), offers many useful tips. **"The Mature Traveler"** (✉ Box 50400, Reno, NV 89513, ☎ 702/786–7419; $29.95), a monthly newsletter, covers all sorts of travel deals.

SIGHTSEEING

The following are among the major companies that operate sightseeing tours on Maui. For descriptions of their different tours, *see* Smart Travel Tips A to Z.

AERIAL TOURS

The best Maui operators include **Blue Hawaiian Helicopters** (✉ Kahului Heliport, Hanger 105, Kahului 96732, ☎ 808/871–8844), **Hawai'i Helicopters** (✉ Kahului Heliport, Hangar 106, Kahului 96732, ☎ 808/877–3900 or 800/346–2403 from the Mainland), **Maui Helicopters** (✉ Box 1002, Kīhei 96753, ☎ 808/879–1601 or 800/367–8003 from the Mainland), and **Kenai Helicopters** (✉ Box 685, Pu'unēnē 96784, ☎ 808/871–6483 or 800/622–3144).

ART TOURS

Maui Art Tours (✉ Box 1058, Makawao 96768, ☎ 808/572–7132).

ASTRONOMY TOURS

Take a star-gazing trip with **Astronomy Tours Maui** (✉ 1597 'A'ā St., Lahaina 96761, ☎ 808/667–9080).

BICYCLE TOURS

Cruiser Bob's Original Haleakalā Downhill (✉ 99 Hāna Hwy., Box B, Pā'ia 96779, ☎ 808/579–8444), **Maui Downhill Bicycle Safaris** (✉ 199 Dairy Rd., Kahului 96732, ☎ 808/871–2155 or 800/535–2453) and **Maui Mountain Cruisers** (✉ Box 1356, Makawao 96768, ☎ 808/871–6014 or 800/232–6284) all offer bike tours.

HIKING TOURS

Crater Bound (✉ Box 265, Kula 96790, ☎ 808/878–1743) specializes in treks into Haleakalā's craters, with tents and gear carried in ahead of the hikers, on pack horses. **Hike Maui** (✉ Box 330969, Kahului 96733, ☎ 808/879–5270) is owned by naturalist Ken Schmitt, who guides some 50 different hikes himself. **Maui-Anne's Island Photography Tours** (✉ Box 2250, Kīhei 96753, ☎ 808/874–3797) offers hiking trips with a focus on photography. **Maui Fun Centers** (✉ 2191 S. Kīhei Rd., Kīhei 96753, ☎ 808/874–3773) offers van and bicycle tours, as well as hiking tours, for energetic visitors.

HORSEBACK TOURS

Mauian Frank Levinson started **Adventures on Horseback** (✉ Box 1771, Makawao 96768, ☎ 808/242–7445) a few years back with five-hour outings into secluded parts of Maui. **Charley's Trail Rides & Pack Trips** (✉ c/o Kaupō Store, Kaupō 96713, ☎ 808/248–8209) requires a hardy physical nature, as the overnighters go from Kaupō—a *tiny* village nearly 20 miles past Hāna—up the slopes of Haleakalā to the crater.

HUNTING TOURS

Hunting Adventures of Maui (⊠ 45-B Kau-pakulua Rd., Haʻikū 96708, ☎ 808/572–8214). This is a guided excursion on more than 100,000 acres of private ranch land on Maui, a "fair chase" hunt for Spanish mountain goats and wild boar.

LAND TOURS

Gray Line Hawaiʻi (⊠ 273 Dairy Rd., Kahului 96732, ☎ 800/367–2420 or 808/877–5507) uses air-conditioned motor coaches, limos, and vans. **Polynesian Adventure Tours** (⊠ 431 Alamaha St., Suite 3, Kahului 96732, ☎ 800/622–3011 or 808/877–4242) and **Roberts Hawaiʻi Tours** (⊠ Box 247, Kahului 96732, ☎ 808/871–6226) both offer full schedules of a variety of tours. **TransHawaiian Services** (⊠ 720 Iwilei Rd., Suite 101, Honolulu 96817, ☎ 800/533–8765) is one of the island's largest tour operators. **No Ka Oi Scenic Tours** (⊠ Box 1827, Kahului 96732, ☎ 808/871–9008) specializes in a Hāna tour.

PERSONAL GUIDES

Rent-a-Local (⊠ 333 Dairy Rd., Kahului 96732, ☎ 808/877–4042 or 800/228–6284). This is *the* best way to see Maui through the eyes of the locals. **Temptation Tours** (⊠ 211 ʻĀhinahina Pl., Kula 96790, ☎ 808/877–8888) specializes in full-day exclusive tours to Haleakalā and Hāna.

WALKING TOURS

The **Lahaina Restoration Foundation** (⊠ Baldwin Home, 696 Front St., Lahaina, ☎ 808/661–3262) has published a walking-tour map for interested visitors. These are all sights you could find yourself, but the map is free, and it makes the walk easier.

GROUPS

A major tour operator specializing in student travel is **Contiki Holidays** (⊠ 300 Plaza Alicante, Suite 900, Garden Grove, CA 92640, ☎ 714/740–0808 or 800/466–0610).

HOSTELING

In the United States, contact **Hostelling International–American Youth Hostels** (⊠ 733 15th St. NW, Suite 840, Washington, DC 20005, ☎ 202/783–6161 or 800/444–6111 for reservations at selected hostels, FAX 202/783–6171); in Canada, **Hostelling International–Canada** (⊠ 205 Catherine St., Suite 400, Ottawa, Ontario K2P 1C3, ☎ 613/237–7884); and in the United Kingdom, the **Youth Hostel Association of England and Wales** (⊠ Trevelyan House, 8 St. Stephen's Hill, St. Albans, Hertfordshire AL1 2DY, ☎ 01727/855215 or 01727/845047). Membership (in the U.S., $25; in Canada, C$26.75; in the U.K., £9.30) gives you access to 5,000 hostels in 77 countries that charge $5–$30 per person per night.

ID CARDS

To be eligible for discounts on transportation and admissions, get either the **International Student Identity Card,** if you're a bona fide student, or the **GO 25: International Youth Travel Card,** if you're not a student but under age 26. Each includes basic travel-accident and illness coverage, plus a toll-free travel hot line. In the United States, either card costs $18; apply through the Council on International Educational Exchange (☞ Organizations, *below*). In Canada, cards are available for $15 each ($16 by mail) from Travel Cuts (☞ Organizations, *below*), and in the United Kingdom for £5 each at student unions and student travel companies.

ORGANIZATIONS

A major contact is the **Council on International Educational Exchange** (mail orders only: ⊠ CIEE, 205 E. 42nd St., 16th Floor, New York, NY 10017, ☎ 212/661–1450), with walk-in locations in Boston (⊠ 729 Boylston St., 02116, ☎ 617/266–1926), Miami (⊠ 9100 S. Dadeland Blvd., 33156, ☎ 305/670–9261), Los Angeles (⊠ 10904 Lindbrook Dr., 90024, ☎ 310/208–3551), 43 other college towns in the U.S., and in the United Kingdom (⊠ 28A Poland St., London W1V 3DB, ☎ 0171/437–7767). Twice per year, it publishes *Student Travels* magazine. The CIEE's Council Travel Service offers domestic air passes for bargain travel within the United States and is the exclusive U.S. agent for several student discount cards.

The **Educational Travel Centre** (⊠ 438 N. Frances St., Madison, WI 53703, ☎ 608/256–5551 or 800/747–5551, FAX 608/256–2042) offers rail passes and low-cost airline tickets, mostly for flights that depart from Chicago.

In Canada, contact **Travel Cuts** (⊠ 187 College St., Toronto, Ontario M5T 1P7, ☎ 416/979–2406 or 800/667–2887).

T

TAXIS

For short hops between hotels and restaurants, this can be a convenient way to go, but you'll have to call ahead. Even busy West Maui doesn't have curbside taxi service. **West Maui Taxi** (⊠ 761 Kumukahi, Lahaina, ☎ 808/667–2605) and **Yellow Cab of Maui** (⊠ Kahului Airport, ☎ 808/877–7000) both service the entire island, but you'd be smart to consider using them just for the areas where they're located. **Ali'i Cab** (⊠ 475 Kū'ai Pl., Lahaina, ☎ 808/661–3688) specializes in West Maui, while **Kīhei Taxi** (⊠ Kīhei, ☎ 808/879–3000) serves Central Maui.

TOUR OPERATORS

Among the companies that sell tours and packages to Maui, the following are nationally known, have a proven

reputation, and offer plenty of options.

GROUP TOURS

Globus (⊠ 5301 S. Federal Circle, Littleton, CO 80123-2980, ☎ 303/797–2800 or 800/221–0090, FAX 303/795–0962) and **Tauck Tours** (⊠ Box 5027, 276 Post Rd. W, Westport, CT 06881, ☎ 203/226–6911 or 800/468–2825, FAX 203/221–6828).

FIRST CLASS➤ **Caravan Tours** (⊠ 401 N. Michigan Ave., Chicago, IL 60611, ☎ 312/321–9800 or 800/227–2826), **Collette Tours** (⊠ 162 Middle St., Pawtucket, RI 02860, ☎ 401/728–3805 or 800/832–4656, FAX 401/728–1380), and **Mayflower Tours** (⊠ Box 490, 1225 Warren Ave., Downers Grove, IL 60515, ☎ 708/960–3430 or 800/323–7064).

BUDGET➤ **Cosmos** (☞ Globus, *above*).

PACKAGES

Hawai'i's top sources of independent vacation packages are **Classic Hawai'i** (⊠ 1 N. 1st St., 3rd floor, San Jose, CA 95113, ☎ 800/221–3949), **Haddon Holidays** (⊠ 1120 Executive Plaza, #375, Mt. Laurel, NJ 08054, ☎ 609/273–8778 or 800/257–7488), **Pleasant Hawaiian Holidays** (⊠ 2404 Townsgate Rd., West Lake Village, CA 91361, ☎ 818/991–3390 or 800/242–9255).

Many tour operators and airlines sell Hawai'i vacations. Contact **American Airlines Fly**

AAway Vacations (☎ 800/321–2121), **Continental Vacations** (☎ 800/634–5555), **Delta Dream Vacations** (☎ 800/872–7786), **United Vacations** (☎ 800/328–6877). **Gogo Tours**, based in Ramsey, New Jersey, sells Hawai'i packages only through travel agents.

Regional operators specialize in putting together Maui packages for travelers from their local area. Arrangements include charter or scheduled air. Contact **Apple Vacations** (⊠ 25 N.W. Point Blvd., Elk Grove Village, IL 60007, ☎ 708/640–1150 or 800/365–2775), **Friendly Holidays** (⊠ 1983 Marcus Ave., Lake Success, NY 11042, ☎ 800/344–5687), and **TWA Getaway Vacations** (☎ 800/438–2929).

Contact **Amtrak**'s Great American Vacations (☎ 800/321–8684). For independent self-drive itineraries, contact **Budget WorldClass Drive** (☎ 800/527–0700; in the U.K., 0800/181181).

FROM THE U.K.

Some of the tour operators that offer packages to Maui are **British Airways Holidays** (⊠ Astral Towers, Betts Way, London Rd., Crawley, West Sussex RH10 2XA, ☎ 01293/518–022), **Kuoni Travel** (⊠ Kuoni House, Dorking, Surrey RH5 4AZ, ☎ 01306/742–222), **Americana Vacations Ltd.** (⊠ Morley House, 320 Regent St., London W1R 5AD, ☎ 0171/637–7853), and **Key to America** (⊠ 1–3 Station Rd.,

Ashford, Middlesex TW15 2UW, ☎ 01784/248–777).

Independent travelers should contact **Trailfinders** (✉ 42–50 Earls Court Rd., London W8 7RG, ☎ 0171/937–5400; 58 Deansgate, Manchester M3 2FF, ☎ 0161/839–6969).

THEME TRIPS

ADVENTURE➤ **American Wilderness Experience** (✉ Box 1486, Boulder, CO 80306, ☎ 303/444–2622 or 800/444–3833, FAX 303/444–3999) has hiking, snorkeling, and camping trips on Maui.

GOLF➤ **Stine's Golftrips** (✉ Box 2314, Winter Haven, FL 33883-2314, ☎ 941/324–1300 or 800/428–1940, FAX 941/325–0384) sells resort-based golf packages that include confirmed tee times and golfing fees and lessons.

LEARNING➤ **Hawaiian Heart of the Jungle Journeys** (✉ Box 1567, Makawao, Maui, HI 96768, ☎ 808/572–5083) takes you walking through a bamboo forest, hiking across lava fields, and swimming in freshwater pools.

VILLA RENTALS➤ Contact **Villas International** (✉ 605 Market St., San Francisco, CA 94105, ☎ 415/281–0910 or 800/221–2260, FAX 415/281–0919).

WALKING➤ For soft adventures, contact **Country Walkers** (✉ Box 180, Waterbury, VT 05676-0180, ☎ 802/244–1387 or 800/464–9255, FAX 802/244–5661). **Walking the World** (✉ Box 1186, Fort Collins, CO 80522, ☎ 303/225–0500) specializes in Hawaiian hiking tours for travelers ages 50 and older.

ORGANIZATIONS

The **National Tour Association** (✉ NTA, 546 E. Main St., Lexington, KY 40508, ☎ 606/226–4444 or 800/755–8687) and the **United States Tour Operators Association** (✉ USTOA, 211 E. 51st St., Suite 12B, New York, NY 10022, ☎ 212/750–7371) can provide lists of members and information on booking tours.

PUBLICATIONS

Contact the USTOA (☞ Organizations, *above*) for its **"Smart Traveler's Planning Kit."** Pamphlets in the kit include the "Worldwide Tour and Vacation Package Finder," "How to Select a Tour or Vacation Package," and information on the organization's consumer protection plan. Also get copy of the Better Business Bureau's **"Tips on Travel Packages"** (✉ Publication 24-195, 4200 Wilson Blvd., Arlington, VA 22203; $2). The National Tour Association will send you **"On Tour,"** a listing of its member operators, and a personalized package of information on group travel in North America.

TRAVEL AGENCIES

For names of reputable agencies in your area, contact the **American Society of Travel Agents** (✉ ASTA, 1101 King St., Suite 200, Alexandria, VA 22314, ☎ 703/739–2782), the

Association of Canadian Travel Agents (✉ Suite 201, 1729 Bank St., Ottawa, Ontario K1V 7Z5, ☎ 613/521–0474, FAX 613/521–0805) or the **Association of British Travel Agents** (✉ 55-57 Newman St., London W1P 4AH, ☎ 0171/637–2444, FAX 0171/637–0713).

TRAVEL GEAR

For travel apparel, appliances, and other travel necessities, get a free catalog from **Magellan's** (☎ 800/962–4943, FAX 805/568–5406), **Orvis Travel** (☎ 800/541–3541, FAX 703/343–7053), or **TravelSmith** (☎ 800/950–1600, FAX 415/455–0554).

V

VISITOR INFORMATION

Contact the **Hawai'i Visitors Bureau** (HVB) in the **United States** at ✉ 350 5th Ave., Suite 1827, New York, NY 10118, ☎ 212/947–0717 or 800/525–6284, FAX 212/947–0725.

In the **United Kingdom**, contact the **HVB** at ✉ Box 208, Sunbury, Middlesex, TW16 5RJ, ☎ 0181/941–4009. Send a £2 check or postal order for an information pack.

IN HAWAI'I

You can reach the **HVB** on Maui at ✉ 1727 Wili Pa Loop, Wailuku, HI 96793, ☎ 808/244–3530, FAX 808/244-1337.

W

WEATHER

For current conditions and forecasts, plus the

local time and helpful travel tips, call the **Weather Channel Connection** (☎ 900/932–8437; 95¢ per minute) from a Touch-Tone phone.

The *International Traveler's Weather Guide* (✉ Weather Press, Box 660606, Sacramento, CA 95866, ☎ 916/974–0201 or 800/972–0201; $10.95 includes shipping), written by two meteorologists, provides month-by-month information on temperature, humidity, and precipitation in more than 175 cities worldwide.

THE GOLD GUIDE / IMPORTANT CONTACTS

SMART TRAVEL TIPS A TO Z

Basic Information on Traveling in Maui & Savvy Tips to Make Your Trip a Breeze

A

AIR TRAVEL

If time is an issue, **always look for non-stop flights,** which require no change of plane. If possible, **avoid connecting flights,** which stop at least once and can involve a change of plane, even though the flight number remains the same; if the first leg is late, the second waits.

AIRPORT TRANSFERS

Most major hotels provide shuttle service from Kahului Airport; **ask when booking your room if airport transfers are included** in your rate.

ALOFT

AIRLINE FOOD➤ If you hate airline food, **ask for special meals when booking.** These can be vegetarian, low-cholesterol, or kosher, for example; commonly prepared to order in smaller quantities than standard fare, they can be tastier.

JET LAG➤ To avoid this syndrome, which occurs when travel disrupts your body's natural cycles, try to maintain a normal routine. At night, **get some sleep.** By day, move about the cabin to **stretch your legs, eat light meals, and drink water—not alcohol.**

SMOKING➤ Smoking is banned on all flights of less than six hours' duration within the United States and on all Canadian flights; the ban also applies to domestic segments of international flights aboard U.S. and foreign carriers.

CUTTING COSTS

The Sunday travel section of most newspapers is a good place to look for deals.

MAJOR AIRLINES➤ The least-expensive airfares from the major airlines are priced for round-trip travel and are subject to restrictions. Usually, you must **book in advance and buy the ticket within 24 hours** to get cheaper fares, and you may have to **stay over a Saturday night.** The lowest fare is subject to availability, and only a small percentage of the plane's total seats is sold at that price. It's smart to **call a number of airlines,** and **when you are quoted a good price, book it on the spot**—the same fare may not be available on the same flight the next day. Airlines generally allow you to change your return date for a $25 to $50 fee. If you don't use your ticket, you can apply the cost toward the purchase of a new ticket, again for a small charge. However, most low-fare tickets are nonrefundable. To get the lowest airfare, **check different routings.** If your destination has more than one gateway, compare prices to different airports.

FROM THE U.K.➤ To save money on flights, **look into an APEX or Super-Pex ticket.** APEX tickets must be booked in advance and have certain restrictions. Super-PEX tickets can be purchased right at the airport.

CONSOLIDATORS➤ Consolidators buy tickets for scheduled flights at reduced rates from the airlines, then sell them at prices below the lowest available from the airlines directly—usually without advance restrictions. Sometimes you can even get your money back if you need to return the ticket. Carefully read the fine print detailing penalties for changes and cancellations. If you doubt the reliability of a consolidator, **confirm your reservation with the airline.**

DIVERS' ALERT

Scuba divers take note: **Do not fly within 24 hours of scuba diving.**

B

BUSINESS HOURS

Banks on Maui are generally open Monday–Thursday 8:30–3, Friday 8:30–6.

Shops are usually open seven days a week, 9–5. Shopping centers tend to stay open later (until 9 on certain days).

C

CAMERAS, CAMCORDERS, & COMPUTERS

LAPTOPS

Before you depart, **check your portable computer's battery;** at security you may be asked to turn on the computer to prove that it is what it appears to be. At the airport, you may prefer to **request a manual inspection,** although security X-rays do not harm hard-disk or floppy-disk storage.

PHOTOGRAPHY

If your camera is new or if you haven't used it for a while, **shoot and develop a few rolls of film** before you leave. Always **store film in a cool, dry place**—never in your car's glove compartment or on the shelf under the rear window.

Select the right film for your purpose—**use print film if you plan to frame or display your pictures,** but **use slide film if you hope to publish your shots.** Also, **consider black-and-white film** for different and dramatic images. For best results, **use a custom lab** for processing; use a one-hour lab only if time is a factor.

The chances of your film growing cloudy increase with each pass through an X-ray machine. To protect against this, carry it in a clear plastic bag and **ask for hand inspection at security.** Such requests are virtually always honored at U.S. airports. Don't depend on a lead-lined bag to protect film in checked luggage—the airline may increase the radiation to see what's inside.

Keep a skylight or haze filter on your camera at all times to protect the expensive (and delicate) lens glass from scratches. Better yet, **use an 81B warming filter,** which—unlike skylight or haze filters—really works in overcast conditions and will pump up those sunrises and sunsets.

VIDEO

Before your trip, **test your camcorder, invest in a skylight filter to protect the lens, and charge the batteries.** (Airport security personnel may ask you to turn on the camcorder to prove that it's what it appears to be.) The batteries of most newer camcorders can be recharged with a universal or worldwide AC adapter-charger (or multivoltage converter), whether the voltage is 110 or 220. All that's needed is the appropriate plug.

Videotape is not damaged by X-rays, but it may be harmed by the magnetic field of a walk-through metal detector, so **ask that videotapes be hand-checked.**

CAR RENTAL

CUTTING COSTS

To get the best deal, **book through a travel agent who is willing to shop around.** When pricing cars, **ask where the rental lot is located.** Some off-airport locations offer lower rates— even though their lots are only minutes away from the terminal via complimentary shuttle. You also may want to **price local car-rental companies,** whose rates may be lower still, although service and maintenance standards may not be as high as those of a national firm. Ask your agent to **look for fly-drive packages,** which also save you money, and **ask if local taxes are included** in the rental or fly-drive price. These can be as high as 20% in some destinations. Don't forget to find out about required deposits, cancellation penalties, drop-off charges, and the cost of any required insurance coverage.

Also **ask your travel agent about a company's customer-service record.** How has it responded to late plane arrivals and vehicle mishaps? Are there often lines at the rental counter, and—if you're traveling during a holiday period—does a confirmed reservation guarantee you a car?

INSURANCE

When driving a rented car, you are generally responsible for any damage to or loss of the rental vehicle, as well as any property damage or personal injury that you cause. Before you rent, **see what coverage you already have** under the terms of your personal auto insurance policy and credit cards.

For about $14 a day, rental companies sell protection, known as a collision- or loss- damage waiver (CDW or LDW), that eliminates your liability for damage to the car; it's always optional and should never be automatically added to your bill.

In most states, the renter's personal auto insurance or other liability insurance covers damage to third parties. Only when the damage exceeds the renter's own insurance coverage does the car-rental company pay. **If you do not have auto insurance or an umbrella insurance policy that covers damage to third parties, purchasing CDW or LDW is highly recommended.**

U.K. CITIZENS

In the United States you must be 21 to rent a car; rates may be higher if you're under 25. To pick up your reserved car you will need the reservation voucher, a passport, a U.K. driver's license, and a travel policy that covers each driver.

SURCHARGES

You'll pay extra for child seats (about $3 per day), compulsory for children under five, and for additional drivers (about $2 per day). Before you pick up a car in one city and leave it in another, **ask about drop-off charges or one-way service fees,** which can be substantial. Note, too, that some rental agencies charge extra if you return the car before the time specified on your contract. To avoid a hefty refueling fee, **fill the tank just before you turn in the car**—but be aware that gas stations near the rental outlet may overcharge.

CHILDREN & TRAVEL

When traveling with children, **plan ahead** and **involve your youngsters** as you outline your trip. When packing, **include a supply of things to keep them busy** en route (☞ Children & Travel *in* Important Contacts A to Z). On sightseeing days, try to **schedule activities of special interest to your children,** like a trip to a zoo or a playground. If you **plan your itinerary around seasonal festivals,** you'll never lack for things to do. In addition, **check local newspapers for special events** mounted by public libraries, museums, and parks.

BABY-SITTING

For recommended local sitters, **check with your hotel desk.**

DRIVING

If you are renting a car, don't forget to **arrange for a car seat when you reserve.**

FLYING

On domestic flights, children under 2 not occupying a seat travel free, and older children are charged at the lowest applicable adult rate.

BAGGAGE➤ In general, the adult baggage allowance applies to children paying half or more of the adult fare.

SAFETY SEATS➤ According to the FAA, it's a good idea to **use safety seats aloft** for children weighing less than 40 pounds. Airline policies vary. U.S. carriers allow FAA-approved models but usually require that you buy a ticket, even if your child would otherwise ride free, since the seats must be strapped into regular seats.

FACILITIES➤ When making your reservation, **request for children's meals or freestanding bassinets** if you need them; the latter are available only to those seated at the bulkhead, where there's enough legroom. If you don't need a bassinet, **think twice before requesting bulkhead seats**—the only storage space for in-flight necessities is in inconveniently distant overhead bins.

LODGING

Most hotels allow children under a certain age to stay in their parents' room at no extra charge; others charge them as extra adults. Be sure to **ask about the cutoff age.**

CRUISES

To get the best deal on a cruise, **consult a cruise-only travel agency.**

CUSTOMS & DUTIES

IN MAUI

Plants and plant products are subject to regulation by the Department of Agriculture, both on entering and leaving Hawai`i. Pineapples and coconuts with the packer's agricultural inspection stamp pass freely; papayas must be treated, inspected, and stamped. All other fruits are banned for export to the U.S. mainland. Flowers pass except for gardenia, rose leaves, jade vine, and mauna loa. Also banned are insects, snails; soil; and coffee, cotton, cacti, sugarcane, and all berry plants.

Leave dogs and other pets at home. A strict 120-day quarantine is imposed to keep out rabies, which is nonexistent in Hawai'i. Many other animals (including iguanas and snakes of any kind) are not allowed at all because non-native escapees can harm the Islands' delicate ecosystems.

Foreign travelers 21 or older, may take into the United States 200 cigarettes or 50 cigars or 2 kilograms of tobacco; 1 liter of alcohol; and duty-free gifts to a value of $100. Be careful not to try to take in meat or meat products, seeds, plants, or fruits. Do not carry illegal drugs.

IN CANADA

If you've been out of Canada for at least seven days, you may bring in C$500 worth of goods duty-free. If you've been away for fewer than seven days but for more than 48 hours, the duty-free allowance drops to C$200; if your trip lasts between 24 and 48 hours, the allowance is C$50. You cannot pool allowances with family members. Goods claimed under the C$500 exemption may follow you by mail; those claimed under the lesser exemptions must accompany you.

Alcohol and tobacco products may be included in the seven-day and 48-hour exemp-

tions but not in the 24-hour exemption. If you meet the age requirements of the province or territory through which you reenter Canada, you may bring in, duty-free, 1.14 liters (40 imperial ounces) of wine or liquor *or* 24 12-ounce cans or bottles of beer or ale. If you are 16 or older, you may bring in, duty-free, 200 cigarettes, 50 cigars or cigarillos, and 400 tobacco sticks or 400 grams of manufactured tobacco. Alcohol and tobacco must accompany you on your return.

An unlimited number of gifts with a value of up to C$60 each may be mailed to Canada duty-free. These do not affect your duty-free allowance on your return. Label the package "Unsolicited Gift— Value Under $60." Alcohol and tobacco are excluded.

IN THE U.K.

From countries outside the EU, including the United States, you may import, duty-free, 200 cigarettes, 100 cigarillos, 50 cigars, or 250 grams of tobacco; 1 liter of spirits or 2 liters of fortified or sparkling wine or liqueurs; 2 liters of still table wine; 60 milliliters of perfume; 250 milliliters of toilet water; plus £136 worth of other goods, including gifts and souvenirs.

D

DISABILITIES & ACCESSIBILITY

The Society for the Advancement of Travel for the Handicapped

has named Hawai'i the most accessible vacation spot for the disabled; the number of ramped visitor areas and specially equipped lodgings in the state attests to its desire to make everyone feel welcome.

When discussing accessibility with an operator or reservationist, **ask hard questions.** Are there any stairs, inside *or* out? Are there grab bars next to the toilet *and* in the shower/tub? How wide is the doorway to the room? To the bathroom? For the most extensive facilities, meeting the latest legal specifications, **opt for newer accommodations,** which more often have been designed with access in mind. Older properties or ships must usually be retrofitted and may offer more limited facilities as a result. Be sure to **discuss your needs before booking.**

DISCOUNTS & DEALS

You shouldn't have to pay for a discount. In fact, you may already be eligible for all kinds of savings. Here are some time-honored strategies for getting the best deal.

DIAL FOR DOLLARS

To save money, **look into "1-800" discount reservations services,** which often have lower rates. These services use their buying power to get a better price on hotels, airline tickets, and sometimes even car rentals. When booking a room, always **call the hotel's local toll-free number** (if one is available) rather than the central reservations number—you'll often get a better price. Ask the reservationist about special packages or corporate rates, which are usually available even if you're not traveling on business.

JOIN A CLUB?

Discount clubs can be a legitimate source of savings, but you must use the participating hotels and visit the participating attractions in order to realize any benefits. Remember, too, that you have to pay a fee to join, so **determine if you'll save enough to warrant your membership fee.** Before booking with a club, **make sure the hotel or other supplier isn't offering a better deal.**

LOOK IN YOUR WALLET

When you **use your credit card to make travel purchases,** you may get free travel-accident insurance, collision damage insurance, medical or legal assistance, depending on the card and bank that issued it. Visa and MasterCard provide one or more of these services, so **get a copy of your card's travel benefits.** If you are a member of the AAA or an oil-company-sponsored road-assistance plan, always **ask hotel or car-rental reservationists for auto-club discounts.** Some clubs offer additional discounts on tours, cruises, or admission to attractions. And don't forget that auto-club membership entitles you to free maps and trip-planning services.

SENIORS CITIZENS

As a senior-citizen traveler, you may be eligible for special rates, but **you should mention your senior-citizen status up front** when booking hotel reservations, not when checking out, and before you're seated in restaurants, not when paying the bill. Note that discounts may be limited to certain menus, days, or hours. When renting a car, **ask about promotional car-rental discounts**—they can net even lower costs than your senior-citizen discount.

STUDENTS

To save money, **look into deals available through student-oriented travel agencies.** To qualify, you'll need to have a bona fide student ID card. Members of international student groups are also eligible (☞ Students *in* Important Contacts A to Z).

DRIVING

Maui, the second-largest island in the state of Hawai'i, with 729 square miles, has some 120 miles of coastline, not all of which is accessible. Less than one-quarter of its landmass is inhabited. **To see the island your best bet is a car;** there is no reliable public transportation.

Maui has several major roads. Highway 30, the Honoapi'ilani Highway, goes from Wailuku in Central Maui around the south of the West Maui mountains and up the west coast past Lahaina, Kā'anapali, and Kapalua. The road from the Pu'unēnē to Kīhei, Wailea, and Mākena is called Highway 311, or the Mokulele Highway. When you reach Kīhei, **you can take Kīhei Road to reach all the lodgings in that town, or you can bypass them on Highway 31 (the Pi'ilani Highway) if you're staying in Wailea or Mākena.** The latter road is the best on the island in terms of driving because it is wide and sparsely traveled. Another main thoroughfare is the Haleakalā Highway (numbered 37, 377, and 378 at different points), which goes between Kahului and Haleakalā. Most of the island's roads have two lanes.

If you're going to attempt the dirt roads between Kapalua and Wailuku or from Hāna to Mākena, **you'll need a four-wheel-drive vehicle.** Be forewarned: Car-rental companies prohibit travel off the pavement, so if you break down, you're on your own for repairs. The only other difficult road on Maui is the Hāna Highway, which runs 56 miles between Kahului and Hāna and includes more twists and turns than a person can count. Take it slow and you should have no problems.

Asking for directions will almost always produce a helpful explanation from the locals, but **you should be prpared for an island term or two.** Instead of using compass directions, Hawai'i residents refer to places as being either *mauka* (toward the mountains) or *makai* (toward the ocean).

I

INSURANCE

Travel insurance can protect your monetary investment, replace your luggage and its contents, or provide for medical coverage should you fall ill during your trip. Most tour operators, travel agents, and insurance agents sell specialized health-and-accident, flight, trip-cancellation, and luggage insurance as well as comprehensive policies with some or all of these coverages. Comprehensive policies may also reimburse you for delays due to weather—an important consideration if you're traveling during the winter months. Some health-insurance policies do not cover preexisting conditions, but waivers may be available in specific cases. Coverage is sold by the companies listed in Important Contacts A to Z; these companies act as the policy's administrators. The actual insurance is usually underwritten by a well-known name, such as The Travelers or Continental Insurance.

Before you make any purchase, **review your existing health and homeowner's policies** to find out whether they cover expenses incurred while traveling.

BAGGAGE

Airline liability for baggage is limited to $1,250 per person on domestic flights. On international flights, it amounts to $9.07 per pound or $20 per kilogram for checked baggage (roughly $640 per 70-pound bag) and $400 per passenger for unchecked baggage. Insurance for losses exceeding the terms of your airline ticket can be bought directly from the airline at check-in for about $10 per $1,000 of coverage; note that it excludes a rather extensive list of items, shown on your airline ticket.

COMPREHENSIVE

Comprehensive insurance policies include all the coverages described above plus some that may not be available in more specific policies. If you have purchased an expensive vacation, especially one that involves travel abroad, comprehensive insurance is a must; **look for policies that include trip delay insurance,** which will protect you in the event that weather problems cause you to miss your flight, tour, or cruise. A few insurers will also sell you a waiver for preexisting medical conditions. Some of the companies that offer both these features are Access America, Carefree Travel, Travel Insured International, and TravelGuard (☞ Insurance *in* Important Contacts A to Z).

FLIGHT

You should **think twice before buying flight insurance.** Often purchased as a last-minute impulse at the airport, it pays a lump sum when a plane crashes, either to a beneficiary if the insured dies or sometimes to a surviving passenger who loses his or her eyesight or a limb. Supplementing the airlines' coverage described in the limits-of-liability paragraphs on your ticket, it's expensive and basically unnecessary. Charging an airline ticket to a major credit card often automatically provides you with coverage that may also extend to travel by bus, train, and ship.

U.K. TRAVELERS

According to the Association of British Insurers, a trade association representing 450 insurance companies, it's wise to **buy extra medical coverage when you visit the United States.** You can buy an annual travel insurance policy valid for most vacations during the year in which it's purchased. If you are pregnant or have a preexisting medical condition make sure you're covered before buying such a policy.

TRIP

Without insurance, you will lose all or most of your money if you cancel your trip regardless of the reason. Especially if your airline ticket, cruise, or package tour is nonrefundable and cannot be changed, it's essential that you **buy trip-cancellation-and-interruption insurance.** When considering how much coverage you need, look for a policy that will cover the cost of your trip plus the nondiscounted price of a one-way airline ticket should you need to return home early. Read the fine print carefully, especially sections that define "family member" and "preexisting medical conditions." Also **consider default or bankruptcy insurance,** which protects you against a supplier's failure to deliver. Be aware, however, that if you buy such a policy from a travel agency, tour operator, airline, or cruise line, it may not cover default by the firm in question.

L
LODGING

APARTMENT, HOUSE & VILLA RENTAL

If you want a home base that's roomy enough for a family and comes with cooking facilities, **consider taking a furnished rental.** This can also save you money, but not always—some rentals are luxury properties (economical only when your party is large). Home-exchange directories list rentals—often second homes owned by prospective house swappers—and some services search for a house or apartment for you (even a castle if that's your fancy) and handle the paperwork. Some send an illustrated catalog; others send photographs only of specific properties, sometimes at a charge; up-front registration fees may apply.

You can rent a house on Maui through several brokers (☞ Lodging in Important Contacts A to Z). There is no average rate; you can expect to find houses for as little as $100 a night or as much as $1,000.

BED & BREAKFASTS

Maui has quite a few bed-and-breakfasts (☞ Lodging in Important Contacts A to Z) and many have separate guest quarters, which allows privacy while still giving you a chance to get to know your hosts. Rates range from $35 a night to more than $150.

CONDOMINIUMS

Maui has condos you can rent through central booking agents (☞ Lodging in Important Contacts A to Z). Most agents represent more than one condo complex, so **be specific about what kind of price, space, facilities, and amenities you want.**

HOME EXCHANGE

If you would like to find a house, an apartment, or some other type of vacation property to exchange for your own while on holiday, **become a member of a home-exchange organization,** which will send you its updated listings of available exchanges for a year, and will include your own listing in at least one of them. Arrangements for the actual exchange are made by the two parties involved, not by the organization.

M
MONEY & EXPENSES

ATMS

CASH ADVANCES➤ Chances are that you can **use your bank card, MasterCard, or Visa at ATMs** to withdraw money from an account or get a cash advance.

Before leaving home, **check on frequency limits** for withdrawals and cash advances.

TRANSACTION FEES➤ On credit-card cash advances you are charged interest from the day you receive the money, whether from a teller or an ATM. Transaction fees for ATM withdrawals outside your local area may be higher than those charged for withdrawals at home.

TAXES

CAR RENTALS➤ A $2/day surcharge and sales tax of 4.17% are added to all car-rental charges.

HOTEL➤ A 6% lodging tax, as well as 4.17% sales tax, is added to hotel bills.

SALES TAX➤ Sales tax (called general excise tax) throughout Hawai'i is 4.17%

TRAVELER'S CHECKS

Whether or not to buy traveler's checks depends on where you are headed; **take cash to rural areas and small towns, traveler's checks to cities.** The most widely recognized checks are issued by American Express, Citicorp, Thomas Cook, and Visa. These are sold by major commercial banks for 1%–3% of the checks' face value—it pays to **shop around.** Both American Express and Thomas Cook issue checks that can be countersigned and used by either you or your traveling companion. Before leaving home, **contact your issuer for**

information on where to cash your checks without a incurring a transaction fee. Record the numbers of all your checks, and keep this listing in a separate place, crossing off the numbers of checks you have cashed.

WIRING MONEY

For a fee of 3%–10%, depending on the amount of the transaction, you can have money sent to you from home through Money-Gram^SM or Western Union (☞ Money Matters *in* Important Contacts A to Z). The transferred funds and the service fee can be charged to a Master-Card or Visa account.

N

NATIONAL PARKS

If you are a frequent visitor, senior citizen, or traveler with a disability, you can **save money on park entrance fees** by getting a discount pass. The Golden Eagle Pass can be a good deal if you plan to visit several parks during your travels. Priced at $25, it entitles you and your companions to free admission to *all* parks for a year. It does not cover additional park fees such as those for camping or parking. Both the Golden Age Passport, for U.S. citizens or permanent residents 62 or older, and the Golden Access Passport, for travelers with disabilities, entitle holders to free entry to all national parks plus 50% off fees for the use of all park facilities and services except those run by private concessionaires. Both pass-

ports are free; you must show proof of age and U.S. citizenship or permanent residency (such as a U.S. passport, driver's license, or birth certificate) or proof of disability. All three passes are available at all national park entrances.

P

PACKING FOR MAUI

You can pack lightly because Maui is casual. Bare feet, bathing suits, and comfortable, informal clothing are the norm. Local-style casual footwear consists of tennis or running shoes, sandals, or rubber slippers. You'll also see a lot of bare feet, but state law requires that footwear be worn in all food establishments. (If you want to be marked as a tourist, wear your shorts with dark shoes and white socks.)

Don't forget your bathing suit. Sooner or later the crystal-clear water tempts even the most sedentary landlubber. Of course, bathing suits are easy to find in Maui. Shops are crammed with the latest styles. **If you wear a bathing cap, bring one;** you can waste hours searching for one.

Probably the most important thing to tuck into your suitcase is sunscreen. It's best to put on sunscreen when you get up in the morning. Don't forget to reapply sunscreen periodically during the day, since perspiration can wash it away. **Consider using sunscreens with a sun-**

protection factor (SPF) of 15 or higher. There are many tanning oils on the market in Maui, including coconut and *kukui* oils, but doctors warn that they merely sauté your skin. Too many Hawaiian vacations have been spoiled by sunburn.

Hats and sunglasses offer important sun protection, too. Both are easy to find in island shops, but if you already have a favorite packable hat or sun visor, bring it with you, and don't forget to wear it.

Bring an extra pair of eyeglasses or contact lenses in your carry-on luggage, and if you have a health problem, **pack enough medication** to last the trip. It's important that you **don't put prescription drugs or valuables in luggage to be checked,** for it could go astray.

CLOTHING

MEN➢ In the Hawaiian Islands there's a saying that when a man wears a suit during the day he's either going for a loan or he's a lawyer trying a case. **Only a few upscale restaurants require a jacket for dinner, and none requires a tie.** Maui regulars wear their jackets on the plane—just in case—and many don't put them on again until the return flight.

WOMEN➢ Sundresses, shorts, and casual tops are fine for daytime. If you have a long slip, bring it for the muumuu you say you won't buy but probably will.

If you don't own a *pareu*, buy one in Maui.

It's simply a length (about 1½ yards long) of light cotton in a tropical motif that can be worn as a beach wrap, a skirt, or a dozen other wrap-up fashions. A pareu is useful wherever you go, regardless of climate. It makes a good bathrobe, so you don't have to pack one. You can even tie it up as a handbag or sit on it at the beach.

LUGGAGE

Airline baggage allowances depend on the airline, the route, and the class of your ticket; ask in advance. In general, on domestic flights you are entitled to check two bags. A third piece may be brought on board, but it must fit easily under the seat in front of you or in the overhead compartment. In the United States, the FAA gives airlines broad latitude regarding carry-on allowances, and they tend to tailor them to different aircraft and operational conditions. Charges for excess, oversize, or overweight pieces vary.

SAFEGUARDING YOUR LUGGAGE➤ Before leaving home, **itemize your bags' contents** and their worth, and label them with your name, address, and phone number. (If you use your home address, cover it so that potential thieves can't see it readily.) Inside each bag, **pack a copy of your itinerary.** At check-in, **make sure that each bag is correctly tagged** with the destination airport's three-letter code. If your bags arrive damaged—or fail to

arrive at all—file a written report with the airline before leaving the airport.

CANADIANS

No passport is necessary to enter the United States.

U.K. CITIZENS

British citizens need a valid passport to enter the United States. If you are staying for fewer than 90 days and traveling on a vacation, with a return or onward ticket, you probably will not need a visa. However, you will need to fill out the Visa Waiver Form, 1-94W, supplied by the airline.

It is advisable that you **leave one photocopy of your passport's data page** with someone at home and keep another with you, separated from your passport, while traveling. If you lose your passport, promptly call the nearest embassy or consulate and the local police; having the data page information can speed replacement.

S

SHIP TRAVEL

No regularly scheduled American ships steam between the Mainland and Maui. Although foreign-owned vessels often ply the Pacific, the Jones Act of 1896 prohibits them from carrying passengers between two U.S. ports unless the ships first stop at an intervening foreign port or carry the passengers to a foreign destination. What that means to

those wishing for the relaxing ways of ship travel is that they can book with one of the major lines passing through Honolulu, but if they wish to sail on to Kahului, they'll need to book another passage, with **American Hawai'i Cruises** (☞ Cruising *in* Important Contacts A to Z).

SIGHTSEEING TOURS

If getting yourself oriented on an island doesn't come easy, **try taking one of a variety of guided tours offered on Maui.** This is a perfect opportunity to benefit from the services of an expert who can point out the sights you're most interested in and explain what it all means. You usually have a choice of touring by land or air. Ground-tour may use air-conditioned buses or smaller vans. Then you've got your minivans, your microbuses, and your minicoaches. The key is how many passengers each will hold. Be sure to **ask how many stops you'll get on your tour,** or you may be disappointed to find that all your sightseeing is done through a window. About seven helicopter companies regularly offer air tours over Maui. If you're at all nervous, **ask about a helicopter company's safety record,** although most are reliable.

Most of the tour guides have been in the business for years; some were born in the Islands and have taken special classes to learn more about their culture and lore. They expect a **tip**

($1 per person at least), but they're just as cordial without one.

The following are descriptions of some different tours offered on Maui. For companies to contact, *see* Sightseeing *in* Important Contacts A to Z.

AERIAL TOURS

CIRCLE ISLAND TOUR➤ Helicopter companies handle this in different ways. Some have fancy names, such as Ultimate Experience or Circle Island Deluxe. Some go for two hours or more. Cost: about $185–$200.

HĀNA/HALEAKALĀ CRATER TOUR➤ This takes about 90 minutes to travel inside the volcano, then down to the Hawaiian village of Hāna. Some companies stop in secluded areas for refreshments, but local residents have had moderate success in getting this stopped. Cost: about $130.

WEST MAUI TOUR➤ Generally a 30-minute helicopter ride over Kā'anapali and Lahaina. Frankly, this is not a very exciting helicopter tour. Cost: about $70–$95.

ART TOURS

Customized tours are available that take creative types into artists' homes for tea and conversation. The cost can be upwards of $150.

ASTRONOMY TOURS

Take a star-studded trip with an astronomer that may lead you to Haleakalā's summit to view the sunset and stars.

BICYCLE TOURS

Some companies will put you on a bicycle at the top of Haleakalā and let you coast down. Safety precautions are top priority, so riders wear helmets and receive training in appropriate bicycle-bell ringing. If you did the Haleakalā downhill on your last visit to Maui, you might want to try some of the new bicycle adventure tours offered by Cruiser Bob.

HIKING TOURS

Hiking in Maui can be a short five-hour outing or a week-long trek. Some tours are specially designed for photography enthusiasts.

HORSEBACK TOURS

At least two companies on Maui now offer horseback riding that's far more appealing than the typical hour-long trudge over a boring trail with 50 other horses. Some tours traverse ocean cliffs on Maui's north shore, along the slopes of Haleakalā, as they pass by streams, through rain forests, and near waterfalls.

HUNTING TOURS

Maui has a year-round hunting season, so hunting tours are always available.

LAND TOURS

CIRCLE ISLAND TOUR➤ This is a big island to tour in one day, so several companies combine various sections of it—either Haleakalā, 'Iao Needle, and Central Maui, or West Maui and its environs. Some stops include the historical sections of the county

seat of Wailuku, while others focus on some of the best snorkeling spots. Call a selection of companies to find the tour that suits you. The cost is usually $50–$80 for adults, half that for children.

HALEAKALĀ SUNRISE TOUR➤ This tour starts before dawn so that visitors get a chance to actually make it to the top of the dormant volcano before the sun peeks over the horizon. Some companies throw in champagne to greet the sunrise. Cost of the six-hour tour starts at $50.

HALEAKALĀ/UPCOUNTRY TOUR➤ Usually a half-day excursion, this tour is offered in several versions by different companies. The trip often includes stops at a protea farm and at Tedeschi Vineyards and Winery, the only place in Hawai'i where wine is made. Cost: about $55 adults, $35 children.

HĀNA TOUR➤ This tour is almost always done in a van, as the winding road to Hāna just doesn't provide a comfortable ride in bigger buses. Of late, Hāna has so many of these one-day tours that it seems as if there are more vans than cars on the road. Still, it's a more relaxing way to do the drive than behind the wheel of your own car. Guides decide where you stop for photos. Cost: $70–$120.

PERSONAL GUIDES

Local guides are available to give you a personal tour of the island. Transportation may be in your own vehicle, and can be tailored to your particular interests.

WALKING TOURS

Walking-tour maps are available for interested visitors. These are all sights you could find yourself, but the maps are usually free, and it makes the walk easier.

T
TELEPHONES

AREA CODES

All Hawaiian island telephones have the area code 808; this area code must be used for interisland calls, as well as calls from other area codes. Many toll-free 800 numbers for hotels and other establishments may not be dialed from within the Islands. For facilities that have both an 808 phone number and an 800 number, use the 808 number once you arrive in Hawai'i. Include the area code when dialing if you are phoning to a different island.

LONG-DISTANCE

The long-distance services of AT&T, MCI, and Sprint make calling home relatively convenient and let you avoid hotel surcharges; typically, you dial an 800 number in the United States.

TOUR OPERATORS

A package or tour to Maui can make your vacation less expensive and more hassle-free. Firms that sell tours and packages reserve airline seats, hotel rooms, and rental cars in bulk and pass some of the savings on to you. In addition,

the best operators have local representatives available to help you at your destination.

BUYER BEWARE

Each year a number of consumers are stranded or lose their money when operators—even very large ones with excellent reputations— go out of business. To avoid becoming one of them, take the time to **check out the operator**— find out how long the company has been in business and ask several agents about its reputation. Next, **don't book unless the firm has a consumer-protection program.** Members of the USTOA and the NTA are required to set aside funds for the sole purpose of covering your payments and travel arrangements in case of default. Nonmember operators may instead carry insurance; look for the details in the operator's brochure—and for the name of an underwriter with a solid reputation. Note: When it comes to tour operators, **don't trust escrow accounts.** Although there are laws governing those of charter-flight operators, no governmental body prevents tour operators from raiding the till.

Next, **contact your local Better Business Bureau and the attorney general's offices** in both your own state and the operator's; have any complaints been filed? Finally, **pay with a major credit card.** Then you can cancel payment, provided that you can document your complaint. Always

consider **trip-cancellation insurance** (☞ Insurance, *above*).

BIG VS. SMALL➤ Operators that handle several hundred thousand travelers per year can use their purchasing power to give you a good price. Their high volume may also indicate financial stability. But some small companies provide more personalized service; because they tend to specialize, they may also be more knowledgeable about a given area.

A GOOD DEAL?

The more your package or tour includes, the better you can predict the ultimate cost of your vacation. Make sure you know exactly what is covered, and **beware of hidden costs.** Are taxes, tips, and service charges included? Transfers and baggage handling? Entertainment and excursions? These can add up.

Most packages and tours are rated deluxe, first-class superior, first class, tourist, or budget. The key difference is usually accommodations. If the package or tour you are considering is priced lower than in your wildest dreams, **be skeptical.** Also, **make sure your travel agent knows the accommodations** and other services. Ask about the hotel's location, room size, beds, and whether it has a pool, room service, or programs for children, if you care about these. Has your agent been there in person or sent others you can contact?

SINGLE TRAVELERS

Prices are usually quoted per person, based on two sharing a room. If traveling solo, you may be required to pay the full double-occupancy rate. Some operators eliminate this surcharge if you agree to be matched up with a roommate of the same sex, even if one is not found by departure time.

USING AN AGENT

Travel agents are excellent resources. In fact, large operators accept bookings made only through travel agents. But it's good to **collect brochures from several agencies** because some agents' suggestions may be skewed by promotional relationships with tour and package firms that reward them for volume sales. If you have a special interest, **find an agent with expertise in that area**; ASTA can provide leads in the United States. (Don't rely solely on your agent, though; agents may be unaware of small-niche operators, and some special-interest travel companies only sell direct.)

TRAVEL GEAR

Travel catalogs specialize in useful items that can **save space when packing** and make life on the road more convenient. Compact alarm clocks, travel irons, travel wallets, and personal-care kits are among the most common items you'll find.

W
WHEN TO GO

A few years back, Hawai'i narrowly missed its chance to be voted the country's best place to live. The reason? The climate was too perfect. Although Upcountry Maui temperatures can drop to as low as 40°F on a chilly night and standing at the peak of Haleakalā is almost always a downright frigid experience, Maui's balmy weather is a boon to year-round vacationing.

Remember, too, this rule of island climatology: The mountains in the island's center stop the rain clouds, which tend to move east to west. These conditions create a wet, cooler climate on the eastern side of the island and leave the western side hot and dry. You'll find the best weather in the West Maui destinations of Kā'anapali and Kapalua and Central Maui's Wailea Resort. Temperatures year-round at the beaches average about 75°F; Upcountry is about 10° cooler. East Maui gets more than 70 inches of rain in an average year; West Maui gets no more than 15.

The island's peak tourist seasons fall between December 15 and Easter and during the summer. At these times, Maui will be more crowded and more expensive. You'll find escalated prices especially in the mid-winter season.

CLIMATE

The following are average maximum and minimum temperatures for certain areas of Maui:

HĀNA

Jan.	79F	26C	May	81F	27C	Sept.	85F	29C
	63	17		65	18		68	20
Feb.	79F	26C	June	83F	28C	Oct.	83F	28C
	63	17		67	19		67	19
Mar.	79F	26C	July	83F	28C	Nov.	81F	27C
	63	17		67	19		67	19
Apr.	79F	26C	Aug.	83F	28C	Dec.	79F	26C
	65	18		68	20		65	18

KĀ'ANAPALI

Jan.	79F	26C	May	81F	27C	Sept.	85F	29C
	65	18		67	19		70	21
Feb.	77F	25C	June	83F	28C	Oct.	85F	29C
	63	17		68	20		70	21
Mar.	79F	26C	July	85F	29C	Nov.	83F	28C
	67	19		72	22		68	20
Apr.	81F	27C	Aug.	85F	29C	Dec.	79F	26C
	65	18		72	22		67	19

THE GOLD GUIDE / SMART TRAVEL TIPS

LAHAINA

Jan.	85F	29C	May	86F	30C	Sept.	88F	31C
	61	16		63	17		70	21
Feb.	83F	28C	June	88F	31C	Oct.	88F	31C
	59	15		65	18		68	20
Mar.	85F	29C	July	88F	31C	Nov.	86F	30C
	63	17		65	18		67	19
Apr.	85F	29C	Aug.	88F	31C	Dec.	83F	28C
	63	17		68	20		65	18

1 Destination: Maui

WELCOME TO THE VALLEY ISLE

MAUI, SAY THE LOCALS, *nō ka 'oi* it's the best, the most, the top of the heap. To those who know Maui well, there's good reason for the superlatives. Maui magic weaves a spell over the 2 million people who visit its shores each year and leaves them wanting more. Often visitors decide to return for good.

In many ways Maui, the second-largest island in the Hawaiian chain, comes by its admirable reputation honestly. The island's 729 square miles contain Haleakalā, a 10,023-foot dormant volcano whose misty summit beckons the adventurous; several villages where Hawaiian is still spoken; more millionaires per capita than nearly anywhere else in the world; three major resort destinations that have set new standards for luxury; Lahaina, an old whaling port that still serves as one of the island's commercial crossroads; and more than 80,000 residents who work, play, and live on what they fondly call the Valley Isle.

Maui residents have had a bit to do with their island's success story. In the mid-1970s, savvy marketers saw a way to improve the island's economy through tourism and started advertising and promoting their "Valley Isle" separately from the rest of the state. They nicknamed West Maui "the Golf Coast," luring heavyweight tournaments that, in turn, brought more visitors. They went after the upscale tourist—hotels were renovated to accommodate a clientele that would pay more for the best. Condominiums on Maui were also refurbished—the word condo no longer meant second-best accommodations. Maui's visitor count swelled, putting it far ahead of that of the other Neighbor Islands.

That quick growth has led to its share of problems. During the busy seasons—from Christmas to Easter and then again during the summer—West Maui can be overly crowded. Although the County of Maui has successfully widened the two-lane road that connects Lahaina and Kā'anapali, the stop-and-go traffic during rush hour reminds some visitors of what they left at home. It's not that residents aren't trying to do something about it—the Kapalua-West Maui Airport, with its free shuttle to and from Kā'anapali, has alleviated some of the heavy traffic between Kahului and Lahaina.

The explosion of visitors seeking out the Valley Isle has also created a large number of businesses looking to make a fast buck from the high-spending vacationers. Lahaina could easily be called the T-shirt capital of the Pacific (in close competition with Waikīkī), and the island has nearly as many art galleries and cruise-boat companies as T-shirts. As in other popular travel destinations, the opportunity to make money from tourists has produced its fair share of schlock.

But then consider Maui's natural resources. Geologists claim that Maui was created between 1 and 2 million years ago by the eruption of two volcanoes, Pu'u kukui and Haleakalā, the former extinct and the latter now dormant; a low central isthmus formed between them and joined them into West and East Maui. The resulting depression between the two is what gives Maui its nickname, the Valley Isle. West Maui's 5,788-foot Pu'u kukui was the first volcano to form, a distinction that gives the area's mountainous topography a more weathered look. Rainbows seem to grow wild over this terrain as gentle mists move quietly from one end of the long mountain chain to the other. Sugarcane gives the rocky region its life, with its green stalks moving in the trade winds born near the summit.

The Valley Isle's second volcano is the 10,023-foot Haleakalā, a mountain so enormous that its lava filled in the gap between the two volcanoes. You can't miss Haleakalā, whose name means House of the Sun, a spectacle that rises to the east, often hiding in the clouds that cover its peak. To Hawaiians, Haleakalā is holy, and it's easy to see why. It's a mammoth mountain, and if you hike its slopes or peer into one of its craters, you'll witness an impressive variety of nature: desertlike terrain butted up against tropical forests; dew-dripping ferns a few steps from the surface of the moon; spiked, alien plants poking their heads out of the soil right near the most elegant and fragrant flowers.

In fact, the island's volcanic history gives Maui much of its beauty. Rich red soil lines the roads around the island—*becoming* the roads in some parts. That same earth has provided fertile sowing grounds for the sugarcane that has for years covered the island's hills. As the deep blue of ocean and sky mingle with the red and green of Maui's land, it looks as if an artist has been busy painting the scenery. Indeed, visual artists love Maui. Maybe it's the natural inspiration; maybe it's the slower pace, so conducive to creativity.

Farmers also appreciate the Valley Isle. On the slopes of Haleakalā, the volcanic miracle has wrought agricultural wonders, luring those with a penchant for peat moss to plant and watch the lush results. Sweetly scented flowers bloom large and healthy, destined to adorn a happy brow or become a lovely lei. Grapes cultivated on Haleakalā's slopes ripen evenly and deliciously, and are then pressed for wine and champagne. Horses graze languidly on rolling meadows of the best Upcountry grasses, while jacaranda trees dot the hillsides with spurts of luscious lavender. On the eastern slopes of the volcano, lavish rains turn the soil into a jungle.

Maui had no indigenous plants or animals because of its volcanic origins. Birds brought some of the life that would inhabit Maui, as did the waves that washed upon its newly formed shores. Then in about AD 800, Polynesians began to arrive on Maui's shores. They had journeyed from the Marquesas and Society Islands, braving rough waters in their canoes as they navigated by the stars across thousands of miles. These first residents brought animals, such as pigs and chickens, as well as plants, such as breadfruit, yams, coconuts, and bananas.

Not until 1778, when Captain James Cook made his second voyage to the Hawaiian Islands, did the Mauians receive their first visitor. Months earlier, Cook had landed on Kaua'i and Ni'ihau; he had made friends with the Polynesians and left behind bartered goods, as well as dread white man's diseases. When he got to Maui, Cook was surprised to find that the venereal disease running rampant on his ships had preceded him there. Shortly after, Cook pushed on to the Big Island.

Before leaving, however, Cook anchored his ship off the northeast coast of Maui while he hosted Kalani'ōpu'u, the aging chief of the Big Island, who spent a night on the Englishman's HMS *Resolution.* At the time, the Hawaiian Islands were rife with divided kingdoms waging war one against another, and the elderly Kalani'ōpu'u was certainly plotting against Maui's principal chief, Kahekili. How much Cook figured into these strategy sessions is unknown, but the records show that Kalani'ōpu'u was accompanied by his young warrior nephew, Kamehameha.

PERHAPS IT WAS the experience off Maui's coast that eventually fired Kamehameha's ambition to rule more than a tiny section of one island. Kamehameha witnessed that Cook was master of his destiny, and the callow youth, no doubt, wanted the same thing. Years of battle followed as the young chief fought for the right to dominate the Islands. Finally, in 1794, Kamehameha defeated Maui's chief, thereby gaining the Valley Isle as well as its smaller neighboring islands of Moloka'i and Lāna'i. The following year he conquered the Big Island and O'ahu. Kaua'i wouldn't knuckle under, but in 1810 it was won over diplomatically. Kamehameha had earned the right to be king of all the islands. He was called Kamehameha I, or Kamehameha the Great, and the kingdom's headquarters were in Lahaina, on Maui. To this day, you can visit the site of the king's Lahaina palace between the Pioneer Inn and the ocean. The palace itself is long gone, however.

The great king had 21 wives during his lifetime, and the two most notable hailed from Maui. Queen Keōpūolani was Kamehameha's "sacred" wife, the daughter of a traditional brother-sister union that was considered so powerful that Keōpūolani was assured of producing honorable heirs for her husband. Historians believe she was the first Christian convert; she was extremely supportive of the missionaries who came to Hawai'i. Preceded in death by her royal spouse, Queen Keōpūolani is buried in the Waine'e/Waiola Cemetery (on Waine'e Street in Lahaina), next to her second husband, Hawaiian chief Hoapili, who was governor of Maui.

Kamehameha's favorite wife, Ka'ahumanu, also came from Maui. She was tall, statuesque, and politically astute. In fact, after her husband's death in 1819, Queen Ka'ahumanu named herself Hawai'i's first regent when Keōpūolani's eldest son, Liholiho, took the throne; she even continued that role when Liholiho's brother Kau'ikea'ōuli succeeded him. Ka'ahumanu was so powerful that she was instrumental in banning the *kapu* system, the Hawaiian set of rules and standards that had been in force for generations. It was she who insisted that the king move from the Brick Palace in Lahaina to another home in Honolulu.

Not long after Captain Cook landed on Maui, others arrived to take up residence. Missionaries who came from the eastern United States thought Mauians were heathens who needed to be saved, and they diligently tried to convert the residents. The missionaries' job was made even more challenging by the almost simultaneous arrival of whalers from New England. Soon Lahaina developed into the area's most important whaling port, and with the new industry came a lusty lifestyle that included more diseases, wild revelry, and additional motivation for the missionaries to continue their quest.

In 1840 Kau'ikea'ōuli as King Kamehameha III, moved his monarchic capital to Honolulu, but Lahaina continued to be an important city for trade, education, and hearty living. Many of the buildings used during this era still exist in Lahaina and are open to visitors. The Spring House, now located in the Wharf Shopping Center on Front Street, once protected a freshwater source for the missionaries, while the Seamen's Hospital, also on Front Street, was converted by the U.S. government from a royal party residence to a medical facility for sailors.

Along with missionaries and whalers, other new settlers began to come to Maui. The most notable arrivals were businessmen, who viewed the Islands as a place to buy cheap land—or, better yet, to get it for free by befriending a member of the royal family. To the most astute entrepreneurs, sugar, which grew wild on Maui, looked like a good bet for cultivation, and when the Civil War knocked out sugar supplies in the South, the Hawaiian plantations boomed. By the late 1800s,

"King Sugar" had become the new ruler in the Islands.

SOME OF THE MOST prominent leaders in the sugar industry were the grown children of missionaries. On Maui two of the most important businessmen were Samuel Alexander and Henry Baldwin, who joined forces in a sugar dynasty eventually called Alexander & Baldwin. A&B, as it came to be known, was a charter member of Hawai'i's Big Five—the five giant corporations that controlled the Islands economically and politically well into the 20th century. Although the power and influence of the Big Five have waned dramatically in the past few years with the increase of takeovers and buyouts, Alexander & Baldwin remains both Maui's largest private landholder and its largest private employer. The company developed the sunny Wailea Resort and owned it until 1990, as well as all of the island's sugar operations and macadamia-nut farms.

It wasn't until the early 1960s—only a few years after Hawai'i became a state in 1959—that tourism took root on Maui in a major way. That was when Amfac Inc., the largest of the Big Five, opened its major resort destination in West Maui, calling it Kā'anapali. It soon became Hawai'i's second most popular resort area after Waikīkī and was the first to have a master plan. The Royal Lahaina, which opened in 1962, was the first lodging to break ground in the Kā'anapali Resort, which now contains six deluxe hotels and at least a dozen condominiums.

North of Kā'anapali, Maui Land & Pineapple entered into the tourism arena in the mid-1970s when it broke ground for the Kapalua Resort with its 194-room Kapalua Bay Hotel, joined in 1992 by the Ritz-Carlton's 550-room showplace. (Incidentally, Maui Land & Pineapple, like Alexander & Baldwin, is still partly owned by missionaries' descendants.) In Wailea on Maui's south shore Alexander & Baldwin, in partnership with the mainland-based Northwestern Mutual Life Insurance, introduced its Wailea Resort in 1975. During the following decade, the companies put up two hotels and three condominium projects. Four more hotels and six condos have since opened at the resort.

Tourism now accounts for about half of all jobs on the Valley Isle. Beginning in the mid-1800s, the dwindling indigenous population—those Hawaiians whose descendants came from the Marquesas and the Society Islands—were reinforced by labor from Japan, China, Portugal, and the Philippines, so that today's Maui has become a heady stew of ethnicity and culture.

The Valley Isle is full of people ready to share the friendly aloha spirit. If you take the drive to Hāna, around dozens of hairpin curves, across bridges, and past waterfalls, you'll find plenty of folk who still speak the Hawaiian language. Or if you relax on the wharf in historic Lahaina, you can watch transplanted Californians have a great time surfing; most of them find West Maui the best place in the world for working and living. All these residents love their island and will gladly help you have a good time.

By all means, make the effort to meet some locals. Although a fantastic time can be had simply by relaxing on the silky-soft, white-sand beaches, the wonder of Maui is that much, much more awaits your discovery. Don't be surprised if quite a few of your fantasies are actually fulfilled. The Valley Isle hates to let anyone down.

WHAT'S WHERE

West Maui

The extinct volcano Puʻu kukui formed Maui's smaller, western land mass; its balmy leeward shore attracted Kamehameha I, who chose Lahaina for the first capital of his kingdom after he united the Hawaiian Islands. Later years brought missionaries, whalers, and sugar plantations to West Maui, making it an area rich in history. Two of the island's premier resorts, Kāʻanapali and Kapalua, line the coast north of Lahaina.

Central Maui

The isthmus connecting West Maui and East Maui is home to Kahului, Maui's deep-water port, and Wailuku, the county seat. Some historic churches and homes, some of them housing museums, can be found here, as well as the island's largest shopping mall, Kaʻahumanu Center, just minutes from the main airport in Kahului.

Haleakalā and Upcountry

The dormant Haleakalā volcano beckons the eye from every place on Maui. Not surprisingly, the summit and its surrounding crater have views unlike any others on earth. Ranches, nurseries, farms, and a winery on the mountain's fertile slopes give the region an agricultural flavor, neatly encapsulated in the cowboy town of Makawao.

The Road to Hāna

One of the most famous drives in the world, the twisting, turning 55-mile road from Kahului to the tiny eastern shore town of Hāna delights the senses with photoworthy waterfalls and bridges, ginger- and plumeria-scented mists, and fascinating birdsongs. Turn off the radio and the air-conditioner, open the windows, drive slowly, and stop often to take it all in.

Wailea and Kīhei

Stretching along the western shore of East Maui are the family-friendly condos of Kīhei and, farther south, the grande luxe hotels and condos of Wailea, Maui's newest major resort. In addition to five perfect crescent beaches, Wailea has grass- and hard-surface tennis courts, and three (count 'em) first-class golf courses.

PLEASURES AND PASTIMES

Beaches

Enjoy the west coast's family-friendly playgrounds, watch daredevil surfers on the north shore, or contemplate the natural beauty of the sands around Hāna. The choice is yours, but you can't go home and tell your friends you went to Maui and never visited a beach. For swimming, sunning, and people-watching, as well as convenient parking and amenities, the resort beaches of Wailea and Kāʻanapali can't be beat.

Hawaiian Culture and History

It would be a shame to leave Maui without making the acquaintance of at least some of the island's heritage. Take time to visit the Hāna Cultural Center if you drive to the eastern shore town. Tour the Sugar Museum and the Bailey House near Wailuku. Chat with the well-informed guides at the Baldwin Home in Lahaina. You may even want to take one of the programs more and more hotels are offering that focus on Hawaiian culture, including lessons in lei-making, hula, Hawaiian language or music. They're fun, and they'll enrich your enjoyment of what you see and hear as you travel around Maui.

Hiking

Hiking on Maui can be an easy stroll through a botanical garden, a walk along paved and guard-railed paths in 'Īao Valley State Park, or a pack trip into Haleakalā Crater. There's something to suit nearly every age and inclination, from the rugged outdoors-lover to the urbanite who hails cabs for exercise.

Water Sports

Surfing, snorkeling, scuba-diving, sailing, and fishing can be enjoyed year-round on Maui, and lessons are available for almost any water sport you'd like to try. Experienced divers will want to take one of the many snorkel or scuba cruises to the most exotic and challenging offshore dive sites, but Maui's shores offer plenty of colorful and unusual sea-life specimens to delight the underwater eye. If you've never surfed but have always wanted to try, the gentle waters of Lahaina Harbor are a great place to learn, and, yes, you can learn in a single half-day lesson.

NEW AND NOTEWORTHY

Gradually rising visitor counts on Maui have sparked renovations, expansions, and improvements in many hotels and restaurants, as well as some entirely new eateries and attractions. For would-be visitors, the best advice is: Reserve early for any hotel, restaurant, tour, or event that is on your can't-miss list—especially if the event will bring top-ranked college basketball teams to the island at a popular holiday travel time, as the late-November **Maui Invitational Tournament** does.

Among the hotels undergoing renovation, only one, the **Sheraton Maui** in Kā'anapali, closed for its make over. Its all-new incarnation is scheduled to reopen in 1997. And, in addition to its renovation, the **Maui Marriott** now offers the services of licensed massage therapists under a tent on the beach—is that a hedonist's dream or what?

New owners may be waiting in the wings for the **Kapalua Bay Hotel** and Lahaina's lovely **Plantation Inn,** both of which filed for reorganization under Chapter 11 of the bankruptcy laws in 1995. Gerard Reversade, chef and owner of **Gerard's** restaurant on the Plantation's ground floor, says he'll remain at the site, under a long-term lease.

The Kea Lani's authentic Italian bistro, **Caffe Ciao,** keeps growing and winning fans of its wood-fired pizza-oven creations. Boutique wines, from small Italian vineyards, have pointed the way to the next expansion: a poolside, ocean-view wine bar. Instead of trying to expand their renowned Hāli'imaile General Store, Beverly and Joe Gannon opened a second place, **Joe's Bar & Grill,** atop the Wailea Tennis Center's clubhouse, overlooking the center's stadium court.

There's beer on the menu at two other new Maui restaurants. Imported bottle beers—more than 100 of them—are the stars at Pā'ia's **Wunderbar Cafe,** whose eclectic menu includes German specialties and just about anything else that goes well with a brew. Over at the spectacularly renovated Ka'ahumanu Center in Kahului, **Sharktooth Brewery Steakhouse** offers its own made-right-here beer.

Beer-lover or not, you'll want to be stone sober for **Cruiser Bob**'s newest bicycling adventures. The imaginative inventor of the Haleakalā Downhill decided to begin offering new tours, new vistas, and new challenges for cyclists who have already "done the downhill."

FODOR'S CHOICE

No two people will agree on what makes a perfect vacation, but it's fun and helpful to know what others think. We hope you'll have a chance to experience some of Fodor's Choices yourself while visiting Maui. For more information about each entry, refer to the appropriate chapters in this guidebook.

Beaches

★**Hāna Beach.** Though it's not easy to get to, if you want an idea of what Old Hawai'i was like, head for Hāna Beach, or stay at the Hotel Hāna-Maui, and ride the free shuttle.

★**Ho'okipa Beach.** This is the place to watch world-class windsurfing, but not the place to try to learn the sport yourself.

★**Kapalua Beach.** This stretch of resort sand is so well-kept, you almost think the sand won't get into your suit here.

★**Little Mākena Beach.** Although nude sunbathing is illegal on Maui, Little Mākena is best-known for attracting people in search of that all-over tan.

Drives

★**Coming down Mt. Haleakalā.** We recommend that you try to drive to Haleakalā's summit without stopping, to arrive as early as possible, but take your time coming down; the countryside is lovely, and the views are amazing.

★**From Lahaina to Mā'alaea.** The road along the northwest shore offers plenty of good stopping places from which to watch for whales wintering off Maui's coast.

★**The road to Hāna.** This trip is all about the drive, not the destination. If you're pressed for time and can't make it all the way to Hana, at least try and make it halfway. This drive—crossing bridges and passing waterfalls—is one you won't forget, especially if you bring your camera along.

Hotels

★**Four Seasons Resort.** A spectacular setting and impeccable service, plus the beaches, golf, and tennis of Wailea, make this one of Hawai'i's top-rated hotels. *$$$$*

★**Hotel Hāna-Maui.** The fabled eastern shore hideaway of the rich and famous is about as far from the madding crowd as you can get on Maui. *$$$$*

★**Kea Lani Hotel Suites & Villas.** A family-friendly resort with peaceful enclaves for the grown-ups and three terrific restaurants, this property offers celebrities privacy right in Wailea. *$$$$*

★**Kula Lodge.** This Upcountry chalet is completely un-tropical, but cozy and romantic, and a great place to start a trip up Haleakalā. *$$–$$$*

★**Lahaina Hotel.** This tiny (12 rooms), antiques-filled gem of a hotel is smack-dab in the heart of Lahaina. *$$*

Restaurants

★**Raffles.** The pride and joy of the Stouffer Renaissance Hotel celebrates the Islands' Asian connections with Pacific Rim cuisine and stunning artifacts. *$$$$*

★**David Paul's Lahaina Grill.** An innovative menu that changes seasonally, late-afternoon wine tastings, and a loyal clientele from the nearby art galleries keep this popular place growing. *$$$*

★**Gerard's.** Chef-owner Gerard Reversade serves French cuisine at this celebrity favorite; the menu changes daily according to the freshest foods available. *$$$*

★**Hāli'imaile General Store.** This out-of-the-way, one-time camp store just can't stop drawing crowds, and rave reviews, for chef-owner Beverly Gannon's great food. *$$$*

★**Caffe Ciao.** With a wood-fired pizza oven and a wine bar, this authentic Italian bistro overlooks the pool and the ocean at the Kea Lani Hotel in Wailea. *$$*

Sights

★**Haleakalā.** You couldn't miss seeing it if you tried, but take the drive to see it up close.

★**Ho'okipa Beach.** The north shore windsurfers here will earn your respect.

★**'Īao Needle.** You don't have to be a nature-lover to find this rock formation, and the surrounding park, awe inspiring.

★**Lahaina Historic District.** The town is funky and fun, as painless an education as you'll find.

★**Sunsets.** Of course.

FESTIVALS AND SEASONAL EVENTS

DEC.➤ **Bodhi Day.** The traditional Buddhist Day of Enlightenment is celebrated at temples throughout the island. Visitors are welcome at the services. **Christmas.** The hotels outdo one another in extravagant exhibits and events, such as Santa arriving by outrigger canoe.

FEB.–MAR.➤ **Cherry Blossom Festival.** This popular celebration of all things Japanese includes a run, cultural displays, cooking demonstrations, music, and the inevitable queen pageant and coronation ball.

MAR.➤ **Prince Kūhiō Day.** The state holiday on the 26th honors Prince Jonah Kūhiō Kalanianaʻole, a man who might have been a king if Hawaiʻi had not been granted statehood. Instead the man became a respected Territorial representative to the U.S. Congress.

APR.➤ **Art Maui.** The best of a wide variety of media is shown at this prestigious annual event. **Buddha Day.** Flower pageants are staged at temples to celebrate the birth of the Buddha.

MAY➤ **Lei Day.** The annual flower-filled celebration on the first day of May includes music, hula, food, as well as lots of flower garlands on exhibit and for sale, some of them exquisite masterpieces. **Barrio Festival.** This cultural celebration is organized by the Binha Filipino Community. **Junior World Wave Sailing Championships.** Competitors under age 18 come from 15 countries to race the challenging surf at Hoʻokipa Beach.

JUNE➤ **King Kamehameha Day.** Kamehameha united all the islands became Hawaiʻi's first king (making Hawaiʻi the only state to have a royal background). Festivities on June 12 include parades and fairs.

JULY➤ **Kapalua Wine and Food Symposium.** Wine and food experts and enthusiasts gather for formal tastings, panel discussions, receptions and gourmet diners at Kapalua Bay Resort. **Makawao Statewide Rodeo.** On July 4 an old-time Upcountry rodeo is held at the Oskie Rice Arena; the festivities include the annual Makawao Rodeo Parade. **Independence Day.** The national holiday is celebrated with a tropical touch, including fairs, parades, and, of course, fireworks. Special events include the Great Kālua Pig Cook-Off in Maui, with a $1,000 cash prize for the best pig roaster in the state, a pig parade, and good eating.

JULY–AUG.➤ **Bon Odori Season.** Buddhist temples invite everyone to festivals that honor ancestors and feature Japanese Bon dancing.

AUG.➤ **Admission Day.** This local holiday, which is observed on the nearest Friday to the 18th to guarantee a three-day weekend, recognizes Hawaiʻi's statehood.

SEPT.➤ **Taste of Lahaina.** Maui's best chefs compete for top cooking honors, and samples of their entries are sold at a lively open-air party featuring live entertainment. **Maui Writers Conference.** Best-selling authors and powerhouse agents and publishers offer advice—and a few contracts—to aspiring authors and screenwriters at this Labor Day Weekend gathering.

SEPT.–OCT.➤ **Aloha Week Festival.** This traditional celebration, started in 1946, preserves Hawaiian native culture. Crafts, music, dance, pageantry, street parties, and canoe races highlight the festival.

NOV.➤ **Hawaiʻi International Film Festival.** The cinematic feast travels from island to island, showcasing films from the United States, Asia, and the Pacific. **Maui Invitational NCAA Basketball Tournament.** The collegiate competition brings top-ranked Mainland teams to the Lahaina Civic Center. **Kapalua International Champi-** **onship Golf.** Top pro golfers meet at the Kapalua resort for the "Super Bowl" of golf with a purse of over $600,000.

Nā Mele O Maui Festival. Hawaiian arts, crafts, dances, music, and a lūʻau are all part of this cultural event.

2 Exploring Maui

The Valley Isle, as Maui is fondly called, has made an international name for itself with its tropical allure, heady nightlife, and miles and miles of beaches. In east Maui, ferns take over forests, waterfalls cascade down crags, and moss becomes the land's lush carpeting. The rich, fertile slopes of Haleakalā, a dormant volcano in the middle of the island, produce much of Hawai'i's produce, as well as its only wine-producing grapes. In West Maui, "the Golf Coast," beaches are lined with condos, restaurants, and resorts.

YOU'LL FIND PLENTY TO SEE AND DO besides spending time on the beach. To help you organize your time, this guide divides the island into four tours—West Maui, Central Maui, Haleakalā and Upcountry, and the Road to Hāna (East Maui). Each tour lasts from a half day to a full day, depending on how long you spend at each stop. All tours require a car, but they include opportunities for walking.

In getting yourself oriented, first look at a map of Maui. You will notice two distinct circular landmasses, each volcanic in origin, which means that mountains dominate both centers. The smaller lump of land, on the western part of the island, is home to 5,788-foot Pu'u Kukui and the West Maui Mountains, some of whose reaches now grow sugar and pineapple. Occasionally, hardy souls try to hike these mountains, but there are no marked trails, and the views aren't that spectacular. Along the western shore of this landmass is the area known as West Maui, where most of the island's visitor industry has established itself. West Maui is sunny and warm year-round.

The larger landmass of the eastern portion of Maui was created by Haleakalā, the mist-covered peak in the center. One of the best-known mountains in the world, Haleakalā is popular with hikers and sightseers. This larger region of the island is called East Maui, with the areas of Wailea, Kīhei, and Mākena flanking its western shore; Hāna and its wilder environs—past where the pavement stops—sit on the eastern seaboard.

Between the two mountain areas is Central Maui, which was once the ocean until Haleakalā spewed lava into the channel that separated East from West. Central Maui is the location of the county seat of Wailuku, from which the islands of Maui, Lāna'i, Moloka'i, and Kaho'olawe are governed. Most of the island's commerce and industry is based in Central Maui; a majority of Maui's businesspeople work in Kahului and Wailuku.

WEST MAUI

West Maui, anchored by the amusing old whaling town of Lahaina, was the focus of development when Maui set out to become a premier tourist destination. The condo-filled beach towns of Nāpili, Kahana, and Honokōwai are arrayed between the stunning resorts of Kapalua and Kā'anapali, north of Lahaina.

A Good Tour
Numbers in the text correspond to numbers in the margin and on the Exploring Maui and Lahaina maps.

Begin this tour in **Kapalua** ①. If you're not staying at the Kapalua Bay Hotel, have a look around this renowned resort—you may want to have a meal or snack here before you begin the day's exploring. From Kapalua, drive north on the Honoapi'ilani Highway (Highway 30). In less than a mile the road becomes rougher. It was never a good road, and storms now and then make it partly impassable. However, you'll discover some gorgeous photo opportunities along the way, and if you drive nearly as far as you can on the "highway," you'll come to **Kahakuloa** ②. From here, turn around and go back in the direction from which you came—south toward Kā'anapali and Lahaina, past Kapalua and the beach towns of Nāpili, Kahana, and Honokōwai; if you wish to explore these towns, get off the Upper Honoapi'ilani Highway and drive closer to the

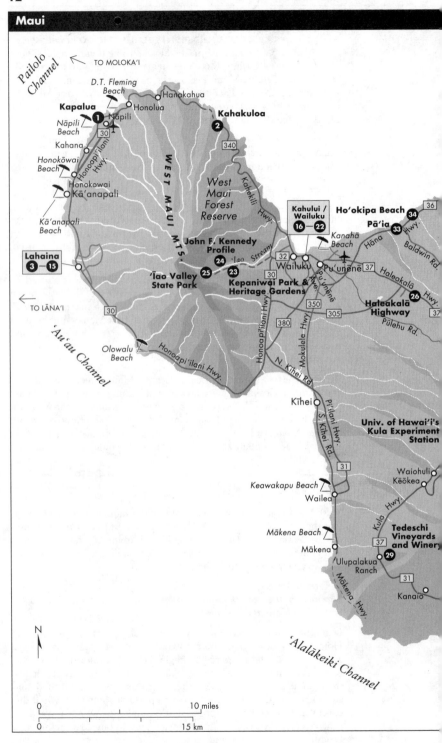

Pailolo Channel

← TO MOLOKAʻI

D.T. Fleming Beach

Kapalua ❶

Hanokahua

Honolua

Nāpili

Nāpili Beach

30

Kahakuloa ❷

Kahana

Honokōwai Beach

Honokowai

Kāʻanapali

340

WEST MAUI MTS

West Maui Forest Reserve

Kahekili Hwy.

Kahului / Wailuku ⓰ — ㉒

Hoʻokipa Beach ㉞ 36

Pāʻia ㉝ *Hāna Hwy.*

Kanahā Beach

Baldwin Rd.

John F. Kennedy Profile ㉔ ʻIao *Stream*

Kāʻanapali Beach

32

Wailuku

Puʻunēnē 37

Haleakalā Hwy.

Lahaina ❸ — ⓯

ʻĪao Valley State Park ㉕ ㉓

Kepaniwai Park & Heritage Gardens

30

Puʻunēnē

Haleakalā Highway ㉖

37

← TO LĀNAʻI

Honoapiʻilani Hwy.

350

305

Pūlehu Rd.

ʻAuʻau Channel

Olowalu Beach

Honoapiʻilani Hwy.

380

Mokulele Hwy.

N. Kīhei Rd.

Kīhei

Piʻilani Hwy.

S. Kīhei Rd.

Univ. of Hawaiʻi's Kula Experiment Station

31

Waiohuli

Keōkea

Keawakapu Beach

Wailea

Kula Hwy.

Mākena Beach

Mākena

Tedeschi Vineyards and Winery

37 ㉙

ʻUlupalakua Ranch

31

Mākena Hwy.

Kanaio

N

0   10 miles

0   15 km

ʻAlalākeiki Channel

PACIFIC OCEAN

'Ulumalu

Rd.

Huelo **35**

36 Kailua

365

360

Puahokamoa
Stream

Kaumahina State
Wayside Park

38

37

390

Kokomo

Honomanū
Valley

39

40 Ke'anae Arboretum

32 Makawao

Wailua

Ke'anae Overlook

41

42 Wailua Lookout

31 Pukalani

377

43

44 Nāhiku

Waikāne
Falls

Haleakalā
Crater Rd.

Kōolau
Forest
Reserve

Pi'ina'au Stream

360

Hāna Hwy.

Wai'ānapanapa
State Park

Hāna
Gardenland

45

46

Park
Headquarters/
Visitor Center

37

378

Leleiwi
Overlook

Halemau'u Trail

Helani Gardens **47**

Hotel Hāna-Maui

49

Hāna Forest Reserve

30

28

Kula Botanical
Gardens

Kalahaku
Overlook

27 Haleakalā
National Park

48 Hāna

Haleakalā

Haleakalā Visitor
Center

Hāmoa

Pu'u 'Ula'ula
Overlook

Kahikinui
Forest Reserve

Kaupō
Trail

Pi'ilani Hwy.

Mū'olea

50 'Ohe'o Gulch

Kīpahulu

31

51 Grave of
Charles Lindbergh

Pi'ilani Hwy.

Kaupō

31

'Alenuihāhā Channel

TO HAWAI'I

water. Two Kā'anapali hotels worth checking out for their beautiful grounds are the Hyatt Regency Maui and the Westin Maui. To reach them, take the third Kā'anapali exit from Honoapi'ilani Highway (the one closest to Lahaina), then turn left on Kā'anapali Parkway. Next, head for **Lahaina** ③. Drive south on Honoapi'ilani Highway, and turn right on Kē Nui Street, then left on Front Street.

Lahaina is best explored on foot, so use the drive along Front Street to get oriented, then park near **505 Front Street** ④ at the southern end of the town's historic and colorful commercial area. It's a short stroll from here to the **Banyan Tree** ⑤, one of the town's best-known landmarks, and next to it is the old **Court House** ⑥ and prison, which is now art galleries. About a half block northwest is the site of Kamehameha's **Brick Palace** ⑦. Anchored at the dock nearby is the **Brig Carthaginian II** ⑧, which is open to visitors. **Pioneer Inn** ⑨ across the street is a good place for an afternoon stop. If you walk from the *Carthaginian II* to the corner of Front and Dickenson streets, you'll find the **Baldwin Home** ⑩ and next door to it, the Master's Reading Room. Wander north or south on Front Street to explore Lahaina's commercial side. At the Wharf Cinema Center, you can see the **Spring House** ⑪ built over a freshwater spring. If you continue north on Front Street, you'll come to **Wo Hing Society** ⑫; walk another block north and you'll find the **Seamen's Hospital** ⑬. If you're finished exploring before dusk with a hankering for another stop or two, walk south down Front Street, make a left onto Dickenson Street, then make a right onto Waine'e Street. Walking south down Waine'e Street will bring you first to **Hale Pa'ahao/Old Lahaina Prison** ⑭, then, one block further south, to the **Waiola Church** ⑮ and Cemetery.

TIMING

You can easily spend a full day checking out the coast's beaches, towns, and resorts. In Lahaina, you can walk the length of Front Street in under 30 minutes if you don't stop along the way; however, it's hard not to be intrigued by the town's colorful shops and historic sites—realistically you'll need at least half a day. If you arrange to spend Friday afternoon exploring Front Street, you can dine in town and hang around for Art Night. The Banyan Tree is a terrific spot to be when the sun sets—mynah birds settle in here for a screeching symphony, which can be an event in itself.

Sights to See

Numbers in the margin correspond to points of interest on the Exploring Maui and Lahaina maps.

★ ⑩ **Baldwin Home.** An early missionary to Lahaina, Ephraim Spaulding, built this plastered and whitewashed coral stone house in 1834–35; in 1836, Dr. Dwight Baldwin—also a missionary—moved in with his family. The house is now run by the Lahaina Restoration Foundation and has been restored and furnished in a decor that reflects the missionary period. You can view the dining room, the living room with the family's grand piano, and Dr. Baldwin's dispensary, including his Hawaiian medical license. ⊠ *696 Front St., Lahaina,* ☎ *808/661–3262.* ☜ *$2.* ⊙ *Daily 9–4:30.*

⑤ **Banyan Tree.** Planted in 1873, this tree is the largest of its kind in the 50th state. The massive tree provides a welcome retreat for the weary who come to sit under its awesome branches; it's also a good meeting place if your group splits up. ⊠ *Front St., between Hotel and Canal Sts., Lahaina.*

⑦ **Brick Palace site.** All that's left of the palace built by King Kamehameha I is a space with several holes sectioned off in front of the Pioneer Inn.

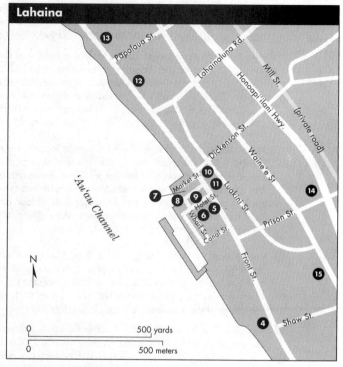

Lahaina

Hawaiʻi's first king lived only one year in the palace because his favorite wife, Kaʻahumanu, refused to stay there. After 70 years, it collapsed. ⊠ *Ocean end of Market St., Lahaina.*

★ **8** **Brig *Carthaginian II*.** This vessel's sailing days are over, but it makes an interesting museum. It was built in Germany in the 1920s and is a replica of the type of ship that brought the New England missionaries around the Horn of South America to Hawaiʻi in the early 1800s. The *Carthaginian II* is the only authentically restored square-rigged brig in the world. ⊠ *At dock opposite north end of Wharf St., Lahaina,* ☎ *808/661–3262.* ⊡ *$3.* ⊙ *Daily 9–4:30.*

6 **Court House.** This old civic building now houses two art galleries—one upstairs and one in what was an old prison in the basement. The Court House, built in 1857 and rebuilt in 1925, retains some of the character of its original purposes, including white-painted iron cell gates downstairs. ⊠ *649 Wharf St., Lahaina,* ☎ *808/661–0111.* ⊡ *Free.* ⊙ *Daily 10–4.*

4 **505 Front Street.** Quaint New England–style architecture characterizes this mall, which houses small shops and restaurants connected by a wooden sidewalk. It isn't as crowded as some other areas in Lahaina, probably because between here and the nearby Banyan Tree, the town turns into a sleepy residential neighborhood and some people walking from the more bustling center of Front Street give up before they reach the mall. Still, the casual eateries lure their share of fun-lovers. ⊠ *At southern end of Front St., near Shaw St., Lahaina,* ☎ *808/667–2514.* ⊙ *Times vary. Most shops 9–6.*

★ **14** **Hale Paʻahao/Old Lahaina Prison.** Here you can see the original coral-block walls that were once the jail for rowdy sailors and whalers. The prison was built between 1852 and 1854 by the prisoners themselves using blocks from the walls of an old fort, which Hale Pa'ahao replaced. The small brown building looks like a chapel. ⊠ *Prison Rd., just off Wainee St., Lahaina,* ☎ *808/661–3262.* ⊠ *Free.* ☉ *Daily 9–5.*

Hale Pa'i/Old Print Shop. This print house published the first Hawaiian-language newspaper. Founded by missionaries in 1837, it now houses the Lahaina Restoration Foundation's extensive archival collection and exhibits depicting Maui's early whaling and missionary days. It's on the grounds of Lahainaluna School. ⊠ *At mountain end of Lahainaluna Rd., Lahaina,* ☎ *808/661–3262.* ⊠ *Free.* ☉ *Mon.–Fri. 10–4.*

OFF THE
BEATEN PATH

JODO MISSION – The largest Buddha outside Japan is the centerpiece of Lahaina's Jodo Mission Cultural Park. The Buddha was placed here to commemorate the arrival of the first Japanese immigrants in 1868. You'll find graveyards, a shrine, a crematorium, and an extensive outdoor meeting area at this park which sits on a parcel of land called Pu'unoa Point. The park is just off Front Street near Māla Wharf. ⊠ *12 Ala Moana, Lahaina,* ☎ *808/661-4304.* ⊠ *Free.*

❷ **Kahakuloa.** This is the wild side of West Maui; true adventurers will find some good hiking trails and terrific snorkeling and swimming. One of the oldest towns on Maui, this tiny fishing village seems lost in time. Many remote villages similar to Kahakuloa used to be tucked away in the valleys of the surrounding area. ⊠ *North end of Honoapi'ilani Hwy.*

❶ **Kapalua.** The Maui Land & Pineapple Company started this resort on the gorgeous white-sand Kapalua Beach in the 1970s. It has two hotels, including the fabulous Kapalua Bay Hotel, some condos, golf courses, and excellent swimming and snorkeling. If you enjoy looking at fancy hotels, the Kapalua Bay Hotel, with its excellent shopping enclave, is worth a look.

★ ❸ **Lahaina.** This little whaling town has a notorious past; there are stories of lusty whalers who met head-on with missionaries bent on saving souls. Both groups journeyed to Lahaina from New England in the early 1800s. At first, Lahaina might look touristy, but there's a lot that's genuine here. Most of the old buildings in Lahaina date from the time it was Hawai'i's capital in the 1800s. Most have been renovated and much of the town has been designated a National Historic Landmark; further restrictions have been imposed on all new buildings, which must resemble structures built before 1920. ⊠ *Off Honoapi'ilani Hwy., about 3 mi south of Kā'anapali.*

NEED A
BREAK?
❾

Both locals and tourists hang out at the **Pioneer Inn** (⊠ 658 Wharf St., Lahaina, ☎ 808/661-3636) in the afternoon. It's a good place to have a drink while taking in the local scene. Built in 1920, the inn was beautifully restored in 1995. Photographs of whaling expeditions and antique whaling equipment recall Lahaina's 19th-century whaling days.

WHALE-WATCHING

THE HUMPBACK WHALES' attraction to Maui is legendary. More than half the North Pacific's humpback population winters in Hawai'i, as they've been doing for years. At one time, thousands of the huge mammals existed, but the world population has dwindled to about 1,500. In 1966 they were put on the endangered-species list, which restricts boats and airplanes from getting too close.

Experts believe the humpbacks keep returning to Hawaiian waters because of the warmth. Winter is calving time for the behemoths, and the whale babies, born with little blubber, probably couldn't survive in the frigid Alaskan waters. No one has ever seen a whale give birth, but the experts studying whales off Maui know that calving is their main winter activity, since the one- and two-ton babies suddenly appear while the whales are in residence.

Whale-watching is not your average spectator sport. Whales are unpredictable, so you must be prepared to wait and watch patiently for a sign of this magnificent animal. During the right time of year on Maui—between November and April—you can see whales breaching and blowing just offshore. Quite a few operations run whale-watching excursions off the coast of Maui, with many boats departing from Lahaina's wharf each day. This allows you to get a closer view; it gives the whale a better vantage point, too. Sometimes, in fact, a curious whale can get so close that it makes the passengers downright nervous. **Pacific Whale Foundation** (⊠ Keālia Beach Plaza, Kīhei 96753, ☎ 808/879–8811) pioneered whale-watching back in 1979 and now runs two boats.

Also offering whale-watching in season are: **Ocean Activities Center** (⊠ 1847 S. Kīhei Rd., Suite 203, Kīhei 96753, ☎ 808/879–4485), **Leilani Cruises** (⊠ 113 Prison St., Lahaina 96761, ☎ 808/661–8397), and **Sentinel Yachts** (⊠ Box 1022, Lahaina 96767, ☎ 808/661–8110). Ticket prices average about $35 adults, $18 children.

🐚 **Lahaina-Kā'anapali & Pacific Railroad.** Affectionately called the Sugarcane Train, this quaint little choo-choo is Hawai'i's only passenger train. It's an 1890s-vintage railway that once shuttled sugar but now moves sightseers between Kā'anapali and Lahaina. This attraction is a big deal for Hawai'i but probably not much of a thrill for those more accustomed to trains. Kids will like it. ⊠ *1½ blocks north of Lahainaluna Rd. stoplight on Honoapi'ilani Hwy., Lahaina,* ☎ *808/661-0089.* 🎫 *$13.* ☉ *Daily 9–5:30.*

🐚 **Lahaina Whaling Museum.** Crazy Shirts' (which is a locally owned chain of high-quality T-shirt shops) owner, Rick Ralston, has opened this repository of more than 800 pieces of whaling memorabilia in his Front Street store. His collection includes carved ivory, harpoons, and old photos. ⊠ *865 Front St.,* ☎ *808/661-4775.* 🎫 *Free.* ☉ *Mon.–Sat. 9 AM–10 PM, Sun. 9–9.*

Master's Reading Room. This is Maui's oldest building, dating from 1833. In the early days, the ground floor was a mission's storeroom, while the reading room upstairs was for sailors. The **Lahaina Restoration Foundation** is housed in this building. Its knowledgeable staff can answer almost any question about the historic sights in town. ⊠ *Corner of Front and Dickenson Sts.,* ☎ *808/661-3262.*

⑬ **Seamen's Hospital.** A royal party house for King Kamehameha III in the 1830s, this property was later turned over to the U.S. government, which used it as a hospital for whaling men. ⊠ *1024 Front St., Lahaina,* ☎ *808/661-3262.* 🎫 *Free.* ☉ *Daily 10–5.*

⑪ **Spring House.** Built by missionaries to shelter a freshwater spring, this historic structure is now home to a huge Fresnel lens, once used in a local lighthouse. ⊠ *At Wharf Cinema Center, 658 Front St., Lahaina.*

NEED A
BREAK?

Dockside ambience given you a yen for a big beefy burger? Head for **Cheeseburger in Paradise** (⊠ Front St. at Lahainaluna Rd., Lahaina, ☎ 808/661-4855). Upcountry locals, who raise their own beef, travel to Lahaina for these $5 behemoths topped with cheddar, mozzarella, or Swiss cheese.

---

⑮ **Waiola Church.** Erected in 1832 by Hawaiian chiefs, the church was originally named Ebenezer by the queen's second husband and widower, Governor Hoapili. It was later named Waine'e, after the district in which it is located. After a few fires and some wind damage, the current structure was put up in 1953 and named Waiola Church. **Waiola Cemetery** is actually older than the neighboring church, dating from the time when Kamehameha's sacred wife Queen Keōpūolani died and was buried there in 1823. ⊠ *535 Waine'e St., Lahaina,* ☎ *808/661-4349.*

🐚 **Whalers Village Museum.** You'll find a 30-foot sperm-whale skeleton and an authentic whaling boat here. The museum's exhibits explore whaling history with photos and artifacts from 1825 to 1860 and information about whale biology. Lectures, films, and special tours are available. ⊠ *On the shore at Kā'anapali Beach Resort, 2435 Kā'anapali Pkwy.,* ☎ *808/661-5992.* 🎫 *Free.* ☉ *Daily 9:30 AM–10 PM.*

⑫ **Wo Hing Society.** This eye-catching building, originally built as a temple in 1912, now contains Chinese artifacts and a historic theater that features Thomas Edison films of Hawai'i, circa 1898. Upstairs is the only public Taoist altar on Maui. ⊠ *858 Front St., Lahaina,* ☎ *808/661-3262.* 🎫 *Free.* ☉ *Daily 9–4:30.*

CENTRAL MAUI

Most Maui visitors give Kahului the go-by, though the shopping malls inevitably catch the eye of tourists driving from the airport to hotels in the south and west. This industrial and commercial town is home to many of Maui's permanent residents, many of whom find their jobs in the area. Kahului was built in the early 1950s as the answer to Alexander & Baldwin's problems. The large company was tired of playing landlord to its many plantation workers and sold land to a developer who promised to create affordable housing. The scheme worked, and Kahului became the first planned city in Hawai'i. Ka'ahumanu Avenue (Highway 32) is Kahului's main street and runs east and west. It's the logical place to begin exploring Central Maui.

A Good Tour
Numbers in the text correspond to numbers in the margin and on the Exploring Maui and Kahului-Wailuku maps.

Begin in **Kahului** ⑯, the commercial center of Maui, which looks nothing like the lush tropical paradise most people envision when they think of Hawaii. Leave here by car and get on Ka'ahumanu Avenue and take a right onto Pu'unēnē Avenue (Highway 350) just after you pass the Kaahumanu Center, Maui's largest shopping mall. Look for the **Alexander & Baldwin Sugar Museum** ⑰ just off Highway 350 as you drive into the town of Pu'unēnē (pronounced poo-oo-nay-nay) in the direction of Wailea. Stop here and take a look around.

Return to Ka'ahumanu Avenue, head toward Wailuku, and take a right onto Kahului Beach Road to see any ships in port at **Kahului Harbor** ⑱. Continue on the beach road until you reach Kanaloa Avenue, make a left to return to Ka'ahumanu Avenue, where you will turn right to reach Wailuku (Ka'ahumanu eventually becomes Wailuku's Main Street). To get a closer look at **Wailuku's Historic District** ⑲, turn right from Main Street onto Market Street, where you can park for free within view of the landmark '**Īao Theater** ⑳. The theater is good place to begin your walking tour. Next door to the theater is Traders of the Lost Art, the first of many amusing shops that line **Market Street** between Vineyard and Main Streets. Then it's a short walk along Main Street to **Ka'ahumanu Church** ㉑, which is on High Street, just around the corner from Main Street. Retrieve your car and return to Main Street, where you'll turn right to drive west, away from Kahului. After a few blocks, on your left, you'll see the **Halehō'ike'ike/Bailey House** ㉒.

From the Bailey House, drive toward the mountains. Main Street turns into 'Īao Valley Road, the air cools, and the hilly terrain gets more lush. Soon you'll come to **Kepaniwai Park and Heritage Gardens** ㉓. As you drive on toward 'Īao Needle, you'll pass to a less imposing landmark called **John F. Kennedy Profile** ㉔. 'Īao Valley Road ends at '**Īao Valley State Park** ㉕, home of the erosion-formed gray and moss-green rock called 'Īao Needle. Here you can end your good tour with a good hike.

TIMING
You can explore Central Maui comfortably in little more than half a day. If you want to combine sightseeing with shopping, this is a good itinerary for it, but you'll need more time. If you're a serious shopper, you may want to pick a day other than Sunday, when many of the shops are closed. Hikers will want to expand their outing to a full day to explore 'Īao Valley State Park, especially in spring, when any plant that can blossom does.

Sights to See
Numbers in the margin correspond to points of interest on the Exploring Maui and Kahului-Wailuku maps.

20

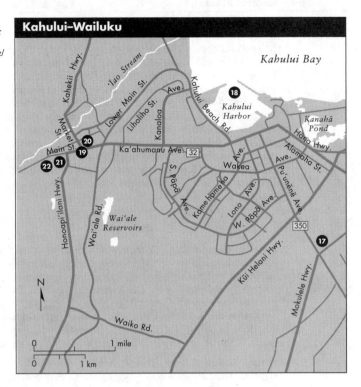

Kahului–Wailuku

★ **⑰ Alexander & Baldwin Sugar Museum.** "A&B," Maui's largest landowner, was one of five companies better known as the Big Five that spearheaded the planting, harvesting, and marketing of the valuable agricultural product sugarcane. Although Hawaiian sugar has been supplanted by cheaper foreign versions—as well as by less costly sugar beets—for many years, the crop was the mainstay of the Hawaiian economy. You'll find the museum in a small, restored plantation manager's house next to the post office and the still-operating sugar mill (at the refinery, black smoke billows up when cane is burning). Historic photos, artifacts, and documents explain the introduction of sugarcane to Hawai'i and how plantation managers brought in laborers from other countries, thereby changing the Islands' ethnic mix. Exhibits also describe the sugar-making process. A stop here is well worth your time. ✉ *3957 Hansen Rd., Pu'unēnē,* ☎ *808/871–8058.* 🎫 *$3.* ☉ *Mon.–Sat. 9:30–4:30.*

㉒ Halehō'ike'ike/Bailey House. This was the home of Edward and Caroline Bailey, two prominent missionaries who came to Wailuku to run the first Hawaiian girls' school on the island, the Wailuku Female Seminary; this school's primary function was to train the girls in the "feminine arts." The school, no longer standing, was next door to the Baileys' house, which they called Halehō'ike'ike (House of Display), but locals always called it the Bailey House (as does the sign out front).

Halehō'ike'ike's construction, between 1833 and 1850, was supervised by Edward Bailey himself. The Maui Historical Society has opened a museum in the plastered stone house with Mr. Bailey's paintings of Wailuku and a small artifacts collection from before and after the missionaries' arrival. Some rooms are decorated with missionary-period furniture. The Hawaiian Room has samples of pre–Captain Cook weaponry and exhibits on the making of tapa cloth. ✉ *2375A Main St., Wailuku,* ☎ *808/244–3326.* 🎫 *$4.* ☉ *Daily 10–4:30.*

⑳ ʻĪao Theater. One of Wailuku's landmarks, this charming art deco-style movie house went up in 1927 and acted as a community gathering spot. When restoration work was completed in 1996 on the building, the Maui Community Theatre, which had temporarily decamped, returned to its Wailuku headquarters, though it still offers performances at other venues as well. Unless there's a play or concert on, you usually can't get inside the theater. ⊠ *68 N. Market St., Wailuku,* ☎ *808/242–6969.*

NEED A BREAK? **Maui Bake Shop & Deli Ltd.** (⊠ 2092 Vineyard St., Wailuku, ☎ 808/242–0064) serves salads, sandwiches, and a daily-changing variety of light entrées, but what you're really going to crave here is the pastries—a feast for the eyes as well as the palate. The pastel-frosted frogs, chicks, rabbits, and mice, made of orange–butter cream cookie dough, are simply irresistible.

★ ㉕ ʻĪao Valley State Park. When Mark Twain saw this park, he dubbed it the Yosemite of the Pacific. Here you'll find the erosion-formed gray and moss-green rock called **ʻĪao Needle,** a spire that rises 1,200 feet from the valley floor. Mist occasionally rises if there's been a rain, making the spot look even more magical. You can take one of several easy hikes from the parking lot across ʻĪao Stream and explore the jungle-like area and study some native plants and flowers. ⊠ *Western end of Hwy. 32,* ▨ *Free.* ☉ *Daily 7–7.*

㉔ John F. Kennedy Profile. The Hawaiians, it sometimes seems, can see something they recognize in every rock formation throughout the Islands. Still, this one does uncannily resemble the profile of the late president. ⊠ *Hwy. 32, about 1 mi east of ʻĪao Valley State Park.*

㉑ Kaʻahumanu Church. It's said that Queen Kaʻahumanu attended services on this site in 1832 and requested that a permanent structure be erected. Builders first tried adobe, which dissolved in the rain, then stone. The present wooden structure, built in 1876, is classic New England style, with white exterior walls and striking green trim. You won't be able to see the interior, however, unless you attend Sunday services. The church conducts a service entirely in Hawaiian language each Sunday at 9 AM. ⊠ *Main and High Sts., Wailuku,* ☎ *808/244–5189.*

⑯ Kahului. As close to a bustling urban center as Maui gets, Kahului is the industrial and commercial hub for the island's year-round residents. Most visitors arrive at the airport here and see all they will see of the town as they drive on to their hotels, unless they stop to explore Maui's largest mall, the Kaʻahumanu Center.

⑱ Kahului Harbor. This is Maui's chief port since it's the island's only deep-draft harbor. American-Hawaiʻi's 800-passenger SS *Independence* and SS *Constitution* each stop here once a week, as do cargo ships and smaller vessels, including the occasional yacht. Surfers sometimes use this spot as a castoff to catch some good waves, but it's not a good swimming beach. ⊠ *Kahului Beach Rd., Kahului.*

OFF THE BEATEN PATH **MAUI SWAP MEET** – This flea market offers the biggest bargains on Maui. You'll see crafts, gifts, souvenirs, fruits, flowers, jewelry, antiques, art, shells, and lots more. ⊠ *Kahului Fairgrounds, Hwy. 35, just off Puʻunēnē Ave., Kahului,* ☎ *808/877–3100.* ▨ *$4 per car.* ☉ *Sat. 6–12.*

㉓ Kepaniwai Park & Heritage Gardens. A memorial to Maui's cultural roots, ethnic displays dot the landscape here. There's an early Hawaiian shack, a New England saltbox, a Portuguese villa with gardens, and dwellings from other cultures such as China and the Philippines. This a good place to picnic, with plenty of facilities available.

However, the peacefulness here belies the history of the area. During his quest for domination, King Kamehameha I brought his troops from the Big Island of Hawai'i to the Valley Isle in 1790 and engaged in a particularly bloody battle against the son of Maui's chief, Kahekili, near Kepaniwai Park. An earlier battle at the site had pitted Kahekili himself against an older Big Island chief, Kalani'ōpu'u. Kahekili vanquished his opponent, but the carnage was so great that the nearby stream became known as Wailuku (water of destruction) and the place where fallen warriors choked the stream's flow was called Kepaniwai (the water dam). ⊠ *'Īao Valley Rd., Wailuku.* 🎫 *Free.* ☉ *Daily 7–7.*

☕ **Maui Tropical Plantation.** A group of visionaries decided to open an agricultural theme park on this former sugarcane field when Maui's once-paramount crop declined severely in importance. A narrated tram ride through the mango, banana, and papaya groves and sugarcane and pineapple fields of the 120-acre preserve familiarizes you with growing processes and plant types. Kids enjoy the historical-characters exhibit, lei-making demonstrations, fruit-testing, coconut-husking, and bird shows. There's a restaurant on the property and a country barbecue (☞ Nightlife *in* Chapter 5) every evening; a Made-on-Maui Marketplace sells fruits and vegetables. ⊠ *On Honoapi'ilani Hwy. just outside Wailuku (Hwy. 30), Waikapu,* ☎ *808/244–7643.* 🎫 *Free to the Marketplace; narrated tour, $8.* ☉ *Daily 9–5.*

Market Street. An idiosyncratic assortment of shops—with proprietors to match—makes this street in Wailuku delightful for strolling (☞ Shopping Areas and Malls *in* Chapter 7).

Wailuku. In ancient times, this was a favored place for the inhabitants of Maui, who maintained two *heiau* (temples) on the hills above. The hills offered a useful vantage to watch for intruders, and villages grew up around the temples to support the cause. But the town really began to grow when the first missionaries arrived in the 1820s. ⊠ *A few mi west of Kahului on Ka'ahumanu Ave.*

🔟 **Wailuku's Historic District.** Much of this area is in the Register of Historic Places, and many of the buildings are being preserved with their wooden facades intact. Overall, the little town is sleepy and belies its function as Maui's county seat. The County Court House is on the corner of Main Street and Honoapi'ilani Highway. From here, Maui's first woman mayor, Linda Lingle, runs the county that includes the islands of Maui, Moloka'i, Lāna'i, and Kaho'olawe. ⊠ *On High, Vineyard, and Market Sts., Wailuku.*

NEED A BREAK?   **Hamburger Mary's** (⊠ 2010 Main St., Wailuku, ☎ 808/244–7776) is a good spot for breakfast, fresh fish, and of course, burgers. The fun, friendly atmosphere is enhanced by a quirky assortment of 1940s collectibles.

HALEAKALĀ AND UPCOUNTRY

The fertile western slopes leading up to majestic Mt. Haleakalā are called Upcountry. This region is responsible for much of Hawai'i's produce—lettuce, tomatoes, and sweet Maui onions—but the area is also a big flower producer. As you drive along you'll notice plenty of natural vegetation, as clumps of cacti mingle with purple jacaranda, wild hibiscus, and towering eucalyptus trees. Carnations are the number-one flower in the area, but the exotic-looking protea are rapidly gaining in popularity.

Upcountry is also fertile ranch land, with such spreads as the 30,000-acre 'Ulupalakua, long famous for raising cattle, and the 20,000-acre Haleakalā Ranch, which throws its well-attended rodeo in Makawao each July 4th. In addition, Tedeschi Vineyards and Winery dominates Hawai'i's only wine-producing region, just a few acres of 'Ulupalakua land.

A Good Tour

Numbers in the text correspond to numbers in the margin and on the Exploring Maui map.

Start in **Kahului.** Make sure you have a full gas tank; there are no service stations on the mountain. Drive on **Haleakalā Highway** (Hwy. 37) ㉖ toward the breath-taking **Mt. Haleakalā** (House of the Sun) in **Haleakalā National Park** ㉗ in the center of East Maui. Try to make the drive up Mt. Haleakalā without stopping since you'll want the best views possible. Watch the signs because Haleakalā Highway will diverge in two directions. If you go straight, the road becomes Kula Highway, which is still Highway 37. Veer to the left, the road becomes Highway 377, the road you want. After about 6 miles, make a left onto Haleakalā Highway. (These directions, although it sounds as if you're backtracking, *were* correct at press time. Beware: The names and numbers on Maui roads change frequently.) The switchbacks begin here. Near the top of the mountain is the **Park Headquarters Visitor Center**—a good spot to stop and stretch your legs. Continuing up the mountain, you'll come to several overlooks, including **Leleiwi Overlook** and **Kalahaku Overlook,** offering vistas you won't see anywhere else in the world. Not far from Kalahaku Overlook you'll find the **Haleakalā Visitor Center.** Eventually you'll reach the highest point on Maui, the **Pu'u 'Ula'ula Overlook.**

Now head back down from the way you came, taking time to see and explore the lower nooks and crannies of Haleakalā. When you reach Highway 377 again, make a left. Go about 2 miles, and you'll come to **Kula Botanical Gardens** ㉘ on your left. Continue on Highway 377, away from Kahului, and you'll soon join Highway 37 again. About 8 miles farther on, you'll reach **Tedeschi Vineyards and Winery** ㉙, where you can sample Hawai'i's only homegrown wines.

Returning the way you came, head north toward Kahului on Highway 37. When you get to the Highway 37/377 fork, bear to the left to stay on Highway 37. This is Kula Highway; another name change will make it Haleakalā Highway again (this isn't as confusing as it sounds). About 2 miles past the fork, you'll see a turnoff to the right called Copp Road. About ½ mile later, turn left onto Mauna Place to visit the **University of Hawai'i's Kula Experiment Station** ㉚.

Retrace your way to Kula Highway and again, head toward Kahului. In about 4 miles you'll come to the bedroom community of **Pukalani** ㉛. If you're pressed for time, you can take Highway 37 from here back to Kahului. Otherwise, head north on Highway 365 toward the paniolo (Hawaiian cowboy) village of **Makawao** ㉜. From Makawao, it's a short drive down toward the ocean on Baldwin Avenue to the Hāna Highway. Make a left on the Hāna Highway to return to Kahului.

TIMING

This can be an all-day outing even without the detours for Tedeschi Vineyards and Makawao. If you start early enough to catch the sunrise from Haleakalā's summit, you'll have plenty of time to enjoy a short hike on the mountain, have lunch in Kula, and end your day with dinner in Makawao. Even if a summit sunrise is not on your agenda, try to get up the mountain early to enjoy the clearest views since the

clouds move over the top of the mountain as early as 11 AM; be prepared for chilly temperatures atop the mountain.

Sights to See

*Numbers in the margin correspond to points of interest on the Exploring
Maui map.*

㉖ **Haleakalā Highway (Highway 37).** On this road, you'll travel from
sea level to an elevation of 10,023 feet in only 38 miles—a feat you
won't be able to repeat on any other car route in the world. It's not a
quick drive, however; it'll take you about two hours—longer if you
can't resist the temptation to stop and enjoy the spectacular views.

★ **㉗** **Haleakalā National Park.** A trip to Maui would not be complete without a visit to this 27,284-acre park, which was dedicated in 1961 to
preserving the area. The centerpiece of the park is **Mt. Haleakalā.** The
10,023-foot dormant volcano is the font from which all of East Maui
flowed, and home now to a wide variety of sights, sounds, and smells;
its terrain, climate, flora, and fauna—not to mention its views—are often
unique, sometimes strange, and always memorable. The crater is actually an "erosional valley," created by centuries of wind and rain chip-
ping away at the mountain's summit (where there may have once been
a small crater), sculpting the dramatic landscape you see today. The small
hills within the valley are volcanic cinder cones, each with a small
crater at its top, and each the site of an eruption. The mountain has terrific camping and hiking opportunities, including a trail that loops
through the crater.

Before you head up Haleakalā, call ☎ 808/871–5054 for the mountain's weather conditions. Extreme gusty winds, heavy rain, and even
snow in winter are not uncommon—even if it is paradise as usual down
at beach level. Because of the high altitude, the mountaintop temperature is often as much as 30 degrees cooler than in sea-level Maui. Be
sure to pack an extra jacket.

You can stop and orient yourself to the volcano's origins and eruption
history at the **Park Headquarters Visitor Center,** (⊠ At the 7,000-ft
elevation on Haleakalā Hwy., ۞ daily 7:30–4). Maps, posters, and other
memorabilia are available at the gift shop here.

Leleiwi Overlook, at about 8,800 feet elevation on Haleakalā, is one
of several lookout areas in the park. There's parking here and the beginning of the Halemau'u Trail, which leads into the valley. If you happen to be at this point in the late afternoon, it's possible you'll experience
a phenomenon called the Brocken Specter. Named after a similar oc-
currence in East Germany's Harz Mountains, the "specter" allows you
to see yourself reflected on the clouds and circled by a rainbow. Don't
wait all day for this, because it's not an everyday thing.

The famous silversword plant grows amid the desertlike surroundings
at **Kalahaku Overlook,** which is at about 9,000 feet elevation on
Haleakalā; in fact, the endangered flowering plant grows in only one
other place in the park, along the Halemau'u Trail, within the crater.
The silversword looks like a member of the yucca family and produces
a stalk 3 to 8 feet tall with several hundred yellow and purple flower
heads. At this lookout, the silversword is kept in an enclosure to protect it from nibbling wildlife and souvenir hunters.

Haleakalā Visitor Center (⊠ At 9,740 feet elevation on Haleakalā, ۞
daily sunrise–3) has exhibits inside and a trailhead that leads to White
Hill, a small crater nearby. This is a short, easy walk that will give you
an even better view of the valley. Short interpretive talks are offered
daily and a 90-minute walk with a ranger guide that goes partly down

Sliding Sands Trail is regularly scheduled; check the center's bulletin board for details.

The highest point on Maui is the **Puʻu ʻUlaʻula Overlook,** which is at the 10,023-foot summit of Haleakalā. Here you'll find a glass-enclosed lookout with a 360-degree view. The building's open 24 hours a day, and this is where visitors gather for the best sunrise view. Sunrise generally begins between 5:45 and 7, depending on the time of year. On a clear day, you can see the islands of Molokaʻi, Lānaʻi, Kahoʻolawe, and the Big Island. On a *really* clear day, you can even spot Oʻahu glimmering in the distance.

On a small hill nearby, you'll see **Science City,** a research and communications center that looks like it's straight out of an espionage thriller. The University of Hawaiʻi and the Department of Defense don't allow visitors to enter the facility, however. The university maintains an observatory here, while the Defense Department tracks satellites. ✉ *Haleakalā National Park entrance off Haleakala Crater Rd. (Hwy. 378), Box 369, Makawao, 96768,* ☎ *808/572–9306.* 🎫 *$4 car fee, $2 per person for hikers/bikers.*

NEED A BREAK?

Kula Lodge (✉ Haleakalā Hwy., Kula, ☎ 808/878–2517) serves hearty breakfasts from 6:30 to 11:30 AM—a favorite with visitors coming down from a sunrise visit to Haleakalā's summit as well as those on their way up for a later morning tramp in the crater. Spectacular ocean views can be seen from the windows of this mountainside lodge (☞ Lodging *in* Chapter 4).

28 Kula Botanical Gardens. Specimens grow somewhat naturally here, and you'll see all kinds of flora that may be unfamiliar. There are koa trees, often made into finely turned bowls and handcrafted furniture, and kukui trees (ancient Hawaiians used the tree's nuts, which are filled with oil, for lighting). In addition, the gardens have Maui's hallmark protea, several varieties of ginger, and stands of bamboo orchid. ✉ *RR 2, Box 288, Upper Kula Rd., Kula,* ☎ *808/878–1715.* 🎫 *$3.* ☉ *Daily 9–4.*

32 Makawao. This tiny town was settled long ago by Portuguese immigrants who were brought to Maui to work the sugar plantations. After their contracts ran out, many moved Upcountry, where their descendants now work the neighboring Haleakalā and ʻUlupalakua ranches. Every Fourth of July, the paniolo set comes out in force for the Makawao rodeo. ✉ *Hwy. 365, East Maui.*

NEED A BREAK?

One of Makawao's most famous landmarks is **Komoda Store & Bakery** (✉ 3674 Baldwin Ave., ☎ 808/572–7261), an old-timey throwback to the town's ranching roots, where customers don cowboy boots—and where you can get a delicious cream puff if you arrive early enough in the day. They make hundreds—and sell out—each day. Cream puffs or no, Komoda's is a nifty little stop, with plenty of tasty snacks as well as all the other trappings of an old-fashioned general store.

OFF THE BEATEN PATH

HUI NOʻEAU VISUAL ARTS CENTER – This nonprofit cultural center is on the old Baldwin estate, just outside the town of Makawao. There are regular exhibitions and audiovisual presentations. ✉ *2841 Baldwin Ave., Makawao,* ☎ *808/572–6560.* 🎫 *Free.* ☉ *Daily 10–4.*

31 Pukalani. There is very little in this town to interest the visitor. It is the first town you'll come to on the Haleakalā Highway (Hwy. 37) after Kahului. Pukalani is a good mid-way point to or from Haleakalā National Park, as there is a gas station and a few fast-food type restaurants.

★ ㉙ **Tedeschi Vineyards and Winery.** You can take a tour of the winery and sample Hawai'i's only homegrown wines here: a pleasant Maui Blush, the Maui Brut-Blanc de Noirs Hawaiian Champagne, and Tedeschi's annual Maui Nouveau. The most unusual wine, Maui Blanc, is made from pineapple concentrate; the winery owners started their operation by buying juice from their neighbor, Maui Land & Pineapple Company. You'll want to taste Maui Blanc before you buy—it's not for everyone. The winery's tasting room is unusual because it once served as the jail for James Makee's Rose Ranch, where the old-time farmer grew sugarcane back in the 1860s. Tedeschi is not far out of the way if you are returning from a visit to Haleakalā, and it's definitely worth a stop. ⊠ *Kula Hwy., 'Ulupalakua Ranch,* ☎ *808/878–6058.* 🎫 *Free.* ☉ *Daily 9–5; tours until 2:30.*

㉚ **University of Hawai'i's Kula Experiment Station.** The station planted the first protea here in the mid-'60s and since then has become the world's foremost protea research and development facility. Within its gates, you'll see as many as 300 varieties of the exotic bloom, most with names to match: Rickrack Banksia, Veldfire Sunburst, Pink Mink, Blushing Bride, and Safari Sunset, to name just a few. You can talk to the growers to find out more about the plants, which were brought to Maui from Australia in 1965 by Dr. Philip Parvin, a University of Hawai'i horticulture professor. Then you can proceed to one of Upcountry Maui's many commercial outlets and buy your favorite blooms. Fresh-cut or dried (protea dry beautifully), these unusual-looking blossoms make great send-home gifts, but fresh flowers leaving Hawai'i must bear an inspection stamp. Most sellers will inspect, pack, and express-ship them for you. ⊠ *Mauna Pl., Kula,* ☎ *808/878–1213.* 🎫 *Free.* ☉ *Weekdays 7–3:30, but you must stop at office and sign a sheet releasing station from any liability; you'll then be given a map.*

THE ROAD TO HĀNA

One of the most dazzling drives on the islands is along the Hāna Highway. You'll pass dozens of waterfalls, cross quaint bridges, and take in some spectacular ocean views. Don't let anyone tell you the Hāna Highway is impassable, frightening, or otherwise unadvisable. Because of all the hype, you're bound to be a little nervous approaching it for the first time. But once you try it, you'll wonder if maybe there's somebody out there making it sound tough just to keep out the hordes. The road isn't a freeway, but it is well maintained. The 55-mile road begins in Kahului, where it is a well-paved highway. The eastern half of the road is challenging, as it is riddled with turns and bridges, but it's not a grueling, all-day drive to Hāna. You will want to stop along the way so you can enjoy the view.

A Good Drive

Numbers in the text correspond to numbers in the margin and on the Exploring Maui map.

Start your trip to Hāna in the little town of **Pā'ia** ㉝, where the main street in town is Hāna Highway. You'll want to begin with a full tank of gas; there are no gas stations along the Hāna Highway, and the stations in Hāna close by 6 PM. Remember that many people—mostly those who live in Hāna—make this trip frequently. You'll recognize them because they're the ones who'll be zipping around every curve; they've seen this so many times before that they don't care to linger. Pull over and let them pass.

If you are setting out on the Road to Hāna and *not* hankering to sample the local fare at the extremely rustic fruit stands and truck markets that will be your only choices along the Hāna Highway, you might also want to purchase a picnic lunch in Pā'ia. Nearly any restaurant in town will pack up whatever you need—perhaps stop off at **Picnics** before you depart.

Your first stop is **Ho'okipa Beach** ㉞, arguably the windsurfing capital of the world, about a mile east of Pā'ia. About 10 miles from Pā'ia, the famous road really begins to twist and turn (as it will for the next 40 miles or so). About 3 miles later you'll come to the first of the Hāna Highway's approximately 65 bridges. The highway's mile markers begin here at **Kākipi Gulch.** All along this stretch of road, waterfalls are abundant. Turn off the radio and the air conditioner and open the windows to enjoy the sounds and smells. There are plenty of places to pull off and park; all are ideal spots to stop and take a picture. You'll want to plan on doing this a few times, as the road's curves make driving without a break difficult. When it's raining, which is often, the drive is particularly beautiful: There are waterfalls everywhere.

As you drive on, you'll pass the small villages of **Huelo** ㉟ and **Kailua** ㊱. At about mile marker 11, you can stop at the bridge over **Puahokamoa Stream** ㊲, where there are more pools and waterfalls. If you'd rather stretch your legs and use a flush toilet, continue on another mile to the **Kaumahina State Wayside Park** ㊳. Near mile marker 13, you'll see **Honomanū Valley** ㊴. Another 4 miles brings you to the **Ke'anae Arboretum** ㊵. Nearby you'll find the **Ke'anae Overlook** ㊶. Coming up is the halfway mark to Hāna. If you've had enough scenery, this is as good a time as any to turn around and head back to civilization. The scenery from here is essentially the same.

Don't expect a booming city when you get to Hāna. It's the road that's the draw. Diehards will want to stick with us. Continue on from mile marker 20 for about ¾ mile to **Wailua Lookout** ㊷. After another ½ mile, you'll hit the best falls on the entire drive to Hāna, **Waikāne Falls** ㊸. At about mile marker 25, you'll see a road that heads down toward the ocean and the village of **Nāhiku** ㊹. Near mile marker 30 watch for Kalo Road; a turn to the right takes you to **Hāna Gardenland** ㊺. It's about half a mile farther to the turnoff for **Hāna Airport.** Near mile marker 31 you'll pass **Wai'ānapanapa State Park** ㊻. Closer to Hāna, you'll come to 60-acre **Helani Gardens** ㊼. **Hāna** ㊽ is just minutes away from Helani Gardens. The fabled **Hotel Hāna-Maui** ㊾ is the town's main attraction and, with its surrounding ranch, the mainstay of Hāna's economy.

Once you've seen Hāna, you might want to drive past the town to the pools at **'Ohe'o Gulch** ㊿. Called the Pi'ilani Highway once past Hāna, the road that spans the 10 miles to the gulch is truly bad—rutted, rocky, and twisting. If you're just sure you've passed the pools because the terrain is so awful, don't give up. These refreshing pools are worth the drive. A lot of people come this far just to see the **Grave of Charles Lindbergh** (51). The world-renowned aviator is buried next to Ho'omau Congregational Church. To reach the church, turn left and drive toward the ocean on the little road you'll find about a mile past 'Ohe'o Gulch.

Unless you've decided to drive completely around east Maui and end up at Mākena, which isn't advisable unless you have a four-wheel-drive vehicle, this is the place to turn around. The drive back isn't nearly as much fun, so you might want to plan on spending plan to spend the night in Hāna (☞ Lodging *in* Chapter 4).

TIMING
With stops, the drive from Pā'ia to Hāna should take you between two and three hours. Lunch in Hāna, hiking, and swimming can easily turn the round trip into a full-day outing. Be sure to plan your trip for daylight hours; there are some poorly lit stretches of Hana Highway that can make night driving difficult. If you take this trip in winter, when the north shore waves are highest, you may have the chance to watch astonishing windsurfing feats at Ho'okipa Beach. Sometimes, though, the winter conditions are too dangerous even for these daredevils.

Sights to See
Numbers in the margin correspond to points of interest on the Exploring Maui map.

51 **Grave of Charles Lindbergh.** The world-renowned aviator chose to be buried here because he and his wife, writer Anne Morrow Lindbergh, spent a lot of time living in the area. He was buried next to Ho'omau Congregational Church in 1974. ⊠ *Ho'omau Congregational Church, Kīpahulu.*

OFF THE
BEATEN PATH

KAUPŌ ROAD – This stretch of road beyond Kīpahulu is near where the pavement stops. Kaupō Road is rough, with more than a few miles of rocky, one-lane terrain not unlike that of the moon; you'll want a four-wheel-drive vehicle for this adventure. Drop-offs plunge far down to the sea and washouts are common. It's a beautiful drive, however, and probably the closest to Old Hawai'i you'll find. Along the way, the little Kaupō Store, about 15 miles past Hāna, sells a variety of essential items, such as groceries, fishing tackle, and hardware; it's also a good place to stop for a cold drink. You'll also pass the renovated Hui Aloha Church, a tiny, wood-frame structure surrounded by an old Hawaiian graveyard. You'll eventually wind up in Mākena.

★ **48** **Hāna.** As you wander around Hāna, keep in mind that this is a company town. Although sugar was once the mainstay of Hāna's economy, the last plantation shut down in the 1940s. In 1946 rancher Paul Fagan built the Hotel Hāna-Maui and stocked the surrounding pastureland with cattle. Suddenly, the ranch and its hotel were putting food on most tables.

The cross you'll see on the hill above the hotel was put there in memory of Fagan. After Fagan died in the mid-1960s, ranch-and-town ownership passed into the hands of 37 shareholders, most of whom didn't care about their property. Then the Rosewood Corporation purchased most of Hāna's valuable land. The company put megamillions into restoring the Hotel Hāna-Maui and began teaching the *paniolo* (cowboy) population all the latest techniques in grazing and breeding. In 1989 Rosewood sold its Hāna holdings to a Japanese company, which appointed Sheraton as manager. Sheraton restored the old hotel and added the plantation-look Sea Ranch health spa across the road, and the isolated resort became a favorite hideaway for health-conscious celebrities. The property was sold again in 1995 to the New York–based Manolis Co., which promptly announced plans to build a golf course on part of the land; some local residents just as promptly announced their opposition to the plan.

Because of the town's size, most of the townspeople are the hands-on suppliers of the services and amenities that make hotel guests happy. Moreover, many locals have worked at the hotel for years; a fascinating family tree that hangs near the lobby shows the relationships of all the employees. If you're at all adventurous, you'll no doubt be able to talk to several of the people who live and work in Hāna. They're candid, friendly, and mostly native Hawaiian—or at least born and raised in Hāna. ⊠ *Off Hāna Hwy. at mi marker 35, East Maui.*

Hāna Airport. Think of Amelia Earhart. Think of Waldo Pepper. If these picket-fenced runways don't turn your thoughts to the derring-do of barnstorming pilots, you haven't seen enough old movies. Only the smallest planes can land and depart here, and when none of them happen to be around, the lonely windsock is the only evidence that this is a working airfield. ⊠ *Hāna Hwy. past mi marker 30,* ☎ *808/248–8208.*

Hāna Cultural Center. You'll find artifacts, quilts, and other Hawaiian memorabilia at this small museum. A knowledgeable staff can explain it all to you. ⊠ *Ukea St., Hana,* ☎ *808/248–8622.*

㊺ Hāna Gardenland. You can wander through 5 acres of anthuriums, orchids, and other tropical treasures on this property, which is Maui's oldest commercial nursery. The proprietors will pack and ship gifts for you, tell you about the craft traditions that lie behind the locally made gift items for sale, and invite you to enjoy a snack or a cup of coffee at the on-site Espresso Cafe. ⊠ *Hāna Hwy. at Kalo Rd.,* ☎ *808/248–7868.* ☉ *Daily 8–6.*

★ ㊼ Helani Gardens. Hāna native Howard Cooper is the proprietor of this 60-acre enclave of plants. Cooper is the crusty old guy you'll find wandering the place or hanging out in his tree house. His wife, Nora, is editor of the *Maui News* in Kahului, but Howard just couldn't bear to leave his beloved Hāna, so Nora commutes. Howard's philosophy of life crops up all over the garden in delightful, hand-painted signs. A tour of Helani Gardens is a self-guided one, but if Howard's around, he'll be glad to show you his favorite plants. ⊠ *Helani Gardens, Box 215, Hāna 96713,* ☎ *808/248–8274.* ⊡ *$2.* ☉ *Daily (weather permitting) 10–4.*

㊴ Honomanū Valley. This enormous valley on the right side of the highway as you drive toward Hāna was carved by erosion during Haleakalā's first dormant period. At the canyon's head, there are 3,000-foot cliffs and a 1,000-foot waterfall, but don't try to reach them. There's not much of a trail, and what does exist is practically impassable. ⊠ *Hāna Hwy. near mi marker 13, Ke'anae).*

★ ㉞ Ho'okipa Beach. There is no better place on this or any other island to watch the world's best windsurfers in action (☞ Beaches *in* Chapter 6). ⊠ *About 1 mi past Pā'ia on Hwy. 36.*

㊾ Hotel Hāna-Maui. This fabled hotel, a favorite of privacy-seeking celebrities, is one of the best hotels in the state—if not the world (☞ Lodging *in* Chapter 4). The newer Sea Ranch cottages across the road are also part of the Hāna-Maui; the cottages were built to look like authentic plantation housing, but only from the outside. ⊠ *Hāna Hwy., Hāna,* ☎ *808/248–8211).*

㉟ Huelo. This sleepy little farm town has two quaint churches, and little else of interest to tourists, but it's a place to meet local residents and learn about a rural lifestyle you might not have expected to find in the Islands. ⊠ *Hāna Hwy. near mile marker 5.*

㊱ Kailua. This small village is home to Alexander & Baldwin's irrigation employees. ⊠ *Hāna Hwy. near mi marker 6.*

㊳ Kaumahina State Wayside Park. The park has a picnic area, rest rooms, and a lovely overlook to the Ke'anae Peninsula. Hardier souls can camp here with a permit. ⊠ *Hāna Hwy. at mi marker 12, Kailua,* ⊡ *Free.*

40 Ke'anae Arboretum. Here is a place that brings order and attaches names to the many plants and trees that are now considered native to Hawai'i. The meandering Pi'ina'au Stream adds a graceful touch to the arboretum. You can take a fairly rigorous hike from the arboretum if you can find the trail at one side of the large taro patch. Be careful not to lose the trail once you're on it; a lovely forest waits at the end of the hike. ✉ *Hāna Hwy. at mi marker 17, Ke'anae, 🎫 Free.*

41 Ke'anae Overlook. From this observation point you'll notice the patchwork-quilt effect the taro farms create below. The ocean provides a dramatic backdrop for the farms; looking inland, there are some awesome views of Haleakalā through the foliage. This is a good spot for photos. ✉ *Hāna Hwy. near mi marker 17, Ke'anae.*

NEED A BREAK?

Just past Ke'anae you can pull over at **Uncle Harry's** (☎ 808/248–7019), a refreshment stand run by Uncle Harry Mitchell offering fruit, home-baked breads, some Hawaiian food, and beverages. Uncle Harry and his family also have souvenirs for sale, and they've opened a small museum next door, including a grass house to demonstrate how their ancestors lived.

44 Nāhiku. This was a popular settlement in ancient times, providing a home to hundreds of natives. Now Nāhiku's population numbers about 80, consisting mostly of native Hawaiians and some back-to-the-land types. Like so many other Hawaiian villages, Nāhiku was once a plantation town. A rubber grower planted trees there in the early 1900s. The experiment didn't work out, so Nāhiku was essentially abandoned. ✉ *Ocean side of Hāna Hwy., near mi marker 25.*

50 'Ohe'o Gulch. Meg Ryan's rhapsody in the 1994 film *I.Q.* about Maui's "seven sacred pools" may have ruined this spot forever, filling visitors with wrong-headed expectations. Here's the straight scoop: Maui residents call this place 'Ohe'o Gulch, and *never* the seven sacred pools; there are many waterfalls well over 100 feet high, but there is no 100-foot-high waterfall that anyone could safely slide down; there are more than seven pools (the actual number depends on rainfall and what you consider a "pool"); and sunbathing and hiking are both popular activities, but swimming here can be hazardous, and there are no lifeguards. From the paved parking lot, you can walk a short way to the first of the pools. Rocks are available for sunbathing, and caves may be explored. In spring and summer, it can get quite crowded here, and it doesn't even thin out when it rains. ✉ *Pi'ilani Hwy., 10 mi south of Hāna.*

★ **33 Pā'ia.** This little town on Maui's north shore was once a sugar-growing enclave, with a mill and plantation camps. The town boomed during World War II when the Marines set up camp nearby. After the war, however, sugar grower Alexander & Baldwin closed its Pā'ia operation, many workers moved on, and the town's population began to dwindle.

In the 1960s, Pā'ia became a hippie town as dropouts headed for Maui to open ethnic shops, bizarre galleries, and unusual eateries. By the late 1970s, windsurfers had discovered nearby Ho'okipa Beach, and turned Pā'ia into the windsurfing capital of the world. You can see this in the youth of the town and in the budget inns that have cropped up to offer cheap accommodations to those who windsurf for a living. Pā'ia is a fun place. ✉ *Junction of Hwy. 390 and Hwy. 36.*

NEED A BREAK?

Apart from windsurfing, what keeps Pā'ia in business these days is feeding Hāna-bound visitors. **Charley's** (✉ 142 Hāna Hwy., ☎ 808/579–9453) is a great spot for breakfast; you can get a good meal here and watch the locals go by.

Picnics. This place specializes in food for the road. They will pack up a tasty snack for your trip, from simple sandwiches to elaborate spreads of salads, fruits, and cheeses. There's no need to order in advance. (☞ Dining *in* Chapter 3). ⊠ *30 Baldwin Ave., Pā'ia,* ☎ *808/579–8021.*

③⑦ Puahokamoa Stream. The bridge over Puahokamoa Stream is the first of many you'll cross en route from Pā'ia to Hāna. It spans pools and waterfalls. If you get out of your car and walk up to the left of the first pool, you'll find a larger pool and get a close-up view of the waterfalls. Picnic tables are available at Puahokamoa Stream, so many people favor this as a stopping point, but there are no rest rooms. ⊠ *Hāna Hwy., at about mi marker 11.*

④⑥ Wai'ānapanapa State Park. With a permit, you can stay in state-run cabins here for less than $20 a night; the price varies depending on the number of people. The park is right on the ocean, and it's a lovely spot to picnic, hike, or swim. An ancient burial site is nearby, and there are at least three heiau, though only one is easily located. Wai'ānapanapa also has one of Maui's only black-sand beaches and has some caves for adventurous swimmers to explore. ⊠ *Hāna Hwy., Hāna, near mi marker 31,* ☎ *808/248–8061.* ☜ *Free.*

④③ Waikāne Falls. Though not necessarily bigger or taller than the other falls, these are the most dramatic—some say the best—falls you'll find on the Road to Hāna. That's partly because the water is not diverted for sugar irrigation; the taro farmers in Wailua need all the runoff. Here is another good spot for photos. ⊠ *Hāna Hwy., just past mi marker 21, Wailua.*

④② Wailua Lookout. From the parking lot, you can see Wailua Canyon, but you'll have to walk up steps to get a view of Wailua Village. The landmark in Wailua Village is a church made of coral, built in 1860. Once called St. Gabriel's Catholic Church, the current Our Lady of Fatima Shrine has an interesting legend surrounding it; as the story goes, a storm washed just enough coral up onto the shore to build the church, but then took any extra coral back to sea. ⊠ *Hāna Hwy., near mi marker 21, Wailua.*

3 Dining

In many of Maui's eateries, Continental classics such as chateaubriand and veal scallopine have given way to dishes such as coconut-chili beef and yellowfin tuna–breadfruit cakes. Although most of the island's food was once shipped in frozen, it is now passé to order goods from the mainland. The island's abundance of ingredients, from some 20 types of wild banana to fresh fish caught off the island's shores, together with Asian and Western techniques has spawned a new style of cooking—contemporary Hawaiian cuisine. The result: exciting and glorious fare.

MAUI CUISINE IS A LOT MORE THAN poi and pineapple at the local lūʻau. It's also more than the burgers and fries doled out at the ubiquitous fast-food chains. Many fine chefs have come to Maui and initiated the trend some call "Hawaiʻi regional cuisine."

In the late 1970s and '80s, Hawaiʻi's chefs disregarded the islands' extensive selection of local produce. Instead, they imported goods from Australia and even from as far away as Europe. In the early '90s, some of Hawaiʻi's top chefs started incorporating these indigenous fruits and vegetables into their dishes, blending classic Asian and Western culinary techniques with the state's distinctive ingredients—creating such dishes as ʻahi (yellowfin tuna) carpaccio, breadfruit soufflé, and papaya cheesecake. This new cooking style came to be known as Hawaii regional cuisine, or contemporary Hawaiian cuisine.

Today, chefs boast of using locally caught fish and the islands' intensely flavored tropical fruits. Of course, many different interpretations of contemporary Hawaiian cuisine have evolved—you'll notice Pacific Rim (Japanese, Southeast Asian, and Californian), Korean, and Portuguese influences. This ever-evolving cuisine, however, is still united by one thing: A strong emphasis on local products.

Of course, you can find plain old local-style cooking on the Valley Isle—particularly if you wander into the less touristy areas of Wailuku or Kahului. Greasy spoons abound—you can get some of the most authentic local food, or what residents call "plate lunch," for very little money. A good plate lunch will fulfill your daily requirement of carbohydrates, with macaroni salad, two scoops of rice, and an entrée of curry stew, teriyaki beef, or kālua (roasted) pig and cabbage.

Some of the island's best restaurants are in hotels, not surprising considering that tourism is the island's number-one industry. Many serve Continental fare. In addition, because many of the upscale hotels sit right on the beach, you'll often have the benefit of a good view.

Except when noted, reservations are not required at Maui restaurants, but it's almost never a bad idea to phone ahead to book a table. Restaurants are open daily unless otherwise indicated.

What to Wear
Few restaurants on Maui require jackets for men. Casual attire is acceptable in all but the fanciest establishments.

CATEGORY	COST*
$$$$	over $50
$$$	$30–$50
$$	$15–$30
$	under $15

Per person for a three course meal, excluding drinks, service, and sales tax (4.17%)

West Maui

American
$$$ ✕ **David Paul's Lahaina Grill.** In the Lahaina Hotel near Front Street's
★ many galleries, this sparkling restaurant opened by chef David Paul Johnson features new American cuisine, a blend of local ingredients and techniques from around the world. The menu is revised nearly daily, according to what's available locally. Kālua duck and Tequila Shrimp

and Firecracker Rice, made mild or spicy at your request, are two of the most popular dishes. A late night bistro menu is available. ⊠ *127 Lahainaluna Rd., Lahaina,* ☎ *808/667–5117. AE, DC, MC, V. No lunch.*

$$$ ✕ **Longhi's.** At this open-air establishment with tile floors and casual ★ wooden tables, proprietor Bob Longhi has gotten a lot of notoriety for the way his young waiters and waitresses pull up a chair and recite the day's menu. But what makes this establishment worth a visit is the food— homemade pasta, desserts whipped up by a full-time pastry chef, fresh fish, and sandwiches you can't get your mouth around. The first floor—where you may spot a celebrity or two—is very inviting; it's a great place to stop and watch the world go by while supping on an enormous burger, pasta with calamari in a spicy red sauce, or prime rib. This is a good choice for breakfast—it opens at 7:30. At night there's dancing on the second floor, where more expensive meals are served. ⊠ *888 Front St., Lahaina,* ☎ *808/667–2288. AE, D, DC, MC, V.*

$$ ✕ **Lahaina Provision Co.** If you like chocolate, this is the place. At 6 PM the Chocoholic Bar opens and until 11 PM you can get chocolate treats of every variety: double-fudge cake, white-chocolate mousse, chocolate-chip cookies, and ice cream with hot fudge, bittersweet chocolate, or white chocolate-coconut sauce. This small restaurant in the Hyatt Regency serves sandwiches and a tasty lunch buffet as well. Dinner is mostly steak and seafood; there's also a well-stocked salad bar. ⊠ *Hyatt Regency Maui, 200 Nohea Kai Dr., Kā'anapali,* ☎ *808/661–1234. AE, D, DC, MC, V.*

$$ ✕ **Leilani's on the Beach.** You'll get a good view of the Kā'anapali Resort at this relaxing, contemporary spot, under the same owners as Kimo's in Lahaina. Baby back ribs, smoked daily; three or four varieties of fresh fish; and steak and lobster are a few of the specialties on the menu. ⊠ *Whalers Village, 2435 Kā'anapali Pkwy., Kā'anapali Beach Resort,* ☎ *808/661–4495. MC, V.*

Contemporary Hawaiian

$$$ ✕ **The Grill & Bar.** The view alone—overlooking Nāpili Bay, with both Moloka'i and Lāna'i visible in the distance—is reason enough to stop here, but you should also come for the wok-charred 'ahi, the sweet rack of lamb, or one of the other delicious dishes on the extensive menu. If you're in the neighborhood during a full moon, stop in for The Grill's monthly "Moonlight Putting Tournament." ⊠ *200 Kapalua Dr., Kapalua,* ☎ *808/669–5653. AE, D, DC, MC, V.*

$$–$$$ ✕ **Avalon Restaurant and Bar.** One of Maui's trendiest restaurants, ★ Avalon is the latest venture for Mark Ellman, the young Californian chef. With white wicker furniture, bright tropical prints on the chairs and tables, palms, ferns, and slowly-turning overhead fans, this spot recalls the days when you arrived by boat to the Islands and found a paradise of swaying palms and hula girls. The menu offers dishes from California, Hawai'i, Mexico, Indonesia, Thailand, Vietnam, and Japan. Ellman's signature items include chili-seared salmon served tiki-style (Ellman's name for ingredients stacked up like heads on a tiki–totem pole) with a four-inch stack of rice, corn, and grilled vegetables and whole 'ōpakapaka (blue snapper) in garlic and black bean sauce. For dessert, try the caramel Miranda—fresh exotic fruits in a homemade caramel sauce with macadamia-nut ice cream. ⊠ *Mariner's Alley, 844 Front St., Lahaina,* ☎ *808/667–5559. AE, D, DC, MC, V.*

$$ ✕ **Hula Grill.** Here, Big Island master chef-restaurateur Peter Merriman brings his magic to the Valley Isle. He turned a space in Whalers Village into a replica of an old Hawaiian beach house; tables both indoors and out look towards the ocean view so that it's easy to forget that you're in a shopping mall. Merriman then went to work on the menu; the man can do no wrong with local ingredients, whether from the ocean or the farm. *Kiawe*-grilled *ono* (mesquite-grilled mackerel-like fish) with pineapple-Maui onion salsa comes with ginger stir-fried brown rice; scallop and lobster potstickers are served with guava plum dipping sauce. Trust the daily specials. ✉ *Whalers Village, 2435 Kā'anapali Pkwy., Kā'anapali,* ☎ 808/661–3894. *AE, MC, V.*

$$ ✕ **Kimo's.** This landmark waterfront eatery in Old Lahaina is hard to beat for atmosphere. From the outdoor lounge and open-air dining room, you get a great view of the harbor, which still looks like the 19th-century whaling port that it was. Additionally, On Wednesday through Sunday nights, a live band plays Hawaiian music. Kimo's home-style fare includes hula pie, a luscious dessert of chocolate mousselike filling encased in an Oreo-cookie crust. A sunset from here is not to be missed. ✉ *845 Front St., Lahaina,* ☎ 808/661–4811. *MC, V.*

$$ ✕ **Lahaina Coolers.** This surf-side bistro specializes in unusual food at reasonable prices. Try the Evil Jungle Pasta (chicken and linguine with peanut sauce) or spinach and feta quesadilla. ✉ *180 Dickenson St., Lahaina,* ☎ 808/661–7082. *AE, MC, V.*

$$ ✕ **Roy's Kahana Bar & Grill.** This is the older of Maui's two Roy Yamaguchi-owned restaurants. Yamaguchi, one of Hawai'i's most celebrated chefs, is often featured on the PBS series *Hawai'i Cooks.* His expanding network of restaurants, which are on Oahu, Kaua'i, and in Asia, and his demanding schedule of guest-chef appearances keep him away from Kahana most of the time, but executive chef Tod Kawachi keeps the menu and the nightly specials up to the master's standards. There's a decidedly Asian-Pacific spin on fish, meats, and pasta here. Spicy Rimfire shrimp with sweet spicy chili sauce is an eye-opener; the accompanying cucumber salad cools things off. ✉ *Kahana Gateway Shopping Center, 4405 Honoapi'ilani Hwy., Kahana,* ☎ 808/669–6999. *AE, D, DC, MC, V.*

$$ ✕ **Roy Yamaguchi's Nicolina.** Right next door to Roy's older restaurant, Nicolina has a personality all its own. The word here is spicy: Grilled Southwestern chicken comes with Anaheim chili hash and smoked tomato sauce, and smoked and peppered duck is accompanied by ginger sweet potatoes and Szechuan Mandarin sauce—you get the idea. Executive chef Jacqueline Lau's imaginative salsas enliven local fish and grilled vegetables. ✉ *Kahana Gateway Shopping Center, 4405 Honoapi'ilani Hwy., Kahana,* ☎ 808/669–5000. *AE, D, DC, MC, V.*

Continental

$$$ ✕ **'Ānuenue Room.** This is the Ritz-Carlton's signature restaurant. Chef Thomas Russell's French and California training, plus his Hawaiian experience, yield what he calls "Hawaiian Provençal" cuisine. The Chef's Signature menu—a preselected three-course dinner for $40—is always available. ✉ *Ritz-Carlton, Kapalua, 1 Ritz-Carlton Dr., Kapalua,* ☎ 808/669–1665. *AE, D, DC, MC, V.*

$$$ ✕ **Bay Club.** The setting makes this Kapalua Resort dining room just
★ the place for a magical candlelight meal: The open-air room, which has richly paneled walls and rattan furniture, occupies a lava-rock promontory overlooking the bay at the far end of Kapalua Beach. The wine list is excellent; and contemporary cuisine includes veal scallopine and fresh fish from the Moloka'i Channel. ✉ *Kapalua Bay Resort, 1 Bay Dr., Kapalua,* ☎ 808/669–5656. *AE, D, DC, MC, V.*

$$$ ✕ **Pineapple Hill.** A spectacular sunset view is one of the best reasons to visit this hillside restaurant in an old plantation house built in 1915 for D. T. Fleming, one of the Hawaiian pineapple industry's founding fathers. The house is high above the Pacific at the end of a drive flanked by towering Norfolk pines and has a large rock fireplace and a delightful waterfall off the patio. Favorite appetizers include stuffed mushrooms, sashimi, and French onion soup; chicken Provençale,

36

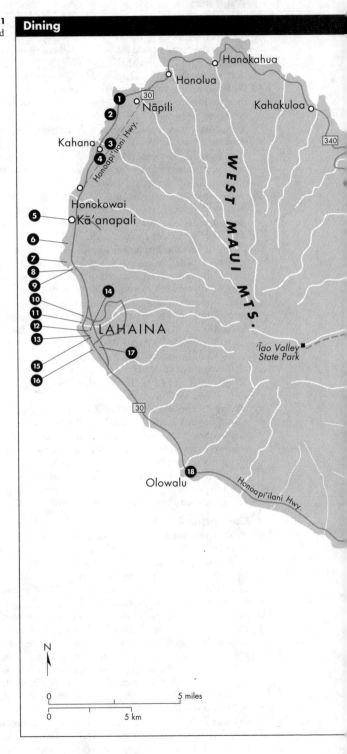

Dining

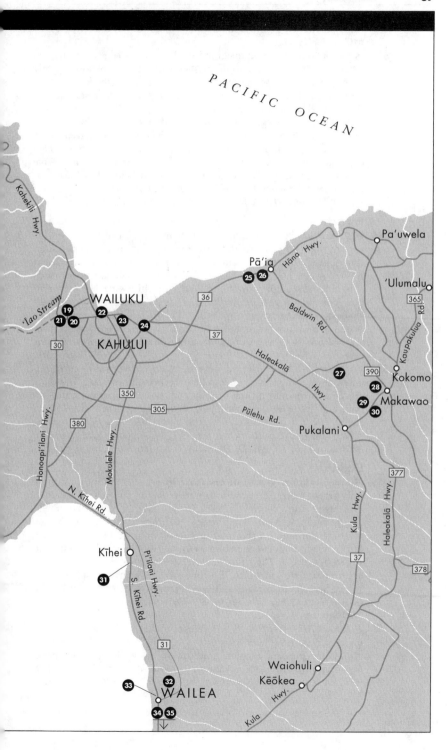

prawns tempura, and Hawaiian teriyaki steak are notable entrées. ⊠ *Kapalua Resort, 1000 Kapalua Dr.,* ☏ *808/669–6129. AE, D, DC, MC, V. No lunch.*

$$$ ✕ **Swan Court.** Descend the grand staircase to the edge of the lagoon where swans glide. A waterfall splashes, and palm fronds sway slightly in the breeze—no less a tastemaker than *Lifestyles of the Rich and Famous* has called Swan Court one of the most romantic restaurants in the world. The menu combines European and Asian flavors and preparations with local vegetables, seafood, and meats, producing the likes of Hunan marinated rack of lamb served with *haricots verts* (green beans) and Maui onion, and Pacific lobster tail with macadamia nuts and Thai chili sauce. Swan Court's extensive wine list has won awards from *Wine Spectator* magazine. The restaurant serves a delicious breakfast buffet. ⊠ *Hyatt Regency Maui, Kā'anapali Beach Resort, 200 Nohea Kai Dr.,* ☏ *808/661–1234. Jacket required. AE, D, DC, MC, V.*

French

$$$ ✕ **Chez Paul.** Four miles south of Lahaina in Olowalu, a mere wide
★ spot in the road provides the setting for this intimate French restaurant. Chez Paul has only 14 tables, each set with a linen tablecloth and fresh flowers. The menu changes daily, but you can always get such specialties as scampi Olowalu, cooked with white wine, herbs, and capers; *poisson beurre blanc,* fresh island fish poached in white wine with shallots, butter, and capers; and veal *à la Normande,* sautéed with green apples in a Calvados sauce. Try the Kahlua cheesecake for dessert. ⊠ *On Hwy. 30, 4 mi south of Lahaina,* ☏ *808/661–3843. Reservations essential. AE, D, MC, V. 2 dinner seatings nightly, at 6:30 and 8:30.*

$$$ ✕ **Gerard's.** Owner Gerard Reversade, one of Hawai'i's most tal-
★ ented chefs, prepares some excellent French dishes here. The daily changing menu may include such specialties as confit of duck and shiitake and oyster mushrooms in puff pastry. The wine list, with 150 varieties, is extensive. This comfortable eatery has plenty of stargazing possibilities—it's a celebrity favorite. ⊠ *174 Lahainaluna Rd., Lahaina,* ☏ *808/661–8939. AE, D, DC, MC, V. No lunch.*

Italian

$$ ✕ **Scaroles Italian Ristorante and Pizzeria.** Scaroles has the look of old Italy that so many American restaurants imitate. You've seen it before, possibly in your own town's best Italian restaurant; you just don't expect to find it in Maui. The entrées—a variety of pastas and chicken and veal plates with a choice of sauces—offer no real surprises either, but the traditional fare may be a welcome relief from all the Asian-inspired fish dishes. The pizza, however, is worth seeking out. Customary toppings are generously distributed over a hearty crust. There's a second Scaroles Ristorante (⊠ 131 Iki Pl. ☏ 808/875–7433) in Wailea. ⊠ *930 Waine'e St., Lahaina,* ☏ *808/661–4466. AE, MC, V.*

Japanese

$$ ✕ **Nikko.** At this *teppan*-style Japanese restaurant, the slicing-and-dicing chef prepares dinner for you at a communal table with a built-in grill. Green peppers, eggplant, and squash—as well as chicken, pork, and beef—are grilled to perfection. ⊠ *Maui Marriott Hotel, Kā'anapali Beach Resort, 100 Nohea Kai Dr.,* ☏ *808/667–1200. AE, D, DC, MC, V.*

Mexican

$$ ✕ **Chico's Cantina.** Although nobody knows for sure, Chico's is usually credited with being the first Mexican restaurant on Maui, and its funky, tropical-cum-south-of-the-border decor looks pretty convincing. The tasty fare runs to the Cal-Mex end of the Mexican cuisine spectrum (lots of veggies, sour cream, and guacamole) with the occasional oddball dish—mango fettucine and smoked chicken—thrown in for good measure. The margaritas come frosty or hand-shaken. On the 5th of every month, the restaurant celebrates "Cinco de Chico" with live music, specialty drinks, half-priced nachos, and a festive atmosphere. ✉ *Whalers Village, Kā'anapali,* ☎ *808/667–2777. AE, D, MC, V.*

$$ ✕ **Compadres Bar & Grill.** All over the islands, branches of this popular restaurant chain serve up Southwest-influenced fare. This one, in the Lahaina Cannery Mall, is casual and convivial. Stews and sautéed items are the standouts here, and everything is reasonably priced to boot. Try the chili Colorado (with its memorably spicy red sauce), or the tequila-grilled chicken *borracho*. There is also a selection of gringo basics. The restaurant's bar is a happening place after dark; locals come to sip margaritas, Mexican beers, spiked coffees, and the obligatory tropical drinks. ✉ *Lahaina Cannery Mall, 1221 Honoapi'ilani Hwy.,* ☎ *808/661–7189. AE, D, MC, V.*

Seafood

$$ ✕ **Erik's Seafood Grotto.** A netful of fresh island fish is available daily at this restaurant and oyster bar in the Kahana Villas Condominiums. Cioppino, a fish stew with garlic, tomato, and white wine is one of the house specialties. Other offerings include seafood curry; local lobster filled with seafood stuffing; and sautéed red snapper with mousseline sauce. For children under 12, Erik's has $9.95 keiki (child) dinners—a petite steak or medley of chicken, fish, and shrimp. ✉ *Kahana Villas, 4242 Lower Honoapi'ilani Hwy., Kahana,* ☎ *808/669–4806. AE, D, MC, V.*

Thai

$$ ✕ **Orient Express.** Red lacquer carvings, splashes of yellow flowers, and a decorative fountain create an Asian atmosphere here. The Kung Pao shrimp, cooked with dried chilies, bamboo shoots, and water chestnuts, is a house specialty. The coconut chicken soup with *kafir* leaves and mushrooms is delicious, as is the satay, made with beef strips marinated in spices and coconut milk, and then speared on bamboo sticks and grilled. Never fear if you can't take the heat—as at most Thai restaurants, you can request spicing mild, medium, or hot. ✉ *Nāpili Shores Resort, 5316 Lower Honoapi'ilani Hwy., Nāpili,* ☎ *808/669–8077. AE, MC, V.*

Central Maui

Chinese

$ ✕ **Ming Yuen.** Locals love this low-key place with unassuming decor, ★ and they'll line up to prove it. The extensive menu is mostly Cantonese cuisine, plus a few Szechuan dishes. The lemon chicken is famous, or you might try the hot-and-sour soup to start and then go for the Kung Pao chicken: chicken stir-fried with chili peppers, garlic, peanuts, and chopped vegetables. The moo shu pork is good. ✉ *162 Alamaha St., Kahului,* ☎ *808/871–7787. D, MC, V.*

German

$$ ✕ **Wunderbar Cafe.** You might not think German food would be a big mover in Maui, but German beer, now, that's another story. Austrian chef Martin Lackner brings Old World techniques to local seafood and organically grown produce. The menu includes traditional schnitzels and wursts as well. An eye-popping selection of German beers includes bottle-brewed Erlinger; there's a story and a pouring ritual to go with that one. ⊠ *89 Hāna Hwy., Pā'ia,* ☎ *808/579–8808. AE, DC, MC, V.*

Japanese

$ ✕ **Ichiban.** If you want Japanese food, this is the best bet. Nothing is fancy here, but you'll find authentic sashimi, teriyaki, and noodle dishes. The shrimp tempura and the combination dish with tempura, teriyaki, and pickled vegetables are both popular. ⊠ *Kahului Shopping Center, 47 Ka'ahumanu Ave., Kahului,* ☎ *808/871–6977. MC, V.*

Steak House

$$ ✕ **Chart House.** One of the nicest dining spots around, this is about as close to the ocean as you can get in a Kahului restaurant. Model ships, boat hulls, and surf prints are all part of the nautical decor. Here, fresh fish is prepared a multitude of ways—sautéed, baked, broiled, or cooked in herbs and spices. Actually though, steak is what this restaurant does best. There's also a well-stocked salad bar. The Chart House is popular with locals after work. ⊠ *500 Pu'unēnē Ave., Kahului,* ☎ *808/877–2476. AE, D, MC, V.*

Thai

$–$$ ✕ **Saeng's Thai Cuisine.** Exotic flowers and a waterfall view enhance the tropical decor at this hot spot, which has received quite a bit of attention since it opened in 1989. Red-curry shrimp and Evil Prince Chicken cooked in coconut sauce with Thai herbs are standout specialties. The spicy vegetarian dishes are also delicious. ⊠ *2119 Vineyard, Wailuku,* ☎ *808/244–1561. MC, V. No lunch Sun.*

$–$$ ✕ **Siam Thai.** This is one of the best places for sampling Thai cuisine in the Islands—and celebrities such as Robert Redford will probably vouch for it. There are some 70 selections on the menu, including several fine vegetarian dishes. The specialties are the curries, which come in red, green, or yellow, and hot, medium, or mild. ⊠ *123 Market, Wailuku,* ☎ *808/244–3817. AE, D, MC, V.*

Vietnamese

$–$$ ✕ **A Saigon Café.** When Jennifer Nguyen took over the space formerly occupied by Naokee's Steak House, she retained some of that establishment's most popular menu offerings. Notable among the Thai, vegetarian, and Vietnamese specialties is Banh Hoi Chao Tom—just ask for "shrimp pops burritos," like everyone else—ground marinated shrimp, steamed and grilled on a "stick" of sugar cane. Your waiter will show you how to assemble these with the basil, mint, cucumber, lettuce, bean sprouts, cake noodle, pickled carrots, and daikon in a rice paper wrapper. Forget neatness—this dish is fun and delicious. ⊠ *1792 Main St., Wailuku,* ☎ *808/243–9560. AE, D, MC, V.*

East Maui

Contemporary Hawaiian

$$$$ ✕ **Raffles.** The pride and joy of the Stouffer Renaissance Wailea Beach
★ Resort pays homage to British colonial elegance with ivory-tone walls, pastel furnishings, and 19th-century Asian artifacts. The sophisticated Pacific Rim menu includes contemporary Hawaiian specialties each week. Try 'ōpakapaka in lobster broth with baby leeks and chervil; roast rack

of lamb with Moloka'i herbs; or sautéed veal medallions with a gin-ger-scallion *beurre blanc.* ✉ *Stouffer Renaissance Wailea Beach Re-sort, 3550 Wailea Alanui Dr.,* ☎ *808/879–4900. Reservations essential. AE, D, DC, MC, V. No lunch. Closed Sun.–Mon.*

$$$ ✕ **Hāli'imaile General Store.** This delightful restaurant was a camp
★ store in the 1920s, but you'd never know it now. The white, green, and peach tin exterior of this restaurant looks a little out of place, sitting proudly in a pineapple field in Upcountry Maui, literally in the mid-dle of nowhere. Owner Beverly Gannon intended to open a deli with only 32 seats—however, it grew to 80 within one week. She has done wonders with this place, turning it into a charming outpost that serves some of the best food in the state. The contemporary menu uses island products that change with the seasons. One of Hāli'imaile's staples is duck prepared in a variety of ways, such as duck smoked with pineap-ple chutney. Other standouts are dynamite barbecued ribs, wild-mush-room pasta, and Asian seafood pasta with two or more kinds of seafood, greens, bean sprouts, and water chestnuts. This is one of Maui's most magnetic restaurants, repeatedly attracting celebrities and a host of other see-and-be-seen types. ✉ *Hāli'imaile Rd., 2 mi north of Pukalani,* ☎ *808/572–2666. MC, V.*

$$$ ✕ **Kea Lani Restaurant at Kea Lani Hotel.** Chef Steve Amaral is nothing
★ if not fussy about fresh ingredients. He grows his own herbs on the grounds of the hotel, and some of the fruits and vegetables he uses are organically grown on-site as well. The staff is always well informed about every selection. Chef Amaral puts the produce to good use in a delicate signature salad, an outstanding tomato and basil soup, and the day's fresh catch prepared with three kinds of wild mushrooms and served with garlic mashed potatoes. The excellent wine list has some imaginative by-the-glass offerings. ✉ *Kea Lani Hotel, 4100 Wailea Alanui Dr., Wailea 96753,* ☎ *808/875–4100. AE, D, DC, MC, V.*

$$$ ✕ **A Pacific Cafe.** Like its namesake on Kaua'i, this restaurant serves
★ chef Jean-Marie Josselin's signature Pacific Rim dishes such as mahimahi with garlic-sesame crust and lime-ginger sauce. The grill yields smoked chicken with Thai rice, pineapple, and preserved lemon-jalapeño mar-malade, and green curry jus. The spacious and comfortable dining room is decorated in shades of deep sea green and copper. ✉ *Azeka Place II, Kīhei,* ☎ *808/879–0069. AE, DC, MC, V. No lunch.*

$$$ ✕ **Prince Court.** Innovative chef Roger Dikon has a way with Hawaii
★ regional cuisine. The menu includes lots of fresh fish and locally grown produce. The champagne brunch, served Sunday 9:30–1:30, is won-derful. The light-filled Prince Court's dining room, in the Maui Prince Hotel, takes advantage of the tropical locale and the marvelous ocean view; cushioned bamboo chairs and tropical plants and flowers remind you where you are in case, for a moment, you lose sight of the water. ✉ *Maui Prince Hotel, Mākena Resort, Mākena,* ☎ *808/874–1111. AE, DC, MC, V. No lunch.*

Italian

$$ ✕ **Caffe Ciao.** What started as little more than a tasteful carryout shop
★ for guests at the Kea Lani Hotel has grown into an authentic and pop-ular Italian bistro—complete with a wine bar and fine list of Italian wines. Fresh, authentic ingredients are used in all the seafood and pasta dishes; and a wood-burning oven turns out delicious pizzas. This, combined with friendly service and pool and ocean views from every outdoor table, complete the picture and turn this casual spot into something special. (And, yes, there's still a take-out shop.) ✉ *Kea Lani Hotel, 4100 Wailea Alanui Dr., Wailea 96753,* ☎ *808/875–4100. AE, D, DC, MC, V.*

$$ ✕ **Casanova Italian Restaurant & Deli.** Owned by three young native Italians and a German brought up in Italy, this Upcountry establishment has expanded into a real restaurant offering the best Italian food on Maui. A wood-fired pizza oven produces a variety of yummy pies; try the *vulcano* with grilled eggplant and smoked mozzarella in tomato sauce. You can also order basic pasta, chicken, or fish dishes with tomato, cream, or mushroom sauce. ✉ *1188 Makawao Ave., Makawao,* ☎ *808/572–0220. D, DC, MC, V.*

Mexican

$ ✕ **Polli's.** Native Arizonan Polli Smith and her husband opened this
★ lively, once entirely vegetarian Mexican cantina in Upcountry Makawao. They've now added meat to the menu, but their meatless tacos, burritos, and enchiladas are just as good. Everything's available à la carte here, or you can get complete dinners, too. The margaritas served here are some of the best in the state. ✉ *1202 Makawao Ave., Makawao,* ☎ *808/572–7808. AE, MC, V.*

Seafood

$$ ✕ **Mama's Fish House.** The fresh fish here is some of the best in the
★ area, so put your car on the Hāna Highway and head toward Pā'ia. About 1½ miles east of town, you'll see a lovely, well-landscaped oceanfront building on your left—this is Mama's, a casual Old Hawaiian-style restaurant serving honest food. You can get fish sautéed in butter, poached in white-wine sauce with mushrooms, or broiled with lemon butter. One recommended dish is Pua Me Hua Hāna—fresh fish sautéed with banana and fresh young coconut in the style of old Hāna. Mama's also serves meat and chicken. ✉ *799 Kaiholo Pl., Kū'au,* ☎ *808/579–8488. Reservations essential. AE, D,MC, V.*

Steak Houses

$$$ ✕ **Joe's Bar & Grill.** This is the second restaurant Beverly and Joe Gannon have opened in Maui. No carbon copy of their deservedly popular Hāli'imaile General Store, this spot overlooking the Wailea Tennis Club's stadium court has a sportive atmosphere. The home cooking—grilled pork chops with sweet potatoes and dried fruit compote, and New York steak with caramelized onions, wild mushrooms, and Gorgonzola—is hearty. ✉ *131 Wailea Ike Pl., Wailea 96753,* ☎ *808/875–7767. MC, V.*

$$ ✕ **Makawao Steak House.** This popular Upcountry dinner house is arguably one of the best steak joints on the island—a tender top sirloin goes for less than $25. The fresh fish and freshly baked bread are just as good. If you really decide to splurge, you can get scampi and lobster. But meat lovers shouldn't miss the steak. ✉ *3612 Baldwin Ave.,* ☎ *808/572–8711. AE, D, DC, MC, V. No lunch.*

Picnics

You'll find plenty of secluded places for a laptop lunch for two on Maui. Also, if you're on your way to Haleakalā or Hāna, you might want to take a picnic along. Many hotels will prepare a picnic for you, or try one of these Maui delis:

✕ **Casanova Italian Restaurant & Deli** (✉ 1188 Makawao Ave., Makawao, ☎ 808/572–0220) packs Italian specialties for the road, for the beach, or for back at the condo, from 8 AM to 6:30 PM.
✕ **Picnics** (✉ 30 Baldwin Ave., Pā'ia, ☎ 808/579–8021) has experience and expertise in packing lunch for the road. Their take-away meals start at $8 per person. A $50 extravaganza for two to four people comes in a basket with a cooler, a tablecloth, and a "Road to Hāna" cassette.

4 Lodging

Maui has it all—from beachside villas to cozy B&Bs. Most of the island's big resorts and hotels are in the west, while lodges and inns are in the east. It takes time to find the perfect home away from home, so be sure to plan ahead.

MAUI HAS THE STATE'S HIGHEST concentration of luxury hotels and condominium units. For the most part, Maui condos are not tacky high-rises with thin walls and cheap appliances, but top-of-the-line units with all the amenities. Many are on the ocean, and you'll get the comforts of a hotel suite without the cost.

The average accommodation cost on Maui is as much as $70 more per night than other Hawaiian islands. Rates depend in part on where you want to stay. West Maui is the tourist center; lodgings here tend to be upscale and rather pricey. However, more rooms are available in this area than anywhere else. Two major resorts anchor West Maui: the Kā'anapali Beach Resort, with its six hotels and seven condominiums, and the Kapalua Bay Resort, with its two hotels and several condo complexes.

Choices are limited in Central Maui. Most of the island's permanent residents live here. Wailuku is the county seat and Kahului is the industrial-commercial center, but neither place has much in the way of accommodations. Kahului has a decent hotel and Mā'alaea Harbor has a few passable condos. There are also hangouts, flophouses, and the like for the windsurfers who seem to have found a permanent home on Maui.

East Maui is a mixed bag. You can find just about any degree of comfort for just about any price. This is partly because the area is huge, encompassing several towns and resorts. The full-service Wailea and Mākena Resorts along the southwestern shore charge fairly steep prices. Reasonably priced condos dot Kīhei, a hodgepodge strip running north from Wailea. (Kīhei is especially popular with families, so it's an easy place for kids to find playmates by the pool.) Upcountry Maui, the area that rises into the clouds of Haleakalā, has a couple of lodges and some bed-and-breakfasts. And Hāna, secluded in the easternmost part of Maui has only a few lodgings, with prices ranging from $ to $$$$.

Except in busy February and August, you should have no trouble getting a room on Maui. When booking your reservations, ask about packages and extras. Some hotels have special tennis, golf, or honeymoon packages. Others have room-and-car packages.

For information on Maui B&Bs and condominium rental agents, *see* Important Contacts A to Z Lodging section *in* Gold Guide.

CATEGORY	COST*
$$$$	over $200
$$$	$125–$200
$$	$75–$125
$	under $75

All prices are for a standard double room, excluding 10.17% tax and service charges.

West Maui

Hotels

$$$$ 🗹 **Embassy Suites.** This all-suite hotel with one- and two-bedroom apartments is north of Kā'anapali. In 1996, a health spa was added, as was a 24-foot water slide to spiff up the 1-acre pool. The rooms are decorated in an olive-and-tan color scheme. Each suite is set up for lānai dining and has two phones (fax- and modem-compatible), ceiling fans, a microwave oven, and a coffeemaker. The rates include a breakfast buffet each morning and a two-hour cocktail party each evening. ⊠ *104*

Kā'anapali Shores Pl., Lahaina 96761, ☎ 808/661–2000 or 800/462–6284, ꜰꜵꜹ 808/667–5821. 413 units. 3 restaurants, air-conditioning, refrigerators, in-room VCRs, pool, sauna, golf privileges, tennis court, health club, beach. AE, D, DC, MC, V.

$$$$ ⊞ **Hyatt Regency Maui.** This lavish property has nine major waterfalls plus several smaller ones and a collection of exotic animals, including penguins. The 750,000-gallon pool is something every honeymooning couple should have access to—there's a swim-up cocktail bar, swinging rope bridge, 130-foot water slide, and secret romantic grotto made more secluded by a waterfall cascading over the opening. An $11 million face-lift to this renowned Maui fantasyland in 1995–96 included improved access for people with disabilities, and some new facilities—an outdoor Jacuzzi, wedding gazebo, and beachfront bar. ⊠ *200 Nohea Kai Dr., Lahaina 96761,* ☎ *808/661–1234 or 800/233–1234,* ꜰꜵꜹ *808/667–4499. 815 rooms with bath. 7 restaurants, 7 bars, air-conditioning, 2 golf courses, 6 tennis courts, health club, beach, library, chapel. AE, D, DC, MC, V.*

$$$$ ⊞ **Maui Marriott.** Although this hotel shares the same beach with the glitzy Hyatt and Westin, it is much more subdued than its neighbors—the Marriot's tone is one of quiet elegance. The large rooms have pastel fabrics and bamboo furniture, and most have ocean views. The open-air lobby, filled with cascading orchids, has fishponds. The best thing about the Marriott, however, is the service. The staff is genuinely friendly and helpful. One of Maui's best Japanese restaurants, Nikko (☞ Chapter 3) is on the ground floor. ⊠ *100 Nohea Kai Dr., Lahaina 96761,* ☎ *808/667–1200 or 800/228–9290,* ꜰꜵꜹ *808/667–8575. 720 rooms with bath. 4 restaurants, 3 lobby lounges, air-conditioning, pool, golf course, 6 tennis courts, beach, dance club. AC, D, DC, MC, V.*

$$$$ ⊞ **Ritz-Carlton, Kapalua.** This Ritz has all the grace, elegance, and service for which the hotel chain is known. The spacious, comfortable rooms have oversize marble bathrooms and lānai; most rooms have ocean views. The hotel's three pools are each on a separate level connected by waterfalls. Guests on the Club floors have a private concierge and lounge with complimentary snack and beverage service all day long. ⊠ *1 Ritz-Carlton Dr., Kapalua 96761,* ☎ *808/669–6200 or 800/241–3333,* ꜰꜵꜹ *808/669–2028. 550 rooms with bath. 4 restaurants, 5 lobby lounges, air-conditioning, 3 pools, beauty salon, golf course, 10 tennis courts, health club, beach, shops, children's programs. AE, D, DC, MC, V.*

$$$$ ⊞ **Westin Maui.** This hotel is for active people who like to be out and about and don't spend much time in their rooms, which are rather small for the price. The lush grounds are another enticement not to stay indoors. There are more than 15 waterfalls and several lagoons filled with exotic birds. The hotel's impressive art collection, worth about $2 million, includes many Asian and Pacific works. ⊠ *2365 Kā'anapali Pkwy., Lahaina 96761,* ☎ *808/667–2525 or 800/228–3000,* ꜰꜵꜹ *808/661–5831. 761 rooms with bath. 3 restaurants, 4 lobby lounges, air-conditioning, 5 pools, beauty salon, hot tub, health club, beach, shops, children's programs. AE, D, DC, MC, V.*

$$$–$$$$ ⊞ **Kapalua Bay Hotel.** Surrounded by pineapple fields in a wonder-
★ fully secluded spot, this is one of the finest hotels in the state—it has a real Maui feel to it. The exterior is all understated white and natural wood; the open lobby, filled with flowering vanda and dendrobium orchids, has a fine view of the ocean beyond; rooms are spacious; and the staff is very helpful. The hotel, which is part of the Kapalua Bay Resort, hosts dedicated golfer celebrities who want to be left alone (both of the resort's golf courses were designed by Arnold Palmer) and some of the world's richest folks. A shopping plaza just outside the main hotel entrance has some of the island's finest restaurants and boutiques. ⊠ *1 Bay Dr., Kapalua 96761,* ☎ *808/669–5656 or 800/367–8000,* ꜰꜵꜹ

Lodging

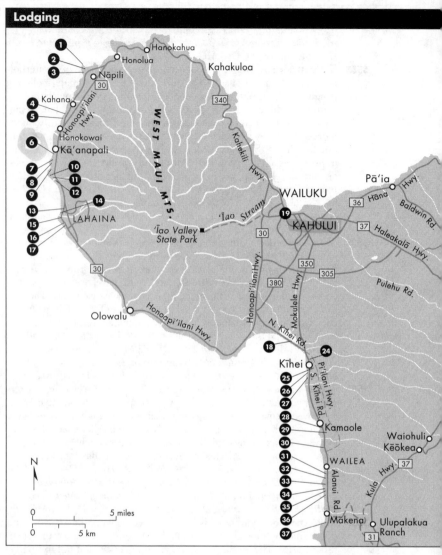

Aloha Cottages, **22**
Aston Wailea Resort, **33**
Embassy Suites, **5**
Four Seasons Resort, **36**
Grand Wailea, **34**
Hale Kama'ole, **29**
Heavenly Hāna Inn, **21**
Hotel Hāna-Maui, **23**
Hyatt Regency Maui, **12**
Kā'anapali Ali'i, **10**

Kā'anapali Beach Hotel, **7**
Kama'ole Sands, **28**
Kapalua Bay Hotel and Villas, **2**
Kea Lani Hotel Suites and Villas, **35**
Koa Resort, **25**
Kula Lodge, **20**
Lahaina Hotel, **14**
Luana Kai Resort, **26**
Mana Kai-Maui, **30**
Maui Beach, **19**
Maui Islander, **16**

Maui Lu Resort, **24**
Maui Marriott, **11**
Maui Prince, **37**
Maui Sunset, **27**
Nani Kai Hale, **18**
Nāpili Kai Beach Club, **3**
Papakea Beach Resort, **4**
Pioneer Inn, **17**
Plantation Inn, **15**
Pu'unoa Beach Estates, **13**

Ritz-Carlton Kapalua, **1**
Royal Lahaina Resort, **6**
Stouffer Renaissance Wailea Beach Resort, **31**
Wailea Villas, **32**
Westin Maui, **9**
Whaler on Kā'anapali Beach, **8**

PACIFIC OCEAN

Pa'uwela

'Ulumalu Rd.
365
Huelo
Kailua
360

390 Kokomo
Makawao
Pukalani
377

Wailua

Nāhiku

360 Hāna Hwy.

Kula Hwy.
Haleakalā Hwy.
20
37
378

Haleakalā
Crater Rd.

Pi'ina'au Stream

Haleamau'u Trail

Haleakalā

Haleakalā
National Park

Kaupō Trail

Kaupō
31

21
22
HĀNA
23

Hāmoa

Pi'ilani Hwy.

Mū'olea

Kīpahulu

808/669–4694. 194 rooms with bath. 3 restaurants, air-conditioning, 2 pools, 2 18-hole golf courses, 6 tennis courts, beach, shops. AE, D, DC, MC, V.

$$$ ⊞ **Kāʻanapali Beach Hotel.** This hotel is right in the midst of all the Kāʻanapali action. And its rates are much more reasonable than those of its neighbors. Instead of glitz and flash, you'll find a comfortable hotel with a friendly Hawaiian staff. The hotel conducts complimentary classes in hula, lei making, ʻukulele playing, and more. ⊠ *2525 Kāʻanapali Pkwy., Lahaina 96761,* ☎ *808/661–0011 or 800/657–7700,* FAX *808/667–5978. 430 rooms with bath. Restaurant, lobby lounge, air-conditioning, pool, golf course, beach, shops. AE, DC, D, MC, V.*

$$$ ⊞ **Nāpili Kai Beach Club.** Ten beautifully landscaped, oceanfront acres
★ on one of the finest beaches in Maui attract a loyal following each year to what the owners call "Maui's Most Hawaiian Resort." The Japanese-style rooms have shoji doors that open onto beachfront lānai. Most rooms have kitchenettes; all have refrigerators and coffeemakers. There are packages that include a car, breakfast, and other extras for guests who stay five nights or longer. ⊠ *5900 Lower Honoapiʻilani Rd., Nāpili Bay 96761,* ☎ *808/669–6271 or 800/367–5030,* FAX *808/669–5740. 162 rooms with bath. 4 pools, hot tub, 2 putting greens, tennis court, beach. MC, V.*

$$$ ⊞ **Royal Lahaina Resort.** The lānai at this Outrigger property have stunning ocean or golf-course views that are worth the price of the room. What distinguishes the Royal Lahaina are the two-story ocean cottages, each divided into four units. The rooms open to the trade winds on two sides; the upstairs units have a private lānai, while those downstairs share one. Bedrooms have small comforts such as throw pillows. A new wedding gazebo in the cottage courtyard has a walkway lined with stepping stones, each engraved with the name of a couple married there and their wedding date. ⊠ *2780 Kekaʻa Dr., Lahaina 96761,* ☎ *808/661–3611 or 800/447–6925,* FAX *808/661–3538. 592 rooms with bath. 3 restaurants, air-conditioning, 3 pools, golf course, tennis court, beach, shops, chapel. AE, D, DC, MC, V.*

$$ ⊞ **Lahaina Hotel.** In this once-derelict hotel, rooms are decked out with
★ antique beds, wardrobes, and chests. Delightful country print curtains and spreads decorate the rooms. The transformation was masterminded by Honolulu businessmen Rick Ralston (also responsible for the rebirth of the Mānoa Valley Inn on Oʻahu) and Alan Beall. David Paul's Lahaina Grill, downstairs, is a trendy scene (☞ Chapter 3). ⊠ *127 Lahainaluna Rd., Lahaina 96761,* ☎ *808/661–0577 or 800/669–3444,* FAX *808/667–9480. 12 rooms with bath. Restaurant. AE, D, MC, V.*

$$ ⊞ **Maui Islander.** An alternative to the pricey West Maui resorts, the Islander is in a quieter section of Lahaina, a few blocks from the ocean. Large studios and even bigger one-bedrooms are spread among nine two-story buildings on a 10-acre jungle site filled with palms, banana trees, plumeria trees, and torch ginger. Upstairs rooms have high, open-beam ceilings. Each morning guests are served complimentary coffee. ⊠ *660 Waineʻe St., Lahaina 96761,* ☎ *808/667–9766 or 800/367–5226,* FAX *808/661–3733. 372 rooms with bath. Air-conditioning, pool, tennis court. AE, D, DC, MC, V.*

$$ ⊞ **Pioneer Inn.** Renovation work begun in 1995 and scheduled for completion in 1996 will erase the seaside seediness that the Pioneer was famous for, but the Lahaina Restoration Foundation likes what owner Howard Lennon has done with the place. Blessed with a heart-of-old-Lahaina location, surrounded by commerce and culture, the lawyer-turned-innkeeper concentrated on structural repairs and cleanup that would make his little inn the sort of place "decent" folk would frequent—without destroying the dockside ambience. Rates for the small hotel rooms have increased, but most still rent for under $100 a night. The worn furnishings are spare and amenities few. You might not want to spend your entire vacation here, but for a night or two of bargain-priced historic atmosphere, the place can't be beat. ⊠ *658 Wharf St., Lahaina 96761, ☎ 808/661–3636 or 800/457–5457, FAX 808/667–5708. 50 rooms with bath. Snack bars, pool. AE, D, DC, MC, V.*

$$ 🏨 **Plantation Inn.** The inn resembles a renovated Victorian home on a quiet country street in the heart of Lahaina, within walking distance of the ocean and all the down-to-earth bars, restaurants, and shops in the old whaling port. Each guest room is decorated differently, with antiques, stained glass, brass beds, and ceiling fans. Downstairs is one of Hawaii's best French restaurants, Gerard's, which adds to the romantic European charm of the place (☞ Chapter 3). At press time (winter 1996), this property had just filed for reorganization under Chapter 11, so changes may be afoot; call ahead. ⊠ *174 Lahainaluna Rd., Lahaina 96761, ☎ 808/667–9225 or 800/433–6815, FAX 808/667–9293. 18 rooms with bath; suite available. Restaurant, fans, refrigerators, pool. AE, MC, V.*

Condominiums

$$$$ 🏨 **Kā'anapali Ali'i.** This is a condominium but you'd never know it; the four 11-story buildings are put together so well, you still have the feeling of seclusion. Instead of tiny rooms, you can choose from one- and two-bedroom apartments. Each has a chaise in an alcove, a sunken living room, and a separate dining room. The Kā'anapali Ali'i is maintained like a hotel—with daily maid service, an Activities Desk, and a 24-hour front desk. ⊠ *50 Nohea Kai Dr., Lahaina 96761, ☎ 808/667–1400 or 800/642–6284, FAX 808/661–1025. 264 1- and 2-bedroom units with bath. Air-conditioning, 2 pools, sauna, 18-golf course, 6 tennis courts, beach. AE, D, DC, MC, V.*

$$$$ 🏨 **Kapalua Bay Villas.** Privately owned and individually decorated one- and two-bedroom units may be rented through the Kapalua Bay Hotel. Condos are assigned to one of five luxury categories and regularly inspected to ensure that standards are maintained. A free shuttle to the hotel is available for renters, as are guest rates for golf, tennis, and other hotel amenities. ⊠ *1 Bay Dr., Kapalua 96761, ☎ 808/669–5656 or 800/367–8000, FAX 808/669–4694. 125 units.*

$$$$ 🏨 **Pu'unoa Beach Estates.** You may be looking for the kind of pampering you'll get here. With only eight units in the secluded beachfront property between Kā'anapali and Lahaina, guests can expect iced champagne on arrival, terry cloth robes, fully stocked in-room bars, outdoor hot tubs, daily in-room copies of the *Wall Street Journal,* and a concierge ready to help plan their stay. Prices here, however, are high: A two-bedroom condo *starts* at about $550 a night, which might include a car. Skylit rooms are tastefully furnished with koa-wood bookcases and floral bedspreads. ⊠ *45 Kai Pali Pl., Lahaina 96761, ☎ 808/667–5972 or 800/642–6284, FAX 808/667–5631. 8 units with bath. Pool, sauna, tennis, concierge. AE, MC, V.*

$$$ 🏨 **Papakea Beach Resort.** This resort in Honokōwai is an active place if you consider all the classes held here, such as swimming, snorkeling, and pineapple cutting. Papakea has built-in privacy because its units are spread out among 11 low-rise buildings on some 13 acres of land. You aren't really aware that you're sharing the property with 363 other units. Bamboo-lined walkways between buildings and fish-stocked ponds create a serene mood. There's a two-day minimum stay. ⊠ *3543 Honoapi'ilani Hwy., Lahaina 96761, ☎ 808/669–9680 or 800/367–5637, FAX 808/669–0751. 364 units with bath, including studios and 1- and 2-bedrooms. 2 pools, hot tub, saunas, spas, putting green, 4 tennis courts, beach. AE, MC, V.*

$$$　🏨 **Whaler on Kā'anapali Beach.** In its twin 12-story towers, this property has three good-size unit configurations, from studios to two-bedrooms. Many of the amenities here are real finds in condominium complexes—a 24-hour front desk, tennis courts, an exercise room and sauna, and a small sundries store. Units are elegantly furnished with tropical prints. The best thing about the Whaler, however, is its location; right on one of the state's finest beaches, between the Kā'anapali Beach Hotel and Whalers Village Shopping Center. Restaurants, golf, and tennis are nearby. ✉ *2481 Kā'anapali Pkwy., Lahaina 96761,* ☎ *808/661–4861 or 800/854–8843,* 🅵🅰🆇 *808/661–8315. 360 studio, 1- and 2-bedroom condo units with bath on Kā'anapali Beach. Air-conditioning, pool, sauna, golf, tennis court, exercise room, shops. AE, MC, V.*

Central Maui

Hotels

$$　🏨 **Maui Beach.** This no-frills hotel has decent rooms with modest furnishings. Its primary attraction—especially for business travelers on a tight budget—is its proximity to Kahului Airport and to the business and government offices of Kahului and Wailuku. The restaurant isn't bad—some of the specials can be pretty tasty. ✉ *170 Ka'ahumanu Ave., Kahului 96732,* ☎ *808/531–5235 or 800/367–5004,* 🅵🅰🆇 *808/533–4072 or 800/477–2329. 148 rooms with bath. Restaurant, air-conditioning, pool, airport shuttle. AE, D, DC, MC, V.*

Hostels

$　🏨 **YMCA.** Maui's only youth hostel is in a secluded location, which makes it very inconvenient for a typical bargain hunter (most likely a student), who may not have a car. Run by the YMCA, the hostel is a rustic wooden building on a beautiful peninsula nearly 35 miles from the airport. A separate bathhouse with hot showers is available, and men and women bunk separately, dorm style. Check in between 4 and 6 PM, and bring a bedroll. The maximum stay is five nights and the cost is about $15 per night. *For more information, write to:* ✉ *YMCA, Box 820, Wailuku 96793,* ☎ *808/244–3253.*

East Maui

Hotels

$$$$　🏨 **Aston Wailea Resort.** Formerly the Maui Inter-Continental, this hotel was sold to the Aston chain in 1995. The place still remains luxurious but not overwhelming. All rooms have private lānai and spacious bathrooms; some are right on the beach. The beautiful grounds have paths you can follow through jungles of palm, banana, and torch ginger. You can book sailing and snorkeling excursions at the activities desk. ✉ *3700 Wailea Alanui, Wailea 96753,* ☎ *808/879–1922 or 800/367–2960,* 🅵🅰🆇 *808/874–8331. 516 rooms with bath. 2 restaurants, air-conditioning, 3 pools, hot tub, 3 18-hole golf courses, tennis privileges, beach, shops. AE, D, DC, MC, V.*

$$$$　🏨 **Four Seasons Resort.** This is a favorite Maui hotel among many,
★　partially because of its location: smack dab on one of the Valley Isle's finest beaches with all the amenities of the well-groomed Wailea Resort, including Emerald, the newest golf course, which opened in 1994. The property itself is no less a stunner, with terraces, courtyards, gardens, waterfalls, and fountains. Nearly all the rooms have an ocean view and combine traditional style with tropical touches. You'll find terry cloth robes and Japanese *yukatas* (robes) in each room, and the best service in Hawai'i. ✉ *3900 Wailea Alanui, Wailea 96753,* ☎ *808/874–8000 or 800/334–6284,* 🅵🅰🆇 *808/874–6449. 380 rooms with*

bath. 3 restaurants, 4 bars, pool, 3 golf courses, tennis privileges, health club, shops. AE, D, DC, MC, V.

$$$$ 🏨 **Grand Wailea.** Opulence and luxury are everywhere at this 42-acre
★ resort. Streams meander through magnificent gardens dotted with quiet enclaves that would seem an accident of nature were it not for the hotel-provided swing settees. A 2,000-foot multilevel "canyon riverpool" is part of the property's water park, with tarzan swings, water slides, and grottoes. The feeling of luxury extends to the spacious ocean-view rooms with overstuffed chaise lounges, a comfortable writing desk, natural-wood dining furniture, private lānai, three telephones, and an oversize marble tub. The Spa Grande cossets guests with relaxing and rejuvenating services that could turn even a marathoner into a sybarite—everything from regular aerobics classes to exotic Hawaiian treatments such as an *ali'i* honey steam wrap and *lomilomi* massage are available. ✉ *3850 Wailea Alanui Dr., Wailea 96753,* ☎ *808/875–1234 or 800/233–1234;* FAX *808/879–4077. 761 rooms with bath. 7 restaurants, 12 bars, 3 pools, spa, 3 18-hole golf courses, tennis privileges, beach, shops, children's programs, chapel. AE, D, DC, MC, V.*

$$$$ 🏨 **Heavenly Hāna Inn.** An impressive Japanese gate marks the entrance
★ to this upscale inn. The decor has Japanese overtones and may seem spare by western standards; however, each room has a TV. The furniture was built by Hāna residents who also refinished the suites' wood floors and walls. ✉ *Box 790, Hāna 96713,* ☎ *808/248–8442. 3 suites with bath. No credit cards.*

$$$$ 🏨 **Hotel Hāna-Maui.** This get-away-from-it-all favorite of the rich and
★ famous is surrounded by a 7,000-acre ranch. Many say it's one of the best places to stay in Hawai'i—if not the Western Hemisphere. The guest quarters of this small, secluded hotel are divided among various free-standing wings and the plantation-look Sea Ranch cottages, which surround a state-of-the-art health spa. The spacious and airy rooms have bleached wood floors and tropical-style furniture upholstered in natural fabrics. A shuttle carries guests to a secluded beach nearby. ✉ *Box 9, Hāna 96713,* ☎ *808/248–8211 or 800/321–4262,* FAX *808/248–7264. 96 large units with bath. Restaurant, lobby lounge, 2 pools, spa, tennis courts, horseback riding, jogging, shops, library. AE, D, DC, MC, V.*

$$$$ 🏨 **Kea Lani Hotel Suites & Villas.** This all-suite resort at the southern
★ end of Wailea offers privacy to suit the most reclusive celebrities in oceanside two- and three-bedroom villas—each with its own small pool—but within easy reach of the dining, shopping, and activities of Wailea and West Maui. All accommodations in the main hotel—a seven-story W embracing the villas, pools, and oceanside grounds—are spacious one-bedroom suites with dining lānai, a sofa bed in the living room, wet bar, microwave, coffeemaker, entertainment center . . . all the comforts and necessities of home, plus what may be the most luxurious marble bathrooms on the island. There are three pools—one with games and activities for families, a second with a swim-up bar and slide, and a third reserved for adults who want to swim laps or get away from the kids and spend some time lounging with a good book. ✉ *4100 Wailea Alanui, Wailea 96753,* ☎ *808/875–4100 or 800/882–4100,* FAX *808/875–1200. 413 1-bedroom suites, 37 2- and 3-bedroom villas. 3 restaurants, deli, 2 lobby lounges, air-conditioning, in-room VCRs, 3 pools, wading pool, beauty salon, 2 hot tubs, 3 18-hole golf courses, tennis privileges, health club, beach, shops, children's program. AE, D, DC, MC, V.*

$$$$ 🏨 **Maui Prince.** The attention to service, style, and presentation are apparent from the minute you walk into the delightful open-air lobby of this low-key luxury hotel. Rooms on three levels surround a courtyard and Japanese garden with carefully tended plants and a bubbling stream. Each evening a small ensemble performs chamber music in the courtyard. Room decoration is understated, in tones of mauve and beige. Unfortunately, there's an earth berm between the hotel and the beach—part of the agreement the hotel had to make with the zoning commission and local residents—so an ocean view isn't possible from the first floor. ⊠ *5400 Mākena Alanui Rd., Mākena 96753, ☎ 808/874–1111 or 800/321–6284, ℻ 808/879–8763. 290 rooms with bath. 4 restaurants, air-conditioning, pool, 2 18-hole golf courses, 6 tennis courts, beach, shops. AE, D, DC, MC, V.*

$$$$ 🏨 **Stouffer Renaissance Wailea Beach Resort.** This is the first hotel you'll
★   come to once you enter the stylish Wailea Beach Resort. Most of the hotel's luxury rooms are in a seven-story building on fantastic Mōkapu Beach. The hotel emphasizes Hawaiian flavor, with gigantic contemporary tapestries and gorgeous carpets in the public areas; outside, you'll find gardens of exotic flowers, waterfalls, and reflecting ponds—plenty of activities are available right on the property. Don't miss the hotel's prized restaurant, Raffles (☞ Chapter 3). ⊠ *3550 Wailea Alanui Dr., Wailea 96753, ☎ 808/879–4900 or 800/992–4532, ℻ 808/874–5370. 347 rooms with bath. 4 restaurants, 5 bars, air-conditioning, refrigerators, 2 pools, hot tub, 2 tennis courts, health club, beach, shops, children's programs. AE, D, DC, MC, V.*

$$–$$$ 🏨 **Kula Lodge.** The Kula Lodge isn't your typical Hawaiian place, for
★   two reasons: first, it looks like a chalet property that should grace the Swiss Alps; and second, two of its five units come with a fireplace. However, the lodge is charming and cozy in spite of its nontropical ambience. Set on three wooded acres, it has a spectacular view of the valley and ocean enhanced by the surrounding forest and fields of flowers. The five guest quarters are in two wooden cabins. The rooms do not have phones or TVs. It's a perfect spot for a romantic interlude or for reading a good book next to a roaring fire. The property has an art gallery and a protea co-op that will pack the unusual flowers for you to take home. ⊠ *RR1, Box 475, Kula 96790, ☎ 808/878–2517 or 800/233–1535, ℻ 808/878–2518. 5 units with bath. Restaurant, lobby lounge, shops. MC, V.*

$$ 🏨 **Maui Lu Resort.** The first hotel in Kīhei, this place might remind you
         of a rustic lodge. The main lobby was once the summer home of the original owner, and over the years, the Maui Lu has added numerous wooden buildings and cottages to its 28 acres. Of the 129 rooms, 50 are right on the beach in their own secluded area. The rest are across Kīhei Road on the main property. In addition, 16 large, one-bedroom cottages have a garden setting and screened-in lānai. The decor isn't fancy, but it isn't tacky either. ⊠ *575 S. Kīhei Rd., Kīhei 96753, ☎ 808/879–5881 or 800/922–7866, ℻ 808/922–8785. 129 rooms with bath. Restaurant, lobby lounge, air-conditioning, pool, tennis court, beach, shops. AE, D, DC, MC, V.*

$ 🏨 **Aloha Cottages.** If you want to meet the people in the little town of
        Hāna, check into one of these cottages, run by Fusae Nakamura. Tourism is Mrs. Nakamura's way of earning extra money for her family now that she's retired, and she takes it seriously. The three two-bedroom units and one studio all have kitchens. The rooms are sparsely furnished but clean and adequate. A special touch is the carefully tended fruit trees on the neighboring property—Mrs. Nakamura often supplies her guests with the harvest, which includes papaya, bananas, and avocados. ⊠ *Hāna 96713, ☎ 808/248–8420. 4 cottages with bath. Kitchenettes. No credit cards.*

$ 🏨 **Nani Kai Hale.** This property, at the head of a seemingly endless beach,
        has condominium units and rooms without kitchens in sparkling white, six-story buildings. The pool is better than average, and there's a nice lawn out back, but the main attraction here is the glorious sand. Although there are no restaurants, dining and groceries may be found

within a mile. No phones are available, except for long-term guests. ✉ *73 N. Kīhei Rd., Kīhei 96753,* ☎ *808/879–9120 or 800/367–6032,* FAX *808/875–0630. 46 condo units on the beach. Some hotel rooms available; other units are studios, 1-, and 2-bedrooms, with kitchens. Pool. No credit cards.*

Condominiums

$$$ ☷ **Wailea Villas.** The Wailea Resort opened with three fine condominium buildings, calling them, appropriately, Wailea ʻEkahi, Wailea ʻElua, and Wailea ʻEkolu (Wailea One, Two, and Three)—and now includes three more: Grand Champion, Mākena Surf, and Polo Beach Club. All have beautifully landscaped grounds, large units with exceptional views, and access to one of the island's best beaches. Wailea ʻElua is usually considered the nicest of the properties, with more expensive furnishings and rates to match. The three original villas are an expansive property, with all the amenities of the fine Wailea Resort, including daily maid service and a concierge. ✉ *3750 Wailea Alanui Dr., Wailea 96753,* ☎ *808/879–1595 or 800/367–5246,* FAX *808/874–3554. 270 units in 6 complexes; studio, 1-, 2-, and 3-bedroom apartments. Pools, golf privileges, tennis privileges, beach. MC, V.*

$$–$$$ ☷ **Kamaʻole Sands.** This is a huge property for Kīhei—11 four-story buildings wrap around a grassy slope clustered with swimming and wading pools, a small waterfall, whirlpool baths, and barbecues; it's just across the road from Kīhei Beach. All units have private lānai and laundry facilities. There is a 24-hour front desk, an Activities Desk, and on-property food and beverage. ✉ *2695 S. Kīhei Rd., Kīhei 96753,* ☎ *808/874–8700 or 800/367–5004,* FAX *808/879–3273. 268 studio, 1-, 2-, and 3-bedroom condo units with bath. Restaurant, air-conditioning, kitchens, pool, wading pool, hot tubs, 4 tennis courts. AE, D, DC, MC, V.*

$$ ☷ **Hale Kamaʻole.** This is a good bet if you're hoping to find playmates for your kids. Like other Kīhei condos, Hale Kamaʻole attracts vacationing families from the neighbor islands. The price is right, and the playgrounds, for all ages, are handy. The beach is within strolling distance right across the road. This property's eight buildings are set in a U shape to capture the best ocean views, and there's an attractive lawn. ✉ *2737 S. Kīhei Rd., Kīhei 96753,* ☎ *808/879–2698 or 800/367–2970. 187 1- and 2-bedroom condo units with bath. Air-conditioning, 2 pools, tennis court, playground. No credit cards.*

$$ ☷ **Koa Resort.** This establishment's five two-story buildings face a beautiful lawn that serves as a putting green. Rooms are large and furnished in bamboo and rattan; lānai are lush with bougainvillea. The huge 120-foot-long pool is spanned by a bridge with a diving board. This reasonably priced property is as nice as most in upscale Kāʻanapali. ✉ *811 S. Kīhei Rd., Kīhei 96753,* ☎ *808/879–1161. 54 1-, 2-, and 3-bedroom units with bath. Pool, spa, putting green, tennis court, shuffleboard. MC, V.*

$$ ☷ **Luana Kai Resort.** This resort, right on the beach, has lovely views. The buildings are widely separated allowing guests privacy. Rooms are decorated with rattan furnishings and tropical prints, and you also get a loft in the two- and three-bedroom units. ✉ *940 S. Kīhei Rd., Kīhei 96753,* ☎ *808/879–1268 or 800/669–1127,* FAX *808/879–1455. 113 1-, 2-, and 3-bedroom condominiums. Pool, hot tub, putting green, tennis court, shops. AE, MC, V.*

$$ ☷ **Mana Kai-Maui.** Here you can get a studio without a kitchen, or a one- or two-bedroom unit with a kitchen on the end of one of the nicest beaches in the state, just down the strip from the Stouffer Renaissance Wailea. The decor is modest—what people on the Islands might call typically tropical—but the view of the ocean right outside the lānai overcomes any reservations you might have about the rooms' interiors. The Mana Kai-Maui has a very good beachfront restaurant, open for lunch and dinner. ⊠ *2960 S. Kīhei Rd., Kīhei 96753,* ☎ *808/879–1561 or 800/525–2025,* FAX *808/874–5042. 98 units. Restaurant, lobby lounge, pool, beach, shops. AE, D, DC, MC, V.*

$$ 🖬 **Maui Sunset.** If you want to get in shape on your vacation, this is the place—it has one of the only health spas in a Kīhei condo. There is a whirlpool for soaking away post-exercise aches and pains, as well as a variety of other activities for the sports-minded. You have a choice of spacious one-, two-, and three-bedroom units, which have been decorated in pleasant pastels and are in two five-story concrete-block buildings. ⊠ *1032 S. Kīhei Rd., Kīhei 96753,* ☎ *808/879–0674 or 800/843–5880. 225 condominiums. Air-conditioning, pool, sauna, putting green, tennis court, health club, shuffleboard, volleyball, beach. No credit cards for rooms; prepayment required.*

5 Nightlife and the Arts

Watching a sunset from a tropical perch, taking a moonlight stroll along a near-perfect crescent beach, or dining in a meadow are among the best nightlife options on Maui.

NIGHTLIFE

IGHTLIFE ON MAUI can be of the make-your-own-fun variety. As on all the Neighbor Islands, the pace is a bit slower than what you'll find in Waikīkī.

Dancing, lū'au shows, dinner cruises, and so on are found mainly in the resort areas. Kā'anapali in particular can really get hopping, with myriad activities for visitors of all ages. The old whaling port of Lahaina also parties with the best of them—its Halloween observances are legendary—and attracts a younger, often towheaded crowd who all seem to be visiting from towns on the West Coast. Overall, Wailea and Kapalua appear more sedate, but the Aston Wailea Resort has one of the island's liveliest dance floors at the Inu Inu Lounge, which always seems jammed.

☺ If you're looking for something to do at night with the kids, try **Reach Out to the Stars.** Astronomy buffs can get their fill of stargazing at this unique nightly program run by a real astronomer. A constellation slide show is followed by a look through giant binoculars and a deep-space telescope. ⊠ *Hyatt Regency Maui's Lahaina Tower, 200 Nohea Kai Dr., Kā'anapali,* ☎ *808/661–1234, ext. 3225.* ☉ *Nightly at 8, 9, and 10.* ⊡ *$10.50.*

Bars and Clubs

Comedy
Comedy Club (⊠ Maui Marriott, Kā'anapali Beach Resort, ☎ 808/667–1200). Every Sunday evening is laugh night at the Marriott; owners of the Honolulu Comedy Club have set up a weekly Valley Isle venue. Although the show starts at 8 PM in the Lobby Bar, it's better to get there early since it's caught on in a big way. Tickets are $15.

Contemporary Music
Lost Horizon (⊠ 3550 Wailea Alanui Dr., Wailea, ☎ 808/879–4900). This popular spot in the Stouffer Wailea Beach Resort features live easy-listening music, often Hawaiian. There's some dancing here, but it's on the slow side.

Makai Bar (⊠ Maui Marriott, Kā'anapali Beach Resort, ☎ 808/667–1200). You can listen to Hawaiian music here at this comfortable spot on the Kā'anapali coast.

Molokini Lounge (⊠ Maui Prince Hotel, Mākena Resort, ☎ 808/874–1111). You can see Molokini Island before the sun sets from this bar with a great ocean view. Live, often Hawaiian-themed music is usually played here. There's a dance floor for late-night revelry.

Rock Music
Banana Moon (⊠ Maui Marriott, Kā'anapali Beach Resort, ☎ 808/667–1200). This is a lively spot in the Maui Marriott Hotel, open nightly from 9 to 2. It has high-tech decor and good music, and is an enjoyable place to meet young tourists and hotel employees out for a night on the town.

Hamburger Mary's (⊠ 2010 Main St., Wailuku, ☎ 808/244–7776) has a dance floor so small it's cute, tucked into a corner where the sound system puts out recorded music that's loud enough for the dancers without deafening customers in other parts of the restaurant.

Hard Rock Café (✉ Lahaina Center, 900 Front St., Lahaina, ☎ 808/667–7400). Maui's version of the Hard Rock is popular with young locals and tourists who like their music *loud*.

Inu Inu Lounge (✉ Aston Wailea Resort, ☎ 808/879–1922). There's dancing nightly here starting at 9, with live music—rock, big bands, or golden oldies. This is an active spot for young crowds from Wailea, Kīhei, and Mākena. It also lures groups who are visiting the resort.

Moose McGillycuddy's (✉ 844 Front St., Lahaina, ☎ 808/667–7758). The Moose offers live music Wednesday, Friday, and Saturday nights; otherwise, it's recorded music, but it's played so loud you would swear it's live. This entertaining place tends to draw an early-20s crowd, who come for the burgers and beer and to meet one another.

Planet Hollywood (✉ 744 Front St., Lahaina, ☎ 808/667–7877). There's little in the way of nightlife, especially for younger people, on Maui. This Maui edition of the popular Planet Hollywood chain, though, does provide a party-like atmosphere. You'll find island touches turning up amid the usual showbiz memorabilia. The food includes some local specialties like Maui potato chips and Hawaiian pizza (pineapple is a better pizza topping than you might imagine) enliven the usual pasta, burgers, and rock-music fare.

Spats II (✉ Hyatt Regency Maui, Kā'anapali Beach Resort, ☎ 808/667–7474). This club is open for disco dancing Sunday through Thursday 10 PM–2 AM and Fridays and Saturdays until 4. There's a cover charge on Friday and Saturday nights.

Tsunami (✉ Grand Wailea, 3850 Wailea Alanui Dr., Wailea, ☎ 808/875–1234). You can dance to recorded Top-40 hits here from 9 PM until 4 AM on Saturday night and until 1 AM the other six nights of the week.

Jazz

Pacific'O (✉ 505 Front St., Lahaina, ☎ 808/667–4341). There's only one place to hear live jazz on the beach. It's a mellow, pacific sort of jazz, and it plays till midnight. A little something to accompany the cocktails and jazz? Try the shrimp wontons with Hawaiian salsa—they're a winner.

Dinner and Sunset Cruises

✕ *America II* **Sunset Sail.** The star of this two-hour cruise is the craft itself—a 1987 America's Cup 12-meter class contender that is exceptionally smooth and steady, thanks to its renowned winged keel design. ✉ *Lahaina Harbor, Slip 5, Lahaina 96761,* ☎ *808/667–2195.* 🎫 *$25.*

✕ **Genesis Sailing Charters.** This dinner sail goes for 2½ hours and includes a delicious meal on the 48-foot luxury sailing yacht *Genesis*. The cruise is limited to 20 passengers at a time. ✉ *Box 10697, Lahaina 96761,* ☎ *808/667–5667.* 🎫 *$56.*

✕ *Kaulana* **Cocktail Cruise.** This two-hour sunset cruise (with a bit of whale-watching thrown in, in season) features an island *pūpū* menu (hot and cold hors d'oeuvres), an open bar, and live music. ✉ *Lahaina Harbor, Lahaina 96761,* ☎ *808/871–1144.* 🎫 *$36.*

✕ *Scotch Mist* **Charters.** A two-hour champagne sunset sail is offered on the 25-passenger Santa Cruz 50 sloop *Scotch Mist II*. ✉ *Box 831, Lahaina 96767,* ☎ *808/661–0386.* 🎫 *$35.*

✕ **Windjammer Cruises.** This cruise includes a sit-down meal and live entertainment on the 70-foot, 110-passenger *Spirit of Windjammer,* a three-masted schooner. ✉ *658 Front St., Suite 101, Lahaina 96761,* ☎ *808/661–8600.* 🍽 *$65.*

Lū'au and Polynesian Revues

✕ **Drums of the Pacific.** The Hyatt presents a fine Polynesian revue on the hotel's Sunset Terrace. The all-you-can-eat-and-drink buffet dinner includes fresh fish, prime rib, chicken, and a native lū'au pūpū platter. Afterward, the show features traditional dances and chants from such countries as Tahiti, Samoa, and New Zealand. ✉ *Hyatt Regency Maui, Kā'anapali,* ☎ *808/661–1234, ext. 4420.* 🍽 *$55.* ☉ *Dinner seating Mon.–Sat. begins at 5:15, show at 7.*

✕ **Maui's Merriest Lū'au.** The Aston Wailea's oceanfront lawn is a beautiful spot for a lū'au. The traditional feast begins with a rum-punch welcome and an imu ceremony, and the evening includes colorful Polynesian entertainment. ✉ *Aston Wailea Resort, Wailea,* ☎ *808/879–1922.* 🍽 *$52.* ☉ *Tues., Thurs., Fri., 5:15.*

✕ **Old Lahaina Lū'au.** This is the best commercial lū'au you'll find on Maui—it's small, personal, and authentic. The Old Lahaina Lū'au is held on the beach at 505 Front Street in Lahaina, presumably the former Hawaiian entertainment grounds of the royals. You'll get all-you-can-eat traditional Hawaiian lū'au food: *kālua* (roasted) pork, chicken long rice, lomilomi salmon, haupia (a coconut dessert with the consistency of Jell-o squares), and other items, such as fresh fruit and salad. You'll also get all you can drink. Guests sit either on tatami mats or at tables. Then there's the entertainment, featuring a musical journey from Old Hawai'i to the present with hula, chanting, and singing. The attention to detail here is remarkable. ✉ *505 Front St., Lahaina,* ☎ *808/667–1998.* 🍽 *$56.* ☉ *Mon.–Sat. 5:30–8:30.*

✕ **Wailea Sunset Lū'au.** A five-star hotel, the Stouffer The five-star Stouffer hotel puts on its excellent Hawaiian lū'au once a week. It features open bar, a lū'au buffet, music by a Hawaiian band, and a Polynesian show with dancers performing pieces from around the Pacific—including one dancer wielding a "fire knife." ✉ *Stouffer Wailea Beach Resort, 3550 Wailea Alanui Dr.,* ☎ *808/879–4900. Reservations essential.* 🍽 *$51.* ☉ *Thurs. 5:30–8:30 PM.*

Shows

✕ **Maui Tropical Plantation's Hawaiian Country Barbecue & Rodney Arias Revue.** This Hawaiian country evening with a *paniolo* (cowboy) theme starts with a narrated tram ride through about half of the 120-acre showcase of Hawai'i's leading agricultural crops; then it moves to an all-you-can-eat barbecued steak dinner and open bar. At 6:30, lively entertainers put on a Hawaiian country-and-western variety show; the audience can join in for some square dancing. ✉ *Maui Tropical Plantation, Waikapu,* ☎ *808/244–7643.* 🍽 *$48.95.* ☉ *Tues.–Thurs. 4:30–7:30. AE, MC, V.*

THE ARTS

Most of Maui's cultural activities are community efforts, with theater, film, and symphony productions held in the island's central towns of Kahului and Wailuku. The **Maui Arts and Cultural Center** (✉ Maui Central Park, Kahului, ☎ 808/242–2787) has become the venue for more and more of the island's best live entertainment. The complex includes

It helps to be pushy in airports.

Introducing the revolutionary new TransPorter™ from American Tourister®. It's the first suitcase you can push around without a fight. TransPorter's™ exclusive four-wheel design lets you push it in front of you with almost no effort—the wheels take the weight. Or pull it on two wheels if you choose. You can even stack on other bags and use it like a luggage cart.

Stable 4-wheel design.

TransPorter™ is designed like a dresser, with built-in shelves to organize your belongings. Or collapse the shelves and pack it like a traditional suitcase. Inside, there's a suiter feature to help keep suits and dresses from wrinkling. When push comes to shove, you can't beat a TransPorter™. For more information on how you can be this pushy, call 1-800-542-1300.

Shelves collapse on command.

American Tourister®

Making travel less primitive.®

©1996 American Tourister®

Use your MCI Card® for the easy way to call when traveling.

MCI. Calling Card

415 555 1234 2244
J.D. SMITH

Convenience on the road

- Your MCI Card® number is your home number, guaranteed.
- Pre-programmed to speed dial to your home.
- Call from any phone in the U.S.

MCI.

1 - 8 0 0 - 7 5 4 - 8 9 4 1

the 1,200-seat **Castle Theater,** which hosts classical, country, and world-beat concerts by touring musicians; a 4,000-seat **amphitheater** for large outdoor concerts; and the 350-seat **McCoy Theater** for plays and recitals. Art, crafts, and hula lessons are offered regularly in the center's workshops and studios. For current programs, check the daily newspaper, the *Maui News.*

Film

International Film Festival. This acclaimed salute to celluloid used to be restricted to Honolulu, but now festival films are presented on the Neighbor Islands, including Maui. With support from the East-West Center and local donors, the festival brings together filmmakers from Asia, the Pacific Basin, and North America to view feature films, documentaries, and shorts every November. The films are shown at the Holiday Theaters in the Ka'ahumanu Center and at selected resort hotels. To find out about specific films and dates, call the International Film Festival Office (☎ 808/944–7200) in Honolulu.

Music

Kapalua Music Festival. Since 1982, the music festival has brought some of the world's finest musicians to Maui for several days each summer. Representatives from Juilliard and the Chicago and New York philharmonics, the Tokyo String Quartet, Israeli-born musical director Yishak Schotten, and violinist Joseph Swensen are only a few of those who have performed at the festival. Kapalua usually has special room rates during the festival. ⊠ *J. Walter Cameron Center, 95 Mahalani St., Wailuku 96793,* ☎ *808/244–3771.* ☜ *$10–$25.*

Maui Philharmonic Society. The Society has presented such prestigious performers as Ballet Hispanico, Shostakovich String Quartet, and the New-Age pianist Philip Glass. ⊠ *J. Walter Cameron Center, 95 Mahalani St., Wailuku 96793,* ☎ *808/244–3771.*

Maui Symphony Orchestra (☎ 808/244–5439). The symphony orchestra performs five season concerts and a few special musical sensations as well. The regular season includes a Christmas concert, an opera gala, a classical concert, and two pops concerts outdoors.

Theater

Baldwin Theatre Guild. Dramas, comedies, and musicals are presented by this group about eight times a year. The guild has staged such favorites as *The Glass Menagerie, Brigadoon,* and *The Miser.* Musicals are held in the Community Auditorium, which seats 1,200, while all other plays are presented in the Baldwin High School Mini Theatre. ⊠ *1650 Ka'ahumanu Ave., Kahului,* ☎ *808/242–5821.* ☜ *$8 adults.*

Maui Community Theatre. Now staging about six plays a year, this is the oldest dramatic group on the island, started in the early 1900s. Recent productions included *Fiddler on the Roof, Amadeus,* and the stage version of *The Rocky Horror Show,* with audiences showing up costumed as favorite characters, as they do for screenings of the movie in cities around the world. Each July the group also holds a fund-raising variety show, which can be a hoot. ⊠ *'Iao Theatre, 68 N. Market, Wailuku,* ☎ *808/242–6969.* ☜ *Musicals: $15; nonmusicals: $1–$2 less.*

Maui Youth Theatre. This theater program for children is one of the largest arts organizations in Hawai'i; it takes original plays and ethnic dramas into the schools around the county but also performs about 10 productions a year for the entire community. Plays have included name shows too, such as *Mame*. Performances are held in various locations around the island. ⊠ *Box 518, Puʻunēnē 96784,* ☎ *808/871–7484; box office* ☎ *808/871–6516.* 🎫 *$3–$8.*

6 Outdoor Activities, Beaches, and Sports

Visiting Maui's miles and miles of beaches is not the only activity on the island. You might hang glide, fish, sail, snorkel, surf, or waterski. And though it surprises visitors to this tropical paradise, the paniolo *(cowboy) culture of Upcountry makes horseback riding only natural here.*

BEACHES

MAUI HAS MORE THAN 100 MILES OF COASTLINE. Not all of this is beach, of course, but Maui's striking white crescents do seem to be around every bend. All of Hawai'i's beaches are free and open to the public—even those that grace the front yards of fancy hotels—so you can feel free to make yourself at home on any one of them.

Though they don't appear often, be sure to pay attention to any signs on the beaches. Warnings of high surf or rough currents should be noted. Before you seek shade under a swaying palm tree, watch for careening coconuts. Though the trades seem gentle, the winds are strong enough to knock the fruit off the trees and onto your head. Also be sure to apply sunscreen diligently. Maui is closer to the equator than many suspect, so although you may think you're safe, take it from those who've gotten a beet-red burn in 30 minutes or less—you're not. Drinking alcoholic beverages on beaches in Hawai'i isn't allowed.

West Maui

If you start at the northern end of West Maui and work your way down the coast in a southerly direction, you'll find the following beaches:

D. T. Fleming Beach is one of West Maui's most popular beaches. This charming, mile-long sandy cove is better for sunbathing than for swimming because the current can be quite strong. There are picnic tables, grills, paved parking, and rest-room facilities with showers. ⊠ *Take Hwy. 30 about 1 mi north of the Kapalua Resort.*

Honokōwai Beach is a bust if you're looking for that classic Hawaiian stretch of sand. Still, kids will enjoy the rocks here that have formed a pool. This beach does have showers and picnic tables. ⊠ *Across from Honokōwai Superette at 3636 Lower Honoapi'ilani Rd.*

Fronting the big hotels at Kā'anapali is one of Maui's best people-watching spots, **Kā'anapali Beach.** This is not the beach if you're looking for peace and quiet, but if you want lots of action, spread your towel here. Cruises, windsurfers, and parasails exit off this beach while the beautiful people take in the scenery. Although no facilities are available, the nearby hotels have rest rooms. You're also close to plenty of shops and concessions. ⊠ *Take any of the three Kā'anapali exits from Honoapi'ilani Hwy. Park at any of the hotels.*

Just south of Wailea is **Mākena,** with two good beaches. **Big Beach** is 3,000 feet long and 100 feet wide. The water off Big Beach is fine for swimming and snorkeling. If you walk over the cinder cone at Big Beach, you'll reach **Little Beach,** which is used for nude sunbathing. Officially, nude sunbathing is illegal in Hawai'i, but several bathers who pushed their arrests through the courts had their cases dismissed. Understand, though, that you take your chances if you decide to partake of a favorite local pastime at Little Mākena.

The lovely **Nāpili Beach** is right outside the **Nāpili Kai Beach Club,** a popular condominium for honeymooners. This sparkling white crescent makes a secluded cove perfect for strolling. No facilities are available here unless you're staying at the condo, but you're only a few miles south of Kapalua. ⊠ *5900 Honoapi'ilani Hwy. From upper highway, take cutoff road closest to Kapalua Resort.*

Olowalu Beach is a secluded snorkeling haven. With mask and fins, you'll see yellow tangs, parrot fish, and sometimes the state fish, the *humuhumunukunukuāpua'a*. You can call it a humu if you like. There's no parking here—except right on the road—and no facilities, but it's one of Maui's best sandy spots. ⊠ *South of Lahaina at mi marker 14.*

South of Olowalu you'll find **Wailea's five crescent beaches,** which stretch nearly 2 miles with relatively little interruption by civilization. Several hotels call Wailea home, and more condominiums are under construction. So far the buildings haven't infringed on the beaches in a noticeable way. With any luck, the population boom won't affect this area either. Swimming is good here—the crescents protect the shoreline from rough surf. Few people populate these beaches—mostly hotel guests who have briefly forsaken the pools of the nearby lodgings—which makes Wailea a peaceful haven. ⊠ *Drive south from Kihei, along the western shore of east Maui.*

Central Maui

If you want to see some of the world's finest windsurfers, stop at **Ho'okipa Beach** on the Hana Highway. The sport has become an art—and a career, to some—and its popularity was largely developed right at Ho'okipa. Waves get as high as 15 feet. This is not a good swimming beach, nor the place to learn windsurfing yourself, but plenty of picnic tables and barbecue grills are available. ⊠ *About 1 mi past Pā'ia on Hwy. 36.*

The beaches in Central Maui are far from noteworthy, but if you're staying in the area, try **Kanahā Beach** in Kahului. A long, golden strip of sand bordered by a wide grassy area, this is a popular spot for windsurfers, joggers, and picnicking Maui families. Kanahā Beach has toilets, showers, picnic tables, and grills. ⊠ *In Kahului, take Dairy Rd. toward airport. At Koeheke, make a left and head toward Kahului Bay.*

East Maui

Kaihalulu Beach was once a favorite spot of privacy-seeking nudists. Hāna's red-sand beach has gotten a little less secluded as more people have discovered it, but this is still a gorgeous cove, with good swimming and snorkeling. No facilities are available. ⊠ *Start at Hāna Community Center at end of Hau'oli Rd. and walk along outside of Ka'uiki Hill. The hike won't be easy, but it's worth the effort.*

OUTDOOR ACTIVITIES AND SPORTS

Baseball

Hawai'i Winter Baseball began in 1993 with a two-month season (mid-Oct.–mid-Dec.) and four locally sponsored teams consisting mostly of local players, and a few promising minor leaguers from the Mainland. In 1994 two female pitchers joined the league. The Maui Stingrays (☎ 808/242–2950) play their home games at War Memorial Stadium in Wailuku. Reserved seats cost $6.

Bicycling

Maui's roads are narrow, which can make bicycling a harrowing experience. Some visitors rent a bike just to ride around the resort where they're staying, but going anywhere else requires getting on a two-lane highway. If it looks like something you'd like to try anyway, **A & B Moped**

Rental (✉ 3481 Lower Honoapi'ilani Hwy., Lahaina, ☎ 808/669–0027) is about your only choice. Bikes rent for $15 a day.

Camping and Hiking

Like the other Hawaiian islands, Maui is riddled with ancient paths. These were the roads the Polynesians used to cross from one side of the island home to the other. Most of these paths today are too difficult to find. But if you happen to stumble upon something that looks as if it might have been a trail, chances are good it was used by the ancients. In fact, most trails on Maui are not well marked. Only three areas have clearly marked trailheads. Luckily, they're some of the best hikes on the island.

Haleakalā National Park

This park in Maui's center is a hiking haven—**Haleakalā Crater** itself has several trails. To get yourself oriented, stop at the **Park Headquarters Visitors Center** (✉ Haleakala Crater Rd., 7,000-ft elevation, ☎ 808/572–9306. ☉ Daily 7:30–4) (☞ Chapter 2). As you drive to the top of the 10,023-foot dormant volcano on the Haleakalā Highway, you'll come to **Hosmer Grove** less than a mile after you enter the park. This lovely, forested area has an hour-long nature trail. You can pick up a map at the trailhead and camp without a permit in the campground. There are six campsites, pit toilets, drinking water, and cooking shelters.

There's also **Halemau'u Trail** near the 8,000-foot elevation. The walk to the crater rim is a grassy stroll, then it's a switchback trail nearly 2 miles to the crater floor.

Nearly 4 miles from the trailhead you'll find **Hōlua Cabin,** which you can reserve—at least three months in advance—through the National Park Service (✉ Box 369, Makawao 96768, ☎ 808/572–9306). Nearby, you can pitch a tent, but you'll need a permit that's issued on a first-come, first-served basis at Haleakalā National Park Headquarters Visitors Center (☞ *above*).

If you opt to drive all the way to the top of Haleakalā, you'll find a trail called **Sliding Sands,** which starts at about the 10,000-foot elevation, descending 4 miles to the crater floor. The scenery is spectacular; it's colorful and somewhat like the moon. You can reach the above-mentioned Hōlua Cabin in about 7 miles if you veer off to the left and out of the crater on the Halemau'u Trail. If you continue on the Sliding Sands Trail, however, you'll come to **Kapalaoa Cabin** within about 6 miles, and at about 10 miles you'll hit **Palikū Cabin,** both also available from the park service with at least three months' notice. All three cabins have bunks, firewood, water, and a stove and are limited to 12 people. They can be reached in less than a day's walk. Palikū Cabin has tent camping nearby with toilets and drinking water. Tent permits, again, are issued at park headquarters on the day you want to use them.

Kaupō Gap is a trail you might want to use to hike out of Haleakalā, but it will put you on the northeastern side of the island, along the Hāna Highway. It begins at about 6,400 feet and descends through private ranch land. This is a rough trail—9 miles from Palikū Cabin to Highway 31—and hiking it can take as long as 10 hours. It's all downhill, which is particularly strenuous on already-tired legs and feet.

'Ohe'o Gulch in East Maui is part of Haleakalā National Park, but it's very different from the crater. That's because it's over on the Hāna side of the park—which actually extends far beyond the mountain you see in the clouds. This is a lush, rainy, tropical area. You can reach 'Ohe'o

Gulch by continuing on the Hāna Highway about 10 miles past Hāna; two major trails begin here. The first trail is **Makahiku Falls,** a half-mile jaunt from the parking lot to an overlook. You can go around the barrier and get closer to the falls if you like. From here, you can continue on the second trail for another 1½ miles. You'll dead-end at **Waimoku Falls.** There's camping in this area with no permit required, although you can only stay for three nights. Toilets, grills, and tables are available here, but no water.

Another camping and hiking area is **Polipoli Forest,** on the southern slope of Haleakalā. It was once heavily forested, until cattle and goats chewed away most of the natural vegetation. Starting in about 1930, the government began a program to reforest the area, and soon redwoods, cedars, pines, and cypresses took hold. Because of the elevation, it's a bit cooler here and sometimes wet and misty. But you'll appreciate the peace and quiet.

To reach the forest, drive on Highway 377 past Haleakalā Road to Waipoli Road. Go up the hill until you reach the park. Next to the lot, you'll see a small campground and a cabin you can rent from the Division of State Parks (write far in advance for the cabin to: ⊠ Box 1049, Wailuku 96793, ☎ 808/244–4354; for the campground, you can wait until you arrive in Wailuku, then visit the State Parks office at 54 High St.).

The first trail you'll see at Polipoli is **Redwood Trail,** which starts at the camping area. The elevation here is about 6,200 feet, and the trail winds through groves of redwoods and pines until it ends near the ranger's cabin at about 5,300 feet. This hike will take about an hour.

For terrific views, try the **Haleakalā Ridge Trail.** It's a fairly easy 1.6-mile hike along a semibare ridge. At the end, you'll find a small cave often used for shelter, including overnight camping. Take your camera, because you'll walk along a ridge with some of Hawai'i's best scenery.

If you want to ascend a fairly rough and rocky path, try the **Upper Waiakoa Trail.** It begins at 6,400 feet and extends 7 miles, until you've reached a viewing point at 7,800 feet. This trail isn't an easy stroll, but you'll be rewarded with terrific vistas at the top.

Other areas around Maui are good for hiking, but they're a bit more difficult to find since trailheads aren't always marked. Look for these areas:

'Īao Valley. Drive on 'Īao Valley Road west from the Central Maui town of Wailuku to reach this spot. Here you can drive up to a lookout to see the famous 'Īao Needle. Go up the steps to the viewing point and climb over the railing on the left. Follow the dirt trail going upward. If you climb 2 miles to a plateau behind the 'Īao Needle, you'll find some great views.

Wai'ānapanapa State Park. You'll reach this spectacular park right before you reach Hāna town; you can camp here and take some hikes along the wild coastline. One trail leads from the park along the coast for 3 miles ending at Hāna Bay. Another heads in the opposite direction, past old burial sites. The park has 12 cabins—each with electricity, bathrooms, kitchens, two bedrooms, and linens—that rent for between $10 and $15 per person a night. These cabins must be reserved months in advance through the **Division of State Parks**(⊠ Box 1049, Wailuku 96793, ☎ 808/244–4354). Campsites for 60 people are also available at Wai'ānapanapa. You'll need a permit, but these sites are available free from the state by writing to the above address. At the campground you'll find cold showers, flush toilets, drinking water, and cooking facilities.

Deep-Sea Fishing

If fishing is your sport, Maui is the place for it. You'll be able to throw in hook and bait for fish like *'ahi* (yellowfin tuna), *aku* (a skipjack tuna), barracuda, bonefish, *kawakawa* (bonito), mahimahi, (a dolphin fish—*not* the mammal), Pacific blue marlin, *ono* (wahoo), and *ulua* (jack crevalle). On Maui you can fish throughout the year, and you don't need a license.

Plenty of fishing boats run out of Lahaina and Māʻalaea harbors. If you charter a boat by yourself, expect to spend in the neighborhood of $600 a day. But you can share the boat with others who are interested in fishing on the same day for about $100. Though there are at least 10 companies running boats on a regular basis, these are the most reliable:

Finest Kind Inc. (⊠ Slip 7, Lahaina Harbor, Box 10481, Lahaina 96767, ☎ 808/661–0338); **Hinatea Sportfishing** (⊠ Slip 27, Lahaina Harbor, Lahaina 96761, ☎ 808/667–7548); and **Luckey Strike Charters** (⊠ Box 1502, Lahaina 96767, ☎ 808/661–4606). **Ocean Activities Center** (⊠ 1325 S. Kīhei Rd., Suite 212, Kīhei 96753, ☎ 808/879–4485 or 800/367–8047 ext. 448) can arrange fishing charters as well. You're responsible for finding your own transportation to the harbor.

Fitness Centers

There are more fitness centers in hotels than anywhere else on Maui, and those will probably be the most convenient for you. The **Grand Hyatt Wailea's** Spa Grande is the largest (and grandest) in Hawaiʻi. The **Kea Lani** has state-of-the-art equipment at its fitness center, and a friendly staff to help you get the most out of it. At the Kāʻanapali Resort, the **Hyatt Regency** has a guests-only health spa with all the trimmings and daily aerobics classes. The **Maui Marriott** has a weights room and aerobics with a $3 charge for nonguests, and the **Westin Maui** has a health club with weights, aerobics, and massage. Daily aerobics are offered at Wailea, the Aston Wailea Resort, Grand Wailea, Kea Lani, and Stouffer Renaissance.

Outside the resorts, the **Lahaina Nautilus Center** (⊠ 180 Dickenson St., Suite 201, ☎ 808/667–6100) has a complete fitness center. **World Gym** (⊠ 845 Waineʻe St., Lahaina, ☎ 808/667–0422) specializes in weights. The **Kahana Gym** (⊠ 4310 Lower Honoapiʻilani Hwy., Kahana, ☎ 808/669–7622) specializes in free weights. There are other clubs as well, but they are simply not convenient unless you want to drive to Kahului or Wailuku—about an hour from West Maui and 45 minutes from Wailea.

Golf

Participant

How do you keep your mind on the game in a place like Maui? It's very hard, because you can't ignore the view, but Maui has become one of the world's premier golf-vacation destinations. The island's major resorts all have golf courses, each of them stunning. They're all open to the public, and most lower their greens fees after 2:30 weekday afternoons.

The **Kapalua Golf Club** (⊠ 300 Kapalua Dr., Lahaina, ☎ 808/669–8044) has two 18-holers—the Village Course and the Bay Course—both designed by Arnold Palmer. Kapalua is also well known among television sports watchers. One of the Kapalua Bay Hotel owners is Mark Rolfing, who's made a name for himself as a producer of sporting events (he founded the Kapalua International) and as an announcer on ESPN. Greens fees at Kapalua are $115–$125 for nonguests, $75–$80 for guests. Carts go for $25 and clubs for $45.

The lovely **Mākena Golf Course** (⊠ 5415 Mākena Alanui Rd., Kīhei, ☎ 808/879–3344) features two 18-hole courses, North and South, designed by Robert Trent Jones, Jr. Of all the resort courses, this one is the most remote. At one point golfers must cross a main road, but there are so few cars that this poses no problem. Greens fees are $110 for nonguests, $80 for guests, including a cart.

The **Royal Kā'anapali Golf Courses** (⊠ Kā'anapali Beach Resort, Lahaina, ☎ 808/661–3691) are two of Maui's most famous, due to television exposure. The layout consists of two 18-hole courses, each of which is famous in its own right. The North Course was designed by Robert Trent Jones, Sr., while the South Course architect was Arthur Jack Snyder. Greens fees run $100 for resort guests, $110 for nonguests.

The **Wailea Golf Club** (⊠ 120 Kaukahi St., Wailea, ☎ 808/879–2966) has three courses: the Gold and the Blue, which were designed by Arthur Jack Snyder, and the newer Emerald, designed by Robert Trent Jones, Jr., and named one of the top-10 new courses in the United States by *Golf* magazine in 1995. In his design, Snyder incorporated ancient lava-rock walls and *heiau* (temples) for an even more unusual golfing experience. Greens fees are $130 for nonguests and $90 for guests.

Maui has municipal courses as well, where the fees are lower. Be forewarned, however, that the weather can be cooler and wetter, and the locations may not be as convenient as those you are used to at home. The **Waiehu Municipal Golf Course** (☎ 808/243–7400) is set on the northeast coast of Maui a few miles past Wailuku off Highway 340. Greens fees are $30; carts are $15. Up the hill from Kīhei, the **Silversword Golf Course** (⊠ 1345 Pi'ilani Hwy., Kīhei, ☎ 808/874–0777) charges $69 including a cart.

Tournaments

Maui has a number of golf tournaments, many of which are televised nationally. Especially popular during the last two months of each year, Maui's golf tourneys are of professional caliber and worth watching. For more information and tournament dates, call Rolfing Productions, ☎ 808/669–4844.

The **Isuzu Kapalua International Championship of Golf** held each November at the Kapalua Resort is the granddaddy of them all and now draws big names competing for a $600,000 purse. Kapalua is the host of the **Kirin Cup World Championship of Golf,** with teams representing the U.S. Professional Golf Association (PGA) tour, the European PGA tour, the Japan PGA Tour, and the Australia/New Zealand PGA tour. Golfing greats play on Kapalua's Bay Course for a $1.1 million purse each December.

At Kā'anapali, the **GTE Kā'anapali Golf Classic** pits senior duffers in a battle for a $300,000 purse each December.

Over in Wailea, the **Annual Asahi Beer Kyosan Golf Tournament** has a $100,000 purse. The **LPGA Women's Kemper Open** moved from Kaua'i to Wailea starting with the February 1990 tournament.

Hang Gliding

One company on Maui will strap wings on your back and let you jump off a cliff, but it insists on giving you lessons first. You can also try tandem flights, where an instructor handles all the flying and you just lie back and enjoy. Experienced hang gliders can leap off Haleakalā Crater. Contact **Maui Soaring Supplies** (⊠ RR 2, Box 780, Kula, ☎ 808/878–1271). Beginner lessons start at about $55.

Horseback Riding

You can take a one- or two-hour ride, a daylong tour along scenic trails of Upcountry or an overnight pack trip into Haleakalā Crater.

For a five-hour ride through an unspoiled Maui rain forest, streams, and a secluded waterfall, call **Adventures on Horseback** (⊠ Box 1771, Makawao 96768, ☎ 808/242–7445 or 808/572–6211). Mauian Frank Levinson takes only six riders at a time and provides a picnic lunch. This is a highly recommended way to go horseback riding, as well as tour an often overlooked part of Maui. The cost is $150.

Charley's Trail Rides & Pack Trips (⊠ c/o Kaupō Ranch, Kaupō 96713, ☎ 808/248–8209) requires a stout physical nature—but not a stout physique: riders must weigh under 200 pounds. Charley's overnighters go from Kaupō—a *tiny* village nearly 20 miles past Hāna—up the slopes of Haleakalā to the crater. The cost is $300 per person for parties of four to six, including meals and cabin or campsite equipment. Charges are higher for fewer people.

Kā'anapali Kau Lio (⊠ Box 10656, Lahaina 96761, ☎ 808/667–7896), a West Maui stable, offers a guided three-hour mountain ride above Kā'anapali for $80; it also has a sunset ride for $90.

Mākena Stables (⊠ 7299–A S. Mākena Rd., Kīhei 96753, ☎ 808/879–0244) offers, among other rides, a 5½-hour winery tour with a catered lunch for $140.

Pony Express Tours (⊠ Box 535, Kula 96790, ☎ 808/667–2200) charges $40 for an hour's ride on Haleakalā Ranch or $60 for two hours.

Rainbow Ranch (⊠ Box 10066, Lahaina 96761, ☎ 808/669–4991) charges $35 for an hour-long beginner's plantation ride; a three-hour West Maui picnic ride goes for $90.

Sailing

Because of its proximity to the smaller islands of Moloka'i, Lāna'i, Kaho'olawe, and Molokini, Maui can provide one of Hawai'i's best sailing experiences. Most sailing operations like to combine their tours with a meal, some throw in snorkeling or whale-watching, while others offer a sunset cruise.

If you want to really sail—as opposed to cruising on a motorized catamaran or other vessel—try **Genesis Sailing Charters** (⊠ Box 10697, Lahaina 96761, ☎ 808/667–5667); **Maui–Moloka'i Sea Cruises** (⊠ 831 Eha St., Suite 101, Wailuku 96793, ☎ 808/242–8777); **Sail Hawai'i** (⊠ Box 573, Kīhei 96753, ☎ 808/879–2201); **Scotch Mist Charters** (⊠ Box 831, Lahaina 96767, ☎ 808/661–0386); and **Sentinel Yachts** (⊠ Box 1022, Lahaina 96767, ☎ 808/661–8110).

Scuba Diving and Snorkeling

Believe it or not, Maui is just as scenic underwater as it is above. In fact, some of the finest diving spots in Hawai'i lie along the Valley Isle's western and southwestern shores. If you're a certified diver, you can rent gear at any Maui dive shop simply by showing your PADI or NAUI card. Unless you're familiar with the area, however, it's probably best to hook up with a dive shop for an underwater tour. Additionally, the only really decent shore dive is at Honolua Bay, a marine reserve above Kapalua Resort. The water is usually rough during the winter.

Popular Maui dive shops—stores that deal exclusively in the sale and rental of diving equipment, as well as lessons and certification—include **Capt. Nemo's Ocean Emporium** (⊠ 150 Dickenson St., Lahaina, ☎ 808/661–5555); **Central Pacific Divers** (⊠ 780 Front St., Lahaina, ☎ 808/661–8718); **Dive Maui** (⊠ Lahaina Market Place, Lahaina, ☎ 808/667–2080); **Ed Robinson's Diving Adventures** (⊠ Box 616, Kīhei, ☎ 808/879–3584); and **Lahaina Divers** (⊠ 143 Dickenson St., Lahaina, ☎ 808/667–7496). All provide equipment with proof of certification, as well as introductory dives for those who aren't certified. Introductory boat dives generally run about $80.

Dive shops have their own favorite spots, but we describe places below that we think are better than others. You can consult a dive shop near you for further information.

Cathedrals is a group of pinnacles off the nearby island of Lānaʻi that rise from 60 feet to just below the water's surface. There are fascinating chambers that play games with the sun rays in beautiful ways; the chambers provide a home for moray eels, lobsters, and ghost shrimp, which keep the area well watched.

Honolua Bay, in West Maui, is a marine preserve with many varieties of coral and tame tropical fish, including large ulua, kāhala, barracuda, and manta rays. With depths of 20 to 50 feet, this is a popular spot for introductory dives. Dives are generally given only during the summer months.

Mokuhoʻoniki Rock lies off the east coast of nearby Molokaʻi. During World War II, it was a military bombing target, so there are plenty of interesting artifacts to explore. Large pelagic fish hang around here, such as barracuda, gray reef sharks, and ulua.

Molokini Crater, at ʻAlalākeiki Channel, is a crescent-shaped islet formed by the top of a volcanic crater. This marine preserve's depth range (10–80 feet), combined with the attraction of the numerous tame fish dwelling here that can be fed by hand, makes it a popular introductory dive site.

There are pieces of military equipment for exploring in a couple of locations off Maui: a Sherman tank and landing craft in 60 feet of water off the shore of southwest Maui, and another Sherman tank at 80 feet, offshore from the Mākena Resort.

The same dive companies that take scuba aficionados on tours will take snorkelers as well—for less money. One of Maui's most popular snorkeling spots can be reached only by boat: Molokini Crater, that little bowl of land off the coast of the Mākena Resort. For about $55 you can spend the day at Molokini, with meals provided.

Ocean Activities Center (⊠ 1325 S. Kīhei Rd., Suite 212, Kīhei 96753, ☎ 808/879–4485) does the best job with a Molokini tour, although many other companies offer a Molokini snorkeling tour.

You can also find some good snorkeling spots on your own. Specifically, secluded **Windmill Beach** (⊠ take Hwy. 30 3½ mi north of Kapalua, then turn onto the dirt road to the left) has a superb reef for snorkeling. A little more than 2 miles south of Windmill Beach, another dirt road leads to **Honolua Bay;** the coral formations on the right side of the bay are particularly dramatic. One beach south of the Kapalua Resort, you'll find **Nāpili Bay,** which is also quite good for snorkeling.

Almost the entire coastline from Kā'anapali south to Olowalu offers fine snorkeling. Favorite sites include the area just out from the cemetery north of Wahikuli State Park, near the lava cone called **Black Rock,** on which Kā'anapali's Sheraton Maui Hotel is built (tame fish will take bread from your hand there); and the shallow coral reef at **Olowalu** (south of Olowalu General Store).

The coastline from Kīhei to Mākena is also generally good for snorkeling. The best sites are found near the rocks of **Kama'ole Beach III** in Kīhei and the rocky fringes of Wailea's **Mōkapu, Ulua, Wailea,** and **Polo** beaches.

Between Polo Beach and Mākena Beach (shortly before the turnoff to 'Ulupalakua) is **Five Caves,** where you'll find a maze of underwater grottoes below offshore rocks. This spot is recommended for experienced snorkelers only, since the tides can get rough. At Mākena, the waters around the **Pu'uōla'i** cinder cone provide superb snorkeling.

If you need gear, **Snorkel Bob's** (⌷ 5425 Lower Honoapi'ilani Rd., Nāpili, ☎ 808/669–9603), in the Nāpili Village Hotel, will rent you a mask, fins, and snorkel, and throw in a carrying bag, map, and snorkel tips for as little as $2.50 a day.

Surfing

Although on land it may not look as if there are seasons on Maui, the tides tell another story. In winter the surf's up on the northern shores of the Hawaiian Islands, while summer brings big swells to the southern side. That means the near-perfect winter waves on Maui can be found at **Honolua Bay,** on the northern tip of West Maui. To get there, continue 2 miles north of D. T. Fleming Park on Highway 30 and take a left onto the dirt road next to a pineapple field; a path takes you to the beach.

Next best for surfing is **Ho'okipa Beach Park** (⌷ off Hwy. 36 a short distance east of Pā'ia), where the modern-day sport began on Maui. This is the easiest place to watch surfing because there are paved parking areas and picnic pavilions in the park. A word of warning: The guys who come here are pros, and if you're not, they may not take kindly to your getting in their way.

You can rent surfboards and boogie boards at many surf shops, such as **Indian Summer Surf Shop** (⌷ 193 Lahainaluna Rd., Lahaina, ☎ 808/661–3794); **Second Wind** (⌷ 111 Hāna Hwy., Kahului, ☎ 808/877–7467); **Lightning Bolt Maui** (⌷ 55 Ka'ahumanu Ave., Suite E, Kahului, ☎ 808/877–3484); and **Ole Surfboards** (⌷ 1036 Limahana Pl., Lahaina, ☎ 808/661–3459).

Maui Surfing School (☎ 808/875–0625) guarantees that one two-hour lesson is all it takes to have "anyone who can walk" standing on a surfboard and riding the gentle waves of Lahaina Harbor. The cost is $65 per person (maximum six per class), including equipment rental; group discounts are available.

Tennis

The state's finest tennis facilities are at the **Wailea Tennis Club** (⌷ 131 Wailea Ike Pl., Kīhei, ☎ 808/879–1958), often called "Wimbledon West" because of its grass courts; there are also 11 Plexipave courts and a pro shop. You'll pay between $10 and $12 an hour per person for the hard courts, and between $40 and $60 per court per hour for the grass numbers. Weekday mornings there are clinics to help you improve your groundstrokes, serve, volley, or doubles strategy.

At the Mākena Resort, just south of Wailea, the **Mākena Tennis Club** (⊠ 5415 Mākena Alanui Rd., Kīhei, ☎ 808/879–8777) has six courts. Rates are $5 per person per hour for guests, $8 for nonguests. After an hour, if there's space available, there's no charge.

Over in West Maui, the **Royal Lahaina Tennis Ranch** (⊠ 2780 Keka'a Dr., ☎ 808/661–3611, ext. 2296) in the Kā'anapali Beach Resort offers 11 courts and a pro shop. Guests pay $6 an hour per person, while nonguests are charged $9.

The **Hyatt Regency Maui** (⊠ 200 Nohea Kai Dr., Kā'anapali, ☎ 808/661–1234, ext. 3174) has five courts, with rentals and instruction. Courts go for $12 an hour for singles, $15 for doubles.

Kapalua Tennis Garden (⊠ 100 Kapalua Dr., Kapalua, ☎ 808/669–5677) serves the Kapalua Resort with 10 courts and a pro shop. You'll pay $9 an hour if you're a guest, $10 if you're not.

There are several small tennis facilities around the island, usually one or two courts in smaller hotels or condos. Most of them, however, are open only to their guests. The best free courts anyone can use are the five at the **Lahaina Civic Center** (⊠ 1840 Honoapi'ilani Hwy., Lahaina, ☎ 808/661–4685), near Wahikuli State Park; they're available on a first-come, first-served basis.

Waterskiing

Only one company tows water-skiers off the coast of Maui: **Lahaina Water Ski** (⊠ 104 Wahikuli Rd., Lahaina, ☎ 808/661–5988). For $30 per 15 minutes for one person, $50 per 30 minutes for one to three people, or $90 an hour for one to five people, Lahaina Water Ski provides the boat, driver, and equipment.

Windsurfing

Participant

It's been more than 15 years since Ho'okipa Bay was discovered by boardsailors, but in those years since 1980, the windy beach 10 miles east of Kahului has become the windsurfing capital of the world. The spot has optimal wave-sailing wind and sea conditions and, for experienced windsurfers, can offer the ultimate experience. Other locations around Maui are good for windsurfing as well—Honolua Bay, for example—but Ho'okipa is absolutely unrivaled.

Even if you're a windsurfing aficionado, chances are good you didn't bring your equipment. You can rent it—or get lessons—from these shops: **Kā'anapali Windsurfing School** (⊠ 104 Wahikuli Rd., Lahaina, ☎ 808/667–1964); **Maui Magic Windsurfing School** (⊠ 520 Keolani Pl., Kahului, ☎ 808/877–4816); **Ocean Activities Center** (⊠ 1325 S. Kīhei Rd., Kīhei, ☎ 808/879–4485); and **Maui Windsurfari** (⊠ Box 330254, Kahului, ☎ 808/871–7766). Lessons range from $30 to $60 and can last anywhere from one to three hours. Equipment rental also varies—from no charge with lessons to $20 an hour. For the latest prices and special deals, it's best to call around once you've arrived.

Tournaments

Not many places can lay claim to as many windsurfing tournaments as Maui. The Valley Isle is generally thought to be the world's preeminent windsurfing location, drawing boardsailing experts from around the globe who want to compete on its waves. In April, the **Marui/O'Neil Invitational** lures top windsurfers from at least a dozen countries to vie for a $30,000 purse. The **Hawaiian Pro-Am Speed Slalom Windsurfing Competition** and **Wailea Speed Crossing** take place in September. The **Maui Grand Prix** and the **Aloha Classic Wave Sailing World Championships** are held in October. The **Junior World Wave Sailing Championships,** for kids under 18 from around the world, is in May. All events are held at Hoʻokipa Bay, right outside the town of Pāʻia, near Kahului.

7 Shopping

*You'll enjoy browsing in the shops
that line Front Street in Lahaina
or the boutiques that are packed into
the major resorts. Kahului and Lahaina
also have some good-size shopping
malls.*

WHETHER YOU HEAD for a mall or opt for the boutiques hidden around the Valley Isle, one thing you should have no problem finding is clothing made in Hawai'i. The Hawaiian garment industry is now the state's third-largest industry, after tourism and agriculture.

Maui has an abundance of locally made arts and crafts in a range of prices. In fact, a group that calls itself Made on Maui exists solely to promote the products of its members—items that range from pottery and paintings to Hawaiian teas and macadamia caramel corn. You can identify the group by its distinctive Haleakalā logo.

You'll find some of the same merchandise in gift shops at museums and historic sites. And there's a crafts fair somewhere (check newspapers) almost every weekend on Maui. These have their share of kitsch, but you can almost always find high-quality woodcrafts, jewelry, and aloha wear at attractive prices, and you can "talk story" (chat) with the artists. You'll also find plenty of edible delights besides the usual pineapple or macadamia nuts on Maui—sweet bread, potato chips, and Maui onions are only a few of the possibilities.

Business hours for individual shops on the island are usually 9–5, seven days a week. Shopping centers tend to stay open later (until 9 or 10 at least one night of the week).

SHOPPING AREAS AND MALLS

Central Maui

Ka'ahumanu Center (⊠ 275 Ka'ahumanu Ave., Kahului, ☎ 808/877–3369) has nearly 100 shops and restaurants. Its anchor stores are Liberty House, Sears, and JCPenney; the popular Japanese retailer Shirokiya is worth visiting for its electronic gadgets, unusual kitchen utensils, toys, and other Japanese specialties, which make great gifts for the folks back home. You'll also find many recognizable mainland stores such as Caswell-Massey, Kay-Bee Toys, and Radio Shack. **Maui Hands**(☎ 808/877–0368) a notable specialty shop, is full of prints, jewelry, and high-quality craftwork by local artists (☞ Art, *below*). You might want to stop in at **Camellia Imports** for what the locals call "crack seed," a delicacy that's made from dried fruits, nuts, and sugar. When you're really ready for a shopping break, try the **Sharktooth Brewery Steakhouse** (☎ 808/871–6689), Maui's own entry in the microbrewery craze sweeping the U.S. mainland.

Market Street (⊠ Wailuku) has an eclectic mix of shops. **Requests** (⊠ 10 Market St., ☎ 808/244–9315) offers new music, oldies, '60s memorabilia, and friendly salespeople. **Jovian Gallery** (⊠ 7 Market St., ☎ 808/244–3660) showcases stunning Gima–painted silks and work by other local craftspeople; like her neighbor merchants, Marcia Godinez is happy to chat with visitors, recommend a restaurant, offer advice or directions . . . whatever.

Maui Mall Shopping Center (⊠ Corner of Ka'ahumanu and Pu'unēnē Aves., ☎ 808/877–5523) has 33 stores.

East Maui

Azeka Place Shopping Center (⊠ 1280 S. Kīhei Rd., ☎ 808/879–4449) in Kīhei is large and bustling.

Shopping Centers

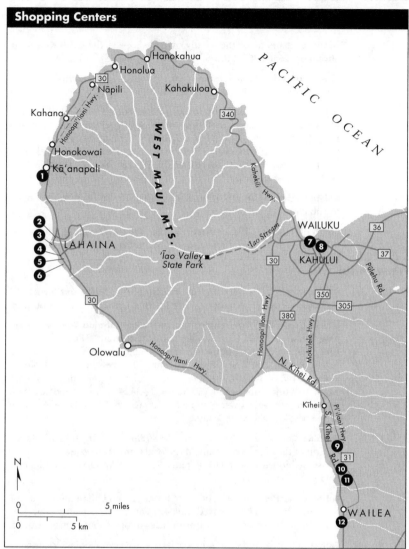

The old Makawao Theater was converted into the **Courtyard** (✉ 3620 Baldwin Ave.), a minimall of galleries and boutiques.

Maui residents favor the locally owned shops at the small **Kamaʻole Shopping Center** (✉ 2463 S. Kīhei Rd., ☎ 808/879–5233).

Makawao's Baldwin Avenue offers good cowboy-town browsing, though some yuppification has set in.

If you want to do some shopping in **Pāʻia** you can find clothing and handcrafted keepsakes in shops like **Alpha & Omega** (✉ 23 Hāna Hwy., ☎ 808/579–8775), **Nuage Bleu** (✉ 76 Hāna Hwy., ☎ 808/579–9792), and **Treasure Corner** (✉ 98 Hāna Hwy., ☎ 808/579–9954), or snacks and sweets at **Peaches & Crumble Baking Co.** (✉ 2 Baldwin Ave., ☎ 808/579–8612).

Rainbow Mall (✉ 2439 S. Kīhei Rd., ☎ 808/879–6144) is another place to rub elbows with Kīhei locals.

South of Kīhei, the Wailea Resort has the **Wailea Shopping Village** (☎ 808/879–4474), with 25 gift shops, boutiques, and restaurants.

West Maui

At the south end of town, New England–style **505 Front Street** (☎ 808/667–2514) has restaurants, snack shops, and a few retail boutiques.

Unlike many shopping centers in Hawaiʻi, the **Lahaina Cannery Shopping Center** (✉ 1221 Honoapiʻilani Hwy., Lahaina, ☎ 808/661–5304) isn't open-air, it's air-conditioned; it's in a building reminiscent of an old pineapple cannery. The center has some 50 shops, including **Dolphin Galleries** (☎ 808/661–5000), featuring sculpture, paintings, and other Maui artwork; **Superwhale** (☎ 808/661–3424) with a good selection of children's tropical wear; and **Kite Fantasy** (☎ 808/661–4766), one of the best kite shops on Maui.

Lahaina Center (✉ 900 Front St., ☎ 808/667–9216) houses Maui's edition of the Hard Rock Cafe, the World Cafe, Arabesque Maui (with classy fashions for women), Banana Republic, Waterwear, and a cinema with four screens.

Lahaina Market Place (✉ corner of Front St. and Lahainaluna Rd., ☎ 808/667–2636), a brick-paved walkway with a dozen quality boutiques and eateries, stretches back from an easy-to-miss Front Street entrance.

Chic and trendy, and nearly double its original size, **Whalers Village** (✉ 2435 Kāʻanapali Pkwy., Kāʻanapali, ☎ 808/661–4567) has grown into a major shopping center with Lahaina Whaling Museum (☞ Chapter 2) and 65 restaurants and shops, including such upscale haunts as Louis Vuitton, Hunting World, Tiffany & Co., and the Chanel Boutique.

The **Wharf Cinema Center** (✉ 658 Front St., ☎ 808/661–8748) has 31 air-conditioned shops and restaurants within a wooden building whose architectural features are nearly obscured by neighboring structures.

SPECIALTY STORES

Art

Maui has more art per square mile than any other Hawaiian island—maybe more than any other U.S. county. Artists love Maui, and they flock here to live and work. There are artists' guilds and co-ops, and galleries galore. Moreover, the town of Lahaina hosts Art Night every Friday starting at 6; galleries open their doors (some serve refreshments), musicians stroll the streets, and Chinese lion dancers parade along the main drag.

In Pāʻia you'll find **Eddie Flotte's Gallery and Studio** (✉ 83 Hāna Hwy., ☎ 808/579–9641), where the artist sells his charming watercolors, which document the sagging town and its people.

Lahaina Galleries has two locations in West Maui (✉ 728 Front St., Lahaina, ☎ 808/667–2152; ✉ Kapalua Resort, ☎ 808/669–0202) and one in the Wailea Resort (✉ Wailea Shopping Village, ☎ 808/879–8850).

Martin Lawrence Galleries (✉ Lahaina Market Place, ☎ 808/661–1788) represents locals and noted mainland artists in a bright gallery where the wry humor of the work on view, including hand-crafted jewelry and sculpture, adds to the cheerful atmosphere of the place.

One of the most interesting galleries on the island is the **Maui Crafts Guild** (✉ 43 Hāna Hwy., Pāʻia, ☎ 808/579–9697). The Guild, in a two-story wooden building alongside the Hāna Highway, is crammed with work by local artists. The best pieces are the pottery and sculpture. Upstairs, antique kimonos and batik fabric are on display.

Maui Hands (✉ Makawao Courtyard, 3620 Baldwin Ave., Makawao, ☎ 808/572–5194, and ✉ Kaʻahumanu Center, 275 Kaʻahumanu Ave., Kahului ☎ 808/877–0368) has paintings, prints, and jewelry by dozens of local artists, including paniolo-themed lithographs by Sharon Shizekawa, who knows whereof she paints: Each year she rides in the Kaupō Roundup.

The **Old Jail Gallery** (✉ 649 Wharf St., across the street from the Pioneer Inn and Lahaina Harbor, ☎ 808/661–0111) in the basement of the old Lahaina Court House sells work by artists who belong to the Lahaina Arts Society. The artists range from watercolorists to specialists in oil and sculpture.

Macario Pascual allows visitors to his **Pascual Art Studio-Gallery** (✉ 551 Waineʻe St., Lahaina, ☎ 808/667–6166).

Flamboyant Italian artist Piero Resta has his **Resta Studios** (✉ 313 W. Kuʻiʻaha Rd., ☎ 808/575–2203) in an old warehouse in the Upcountry town of Haʻikū. Visiting Resta is an experience in itself, but call first.

Sunset Galleries (✉ 758 Front St., Lahaina, ☎ 808/667–9112 and ✉ 156 Lahainaluna Rd., Lahaina, ☎ 808/661–3371) has exclusive rights in Hawaiʻi to sell the work of famous American Indian artist R. C. Gorman, among other artwork.

Traders of the Lost Art (✉ 62 N. Market St., Wailuku, ☎ 808/242–7753) is focused on primitive ritual art from New Guinea and Oceania, the gleanings of owner Tye Hartall's travels in the South Pacific. There's always half-a-store-full of other collectibles too, including bargain-priced aloha shirts at the back of the shop. If Tye's on the road, partner Barry is an equally entertaining storyteller.

Viewpoints (✉ 3620 Baldwin Ave., Makawao, ☎ 808/572–5979) calls itself Maui's only fine-arts collective; this cooperative venture of two dozen Maui painters and sculptors represents a wide variety of styles.

A popular Maui art enclave, **Village Gallery,** now has three locations—one in Lahaina (✉ 120 Dickenson St., ☎ 808/661–4402), one at the Lahaina Cannery Shopping Center (✉ 1221 Honoapiʻilani Hwy., ☎ 808/661–3280), and one in the Embassy Suites (✉ 104 Kāʻanapali Shores

Pl., ☎ 808/667–5115)—featuring such local artists as Betty Hay Free-land, Wailehua Gray, and Margaret Bedell.

As for exclusivity, **Wyland Galleries** (⊠ 697 Front St., Lahaina, ☎ 808/661–7099; ⊠ 711 Front St., Lahaina, ☎ 808/667–2285; ⊠ 136 Dick-enson St., Lahaina, ☎ 808/661–0590) is the only Maui shop to sell the work of Wyland, the marine artist whose favorite technique is a si-multaneous look at scenes from under and above the water. Though the artist continues to decorate Hawai'i's exteriors with his legendary murals, the galleries he operates throughout the state occupy him more and more. These days, the shops offer the work of other marine artists, as well as Wyland's own paintings.

Clothing

Aloha Wear

Andrade offers authentic, high-quality aloha wear in several hotel locations—including the Royal Lahaina, Sheraton Maui, Kapalua Bay, Maui Marriott, and Aston Wailea.

If you want something a bit more brazen—as in louder prints; definitely not what the locals would wear, but something that might work better at a wild party at home—try **Island Muumuu Works** (⊠ 180 Dickenson St., Lahaina, ☎ 808/661–5360; ⊠ Maui Mall Shopping Center, corner of Ka'ahumanu and Pu'unēnē Aves., Kahului, ☎ 808/871–6237).

Islandwear on the Beach (⊠ 505 Front St., Lahaina, ☎ 808/661–8897) has choice selections from such Hawaiian-wear clothiers as Reyn Spooner and Malia.

To find the kind of aloha wear, such as colorful shirts and muumuu dresses, worn by the people who live on Maui year-round, check out **Liberty House.** The store has six locations on the island including three shopping centers—Azeka Place Shopping Center, Ka'ahumanu Center, and Whalers Village (☞ Shopping Centers, *above*)—and three luxury hotels—the Maui Marriott, Stouffer Wailea, and Aston Wailea (☞ Chapter 4, Lodging).

Luana's (⊠ 869 Front St., ☎ 808/667–2275; ⊠ 658 Front St., at the Wharf, ☎ 808/661–0651) has souvenir-style (loud) prints.

Maui Muumuu Factory (⊠ 111 Hāna Hwy., Pā'ia, ☎ 808/871–6672) has plenty of splashy print dresses. Don't expect rock-bottom prices here, despite the "Factory" name, but it's a reliable source for really touristy aloha wear if you haven't time to shop around.

Reyn's (⊠ The Kapalua Bay Hotel, ☎ 808/669–5260; ⊠ Lahaina Can-nery Shopping Center, ☎ 808/661–5356) is an especially good source for the kind of aloha shirts local businessmen wear.

Sears (⊠ Ka'ahumanu Center, 275 Ka'ahumanu Ave., Kahului ☎ 808/877–2221) sells some decent Hawaiian dresses and aloha shirts.

Watumull's (⊠ Lahaina Market Place, corner of Front St. and La-hainaluna Rd., ☎ 808/661–0528) has the moderately priced, gener-ally bold prints favored by tourists; it's a great source for sundresses.

Designer Fashions

Brendi (⊠ Westin Maui, 2365 Kā'anapali Pkwy., Lahaina, ☎ 808/661–7113) has a large selection of designer fashions.

You can't go wrong at Liberty House, especially at its designer-wear boutiques, called **Collections by Liberty House.** There are three locations—

the Hyatt Regency and the Westin Maui, both in Kāʻanapali, and the Maui Prince in Mākena (☞ Chapter 4, Lodging).

Silks Kāʻanapali (⊠ Whalers Village, 2435 Kāʻanapali Pkwy., Kāʻanapali, ☎ 808/667–7133) is a delightful little shop that features hand-painted silk and exotic fashions from the Orient.

Resort Wear
WOMENSWEAR

Apparels of Pauline (⊠ Lahaina Market Place, on corner of Lahainaluna Rd. and Front St.,☎ 808/661–4774), features hand-painted clothing by Maui designers.

Try **Donna's Designs** (⊠ Lahaina Market Place, on corner of Lahainaluna Rd. and Front St., ☎ 808/667–1952).

Imports International (⊠ Wharf Cinema Center, 658 Front St., Lahaina, ☎ 808/661–8987) has skirts, dresses, and novelties imported from hot climates around the world.

Island Casuals (⊠ Lahaina Market Place, on corner of Lahainaluna Rd. and Front St., ☎ 808/667–9156) has locally designed beachwear and sundresses.

In another of Front Street's tucked-away shopping enclaves look for **Joani's Boutique** (⊠ Wharf Cinema Center, 658 Front St, Lahaina, ☎ 808/661–5588) with breezy, colorful styles.

In Pāʻia, **Tropical Emporium** (⊠ 104 Hāna Hwy., ☎ 808/579–8032) is one of the best resort-wear shops.

MENSWEAR

Although stores for women's resort wear are easy to find on Maui, those for men's resort wear are scarcer. Some recommended shops for men's clothing are:

Chapman's (⊠ Hyatt Regency, ☎ 808/661–4121; ⊠ Wailea Shopping Village, (☎ 808/879–3644) carries men's sportswear, including some aloha wear.

Kramer's Men's Wear (⊠ Lahaina Cannery Shopping Center, ☎ 808/661–5377; ⊠ Kaʻahumanu Center, ☎ 808/871–8671).

Reyn's (⊠ Kapalua Bay Hotel, ☎ 808/669–5260) sells its own line of not-so-loud aloha shirts called Reyn's Spooner shirts, which are especially popular with local businessmen.

Food

Many visitors to Hawaiʻi opt to take home some of the local produce: pineapples, papayas, guavas, coconuts, or Maui onions. You can find jams and jellies—some of them Made on Maui products—in a wide variety of tropical flavors. Cook Kwee's Maui Cookies have gained quite a following, as have Maui Potato Chips. Both are available in most Valley Isle grocery stores. Maui has just started growing its own macadamia trees—but it takes seven years before nuts can be harvested! Still, macadamia nuts are a favorite gift back home. Remember that fresh fruit must be inspected by the U.S. Department of Agriculture, so it's safer to buy a box that's already passed muster.

Maui is also the only place in Hawaiʻi that commercially produces its own wine. You can find bottles of Maui Blanc (a pineapple wine—it's not for everyone), Maui Blush, and Maui Brut-Blanc de Noirs Hawaiian Champagne in grocery stores.

Paradise Fruit (⊠ 1913 Kīhei Rd., Kīhei, ☎ 808/879–1723) sells ready-to-ship pineapples, Maui onions, and coconuts.

Take Home Maui (⊠ 121 Dickenson St., Lahaina, ☎ 808/661–8067) will deliver produce free to the airport or your hotel.

You might want to take a drive into Upcountry Maui and visit the **Tedeschi Winery** (☎ 808/878–6058). You can taste before you buy, and let's face it, the ambience here is better than that at a grocery store. ⊠ *To find the winery, take Hwy. 37 from Kahului toward Haleakalā. Continue for about 25 mi, through Pukalani and past the Kula Sanatorium.*

Gifts

By the Bay (⊠ 107 Bay Dr., Kapalua, ☎ 808/669–5227) specializes in shells, coral, and handcrafted jewelry.

Distant Drums (⊠ 125 Bay Dr., Kapalua, ☎ 808/669–5522) has a collection of primitive arts and crafts.

F. W. Woolworth (⊠ Maui Mall, Kahului, ☎ 808/877–3934) has plenty of inexpensive souvenirs.

The **Hilo Hattie Factory Outlet** (⊠ Lahaina Center, ☎ 808/661–8457) is a supermarket for all kinds of souvenirs.

Maui's Best (Ka'ahumanu Center and Wailea Shopping Village, ☎ 808/877–4831) has a wide selection of locally made gifts.

For less expensive gifts try **Maui Gift & Jewelry Factory Outlet** (⊠ 520 Keolani Pl., Kahului, ☎ 808/871–8086), one of Maui's better souvenir shops.

Maui on My Mind (⊠ Lahaina Cannery Shopping Center, ☎ 808/667–5597) offers fine arts and crafts made right on Maui.

Hawaiian Arts and Crafts

Some visiting shoppers are determined to buy only what they can't get anywhere else. The arts and crafts native to Hawai'i can be just the thing. Woods such as koa and milo grow only in certain parts of the world, and because of their increasing scarcity, prices are rising. In Hawai'i, craftsmen turn the exotic woods into bowls, trays, and jewelry boxes that will last for years.

Quilts may not sound Hawaiian, but the way they're done in the 50th state is very different from anywhere else in the world. Missionaries from New England were determined to teach the natives their homespun craft, but—naturally—the Hawaiians adapted quilting to their own style, with many of the designs influenced by local flora.

The **Hāna Cultural Center** (⊠ Ukea St., ☎ 808/248–8622) sells the distinctive island quilts and other Hawaiian crafts.

Technically neither a Hawaiian art nor craft, the fabric produced by **The Island** (⊠ 314 Ano St., Kahului, ☎ 808/871–4450) nevertheless possesses a definite Hawaiian character. A group of well-known Maui artists have formed this textile company, applying its colorful designs to bolts of beautiful print fabric.

John of Maui & Sons (⊠ 810 Ha'ikū Rd., B-6, Ha'ikū, ☎ 808/575–9422), in the Upcountry town of Ha'ikū, is one of the best places to find Hawaiian crafts on Maui. This little family operation turns out some of the most exacting wood products in the Islands.

Lahaina General Store (⊠ 829 Front St., Lahaina, ☎ 808/661–0944) has a few Hawaiian quilts, as well as other local craft items.

Jewelry

In Lahaina, a visit to **Claire the Ring Lady** (⊠ 858–4 Front St., ☎ 808/667–9288) can be a worthwhile jewelry-buying expedition. The somewhat eccentric craftswoman will make an original piece of jewelry for you while you wait.

Haimoff & Haimoff Creations in Gold (☎ 808/669–5213) in the Kapalua Resort features original work of award-winning jewelry designer Harry Haimoff.

Jack Ackerman's The Original Maui Divers (⊠ 640 Front St., ☎ 808/661–0988) has been crafting gold and coral into jewelry for more than 20 years.

Lahaina Scrimshaw (⊠ Whalers Village Shopping Mall, ☎ 808/661–3971) sells Hawaiian heirloom jewelry and tiny carved pendants.

Olah Jewelers (⊠ 839 Front St., Lahaina, ☎ 808/661–4551) displays Australian black opal jewelry designed by Yvette and George Olah.

8 Sidetrip to Lāna'i

Lāna'i's only population center is Lāna'i City, smack in the middle of the island. The town is surrounded by natural wonders: Garden of the Gods, an eerie canyon strewn with colorful boulders, to the northwest; breathtaking Hulopo'e Beach to the south; and Lāna'ihale, the highest point on the island, to the east.

FOR DECADES LĀNA'I WAS KNOWN as the Pineapple Island, with hundreds of acres of fields growing the golden fruit. Today, however, this 140-square-mile island has been renamed "Hawai'i's Private Island," as developers attempt to replace pineapples with people. The island, which was once rarely visited, is now joining most of its sister islands in the tourism business. In the past seven years, Dole Foods Inc., which owns 98% of the island, has opened two upscale hotels, the luxurious 102-room Lodge at Kō'ele and the 250-room Mānele Bay Hotel. Despite these new additions, Lāna'i—the third smallest of the islands—still remains the most remote and intimate destination in Hawai'i.

By Marty
Wentzel

Lāna'i's sole population center is called Lāna'i City, an old plantation town with 2,300 residents, whose tiny houses have colorful facades, tin roofs, and tidy gardens. With its well-planned grid of paved roads and small businesses, Lāna'i City adds one of the few hints of civilization to a mostly wild island.

Though the weather across much of the island is hot and dry, the Norfolk pines that line Lāna'i City's streets create a cool refuge. While there, you'll encounter some of the people who came from the Philippines to work in Lāna'i's pineapple fields. You'll also notice the many other nationalities as well, from Korean, Chinese, and Japanese to transplanted Mainland *haole* (Caucasians).

Lāna'i City has a few family-run shops and stores, but its options are limited. It also offers a couple of diner-style eateries as well as the charming old Hotel Lāna'i, an 11-room hostelry that serves as a gathering place for locals and tourists alike.

But Lāna'i City is not the real reason for coming to Lāna'i. Visitors should be prepared to spend a lot of time outdoors—Lāna'i has no commercial attractions, no shopping malls, and no bowling alleys. Instead you can visit such sights as the Garden of the Gods, where rocks and boulders are scattered across a crimson landscape as if some divine being placed them there as its own sculpture garden. You can spend a leisurely day at Hulopo'e Beach, where the waters are so clear that within a minute of snorkeling you can see fish the colors of turquoise and jade. And you can drive or hike to the top of Lāna'ihale, a 3,370-foot-high, windswept perch from which you can see nearly every inhabited Hawaiian island.

Although today it is an island that welcomes visitors with its friendly, rustic charm, Lāna'i has not always been so amiable. The earliest Polynesians believed it to be haunted by evil ghosts who gobbled up unsuspecting visitors. In 1836 a pair of missionaries named Dwight Baldwin and William Richards came and went after failing to convert the people of Lāna'i to their Christian beliefs. In 1854 a group of Mormons tried to create the City of Joseph on Lāna'i, but they, too, retreated in 1857 after drought forced them to abandon their endeavors.

One of Lāna'i's more successful visitors was a man named Jim Dole. In 1922 Dole bought the island for $1.1 million and began to grow pineapples on it. He built Lāna'i City on the flatlands where the crater meets the mountains. Then, for shipping pineapples, he planned the harbor at Kaumālapa'u. Four years later, as he watched the first harvest sail away to Honolulu, this enterprising businessman could safely say that Lāna'i's Dole Plantation was a success. As is the case throughout the state, however, pineapple has become an unprofitable crop in the last decade; thus the new emphasis on tourism.

Today, a visit to Lāna'i can be simple or elegant. You can be all alone simply by leaving your hotel. That is, unless you encounter the deer on the hillsides, or the dolphins that come into Mānele Bay to swim with you, or the spirits that linger amid the ancient fishing village of Kaunolū. On the other hand, you can rub elbows with sophisticated travelers during a game of croquet at the Lodge at Kō'ele or a round of golf at one of the island's two championship courses. Bring casual clothes because many of your activities will be laid-back, whether you're riding the unpaved roads in a four-wheel-drive vehicle or having a drink on the front porch of the Hotel Lāna'i. You may want to pack something dressier, too, if you plan to eat at one of the finer restaurants, such as the Mānele Bay Hotel.

With two new golf clubhouses, a revitalized movie house, a spiffy riding arena, a new airport terminal, and construction of luxurious vacation homes, Lāna'i is slowly moving forward. Despite the changes, however, everything on Lāna'i is leisurely and lovely, especially its people. Come, take your time, and enjoy yourself before the island changes too much more.

EXPLORING

Lāna'i is small enough to explore in a couple of days of leisurely travel, depending on how you want to experience it. Most of the island's sights are out of the way; that is, you won't find them in Lāna'i City or along paved roads. You'll have to look to find them, but the search is worth it.

Ask your hotel's concierge for a road and sight map; it's a good resource. Bring along a cooler with drinks and snacks for your explorations, because there are no places to stop for refreshments along the way—unless you return to your hotel or Lāna'i City. Admission to all sights mentioned in this chapter is free.

South and West Lāna'i

Pineapples once blanketed the Pālāwai Basin, the flat area south of Lāna'i City. Today it is used primarily for agriculture and grazing, but it does hold archaeological, historical, and natural treasures worth exploring.

A Good Drive
Numbers in the text correspond to numbers in the margin and on the Lāna'i map.

From Lāna'i City, drive south on Highway 440 a few blocks until you reach a major intersection. Go straight, following the highway west to **Kaumālapa'u Harbor** ①, the island's main seaport.

Backtrack to the intersection, turn right, and take Highway 440 south (also called Mānele Road). At the bottom of the long hill awaits **Mānele Bay** ② with its boat harbor. You can also catch sight of **Sweetheart Rock** here; its sheer 50-foot high cliffs are lovely to look at but impossible to scale. The road ends at the island's only true swimming area at **Hulopo'e Beach** ③ (☞ Beaches, *below*).

Off Highway 440 are some four-wheel drive dirt roads which lead you to **Lu'ahiwa Petroglyphs** ④ and its ancient rock carvings, and the well-preserved archaeological sites of **Kaunolū** ⑤, including **Halulu Heiau** ⑥.

TIMING
Although it's a small area of land, south Lāna'i deserves a full day to explore and enjoy. If you're a fan of water sports, you'll want to spend

half the day at Hulopo'e Beach and use the rest of the day for visiting the other attractions.

Sights To See

Numbers in the margin correspond to points of interest on the Lāna'i map.

❻ Halulu Heiau. The carefully excavated remains of an impressive stone *heiau* (outdoor sacred shrine) attest to the sacred history of this spot; it was actively used as a place of worship by the earliest residents of Lāna'i. As late as 1810, this hilltop site was also considered a place of refuge for wayward islanders. *⊠ Take Hwy. 440 south (Mānele Rd.). When road makes a sharp left turn, continue straight on Kaupili Rd., which leads you through pineapple fields. When you come to the fourth dirt road, take it toward ocean.*

❸ Hulop'e Beach. Lāna'i's only—and best—swimming beach, Hulop'e beckons with its perennially clear waters, great snorkeling reefs, and views of spinner dolphins at play. Shady trees and grassy expanses make it a good picnic spot, and there are showers, rest rooms, and changing facilities. It's a five-minute walk from the Mānele Bay Hotel via a short path. *⊠ Take Hwy. 440, south (Mānele Rd.) to bottom of hill; road dead-ends at beach's parking lot.*

❶ Kaumālapa'u Harbor. Built in 1926 by the Hawaiian Pineapple Company (which later became Dole), this is the principal seaport for Lāna'i. The cliffs flanking the western shore are as high as 1,000 feet. Since Kaumālapa'u is actively used for shipping, no swimming, snorkeling, or other water activities are allowed in the area. *⊠ Take Hwy. 440 west (Kaumālapa'u Hwy.) as far as it goes. Turn left and drive about 7 mi to ocean.*

❺ Kaunolū. Set atop the island's highest sea cliffs, Kaunolū was a fishing village in pre-contact times. A team from Honolulu's prestigious Bishop Museum excavated the ruins of this important Hawaiian archaeological find, including terraces, stone floors, and platforms where 86 houses and 35 shelters once stood. In this area you can also find examples of petroglyphs, a series of intricate rock carvings that have been preserved in tribute to the once-thriving community. Kaunolū has additional significance because Hawai'i's King Kamehameha I sometimes lived here. *⊠ Take Hwy. 440 south (Mānele Rd.). When road makes a sharp left turn, continue straight on Kaupili Rd., which leads you through pineapple fields. Take the 4th dirt road to the ocean.*

❹ Lu'ahiwa Petroglyphs. On a steep slope overlooking the Pālāwai Basin, in the flatlands of Lāna'i, are 34 boulders with ancient rock carvings inscribed on them. Drawn in a mixture of ancient and historic styles by the Hawaiians of the early 19th century, the simple stick-figure drawings represent humans, nature, and life on Lāna'i. *⊠ From Lāna'i City, take Hwy. 440 south for about a mile, until you see an unmarked dirt road that heads left through pineapple fields. At end of that road, walk up unmarked trail to petroglyphs.*

❷ Mānele Bay. Flanked by lava cliffs that are hundreds of feet high, Mānele Bay is the only public boat harbor on Lāna'i, and it was the location of most post-contact shipping until Kaumālapa'u Harbor was built in 1926. Today it hosts a regular influx of small boats whose owners are generally from other Neighbor Islands. The ferry to and from Maui also pulls in here. To the right of the harbor are the foundations of some old Hawaiian houses; in fact, this was the site of ancient Hawaiian villages dating back to AD 900.

Lāna'i

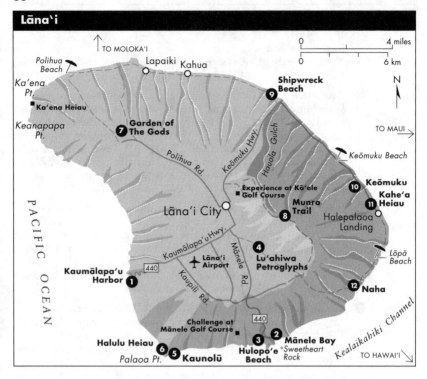

TO MOLOKA'I

Polihua Beach

Lapaiki · Kahua

Ka'ena Pt.

■ Ka'ena Heiau

Keanapapa Pt.

Shipwreck Beach ❾

❼ Garden of The Gods

Polihua Rd.

Keōmuku Hwy.

Hauola Gulch

Keōmuku Beach

TO MAUI →

P A C I F I C   O C E A N

Experience at Kō'ele ■ Golf Course

Lāna'i City ○

Kaumālapa'u Hwy.

Kaumālapa'u Harbor ❶

440

Lāna'i Airport ✈

Lāna'i Airport

Kaupili Rd.

Mānele Rd.

Munro Trail ❽

❹ Lu'ahiwa Petroglyphs

❿ Keōmuku

⓫ Kahe'a Heiau

Halepalaoa Landing

Lōpā Beach

⓬ Naha

Challenge at Mānele Golf Course ■

440

Halulu Heiau

❻ ❺ **Kaunolū**

Palaoa Pt.

Hulopo'e Beach ❸ ❷

Mānele Bay ·Sweetheart Rock

Kealaikahiki Channel

TO HAWAI'I ↘

0 ——— 4 miles
0 ——— 6 km

N

Just offshore you can catch a glimpse of **Sweetheart Rock.** Called Pu'u Pehe in Hawaiian, the rock is an isolated 50-foot-high formation which carries a sad Hawaiian legend—to make a long story short, a man hid his sweetheart there, and later she drowned. ⊠ *Take Hwy. 440 south (Mānele Rd.) to bottom of hill, and look for harbor on your left.*

North and East Lāna'i

With a ghost town and heiau to its credit, the northeast realm of Lāna'i is wild and untamed. The best way to explore its distinctive beauty is by hiking or four-wheel driving, since most of its attractions are accessible only by rugged dirt roads.

A Good Drive

Numbers in the text correspond to numbers in the margin and on the Lāna'i map.

From Lāna'i City, take Keōmuku Highway north. Turn left on the road that runs between the Kō'ele Stables and tennis courts. This leads you to a dirt road, which cuts through hay fields for a couple of miles. At the crossroad, turn right. This road heads upward through an ironwood forest and, 1½ miles beyond, the **Garden of the Gods** ⑦. Red and black lava rocks are scattered across this unique landscape; beyond is a crystal-blue seascape.

Return to the highway, turn left, and follow Keōmuku Highway to the top of the hill. Take a right on the only major dirt road in sight (take caution when it is raining, the roads get very muddy), and you're on your way to the **Munro Trail** ⑧, an 8-mile route that runs over the top of Lāna'ihale.

Keōmuku Highway makes its long descent north to **Shipwreck Beach** ⑨ (☞ Beaches, *below*), an 8-mile expanse of sand where you can stretch your legs and look for washed-up treasures.

There's more excitement if you feel adventurous. A word of caution: Do not continue unless you have a four-wheel-drive vehicle. The going is rough and often muddy.

From the end of the paved road, head southeast (the opposite direction from Shipwreck Beach) along the very bumpy dirt road. Five miles later you will see dozens of tall coconut trees and a run-down old church. This is **Keōmuku** ⑩, an abandoned town where 2,000 people once lived.

A mile and a half farther down the road, you can see the ruins of a heiau called **Kahe'a Heiau** ⑪. The road ends 3 miles later at the remnants of an old Hawaiian fishpond at **Naha** ⑫ and the oft-deserted Lōpā Beach. Here you must turn around and retrace your route—back to Keōmuku Highway.

TIMING

Give yourself a day to tour the north and east reaches of the island. If you're a hiker, you'll want a day just to enjoy the splendors of hiking Lāna'ihale, the mountain that rises above Lāna'i City. A walk along Shipwreck Beach makes a nice morning outing, with stops for shell-collecting, picture-taking, and picnicking.

Since most of the driving is on rugged roads, it takes more time to reach places like the Garden of the Gods and Keōmuku than it does to actually experience them. Relax, on Lāna'i getting there is half the fun.

Sights to See
Numbers in the text correspond to numbers in the margin and on the Lāna'i map.

❼ **Garden of the Gods.** This heavily eroded canyon is scattered with boulders of different sizes, shapes, and colors that seem to have been placed there for some divine purpose. Stop and enjoy this inspiring scenery for a while, for its lunar appearance is unmatched in Hawai'i. Anyone who's a geology buff will want to take photos of the area, which presents magnificent views of the Pacific Ocean, Moloka'i, and on clear days, O'ahu. Stand quietly, and you might spot a deer here. ⊠ *At Kō'ele Stables, take dirt road that cuts through hay fields. 2 mi later, turn right at crossroads and head up through ironwood forest for 1½ mi.*

⑪ **Kahe'a Heiau.** This ancient temple was once a revered place of worship for the people of Lāna'i. Today you must look hard to find its stone platforms and walls, for they have succumbed to an overgrowth of weeds and bushes. ⊠ *Drive east 5 mi on very bumpy dirt road running along island's north shore.*

⑩ **Keōmuku.** In the late 19th century, this busy Lāna'i community of some 2,000 residents served as the headquarter of the Maunalei Sugar Company. When the sugar company failed, Keōmuku shut down in 1901. It was used for cattle and sheep ranching after that, but by 1954 the area was abandoned. You can still go into its ramshackle church, the oldest on the island. There's an eerie beauty about Keōmuku, with its once-stately homes now reduced to weed-infested sites and crumbling stone walls. Dozens of tall coconut trees define the site. ⊠ *5 mi along unpaved road southeast of Shipwreck Beach.*

★ ❽ **Munro Trail.** This 8-mile path winds through a lush tropical rain forest; it was named after George Munro, ranch manager of the Lāna'i

Ranch Co., who began a reforestation program in the 1950s. Use caution if it has been raining, as the roads get very muddy.

The trail winds over the top of Lāna'ihale. This is the high point of the island, at 3,370 feet. Its peak delivers spectacular views of nearly all the Hawaiian Islands. From here, you can see 2,000 feet down into Lāna'i's deepest canyon, Hauola Gulch. ⊠ *From Lodge at Kō'ele, head north on Keōmuku Hwy. for about 1¼ mi, and turn right onto a smaller, tree-lined road. Trailhead is ½ mi past cemetery on your right.*

⑫　**Naha.** The site of an ancient rock-walled fishpond can be seen clearly here at low tide, where the sandy shorelines end and the cliffs begin their rise along the south, west, and north shores of the island. Local fishermen come here to fish, but this is not a good place for swimming due to the dangerous shorebreak and currents. ⊠ *North side of Lāna'i, at end of dirt road heading east.*

★　⑨　**Shipwreck Beach.** Beachcombers come for its shells and washed-up treasures, photographers love the spectacular view of Moloka'i across the channel, and walkers enjoy ambling along this perfect broad stretch of sand—in all a beach with great allure. It's not for swimmers, however. Have a look at the tanker rusting offshore and you'll see that these are not friendly waters. ⊠ *End of Keōmuku Hwy. heading north.*

DINING

Although Lāna'i's restaurant choices are limited, the menus are wide ranging. If you dine at the Lodge at Kō'ele or Mānele Bay Hotel, you'll be treated to ingredients harvested or caught locally, served in upscale surroundings.

Dining in Lāna'i City is a different story; its restaurants have simple food, homey atmospheres, and friendly service.

CATEGORY	COST*
$$$	over $40
$$	$20–$40
$	under $20

Per person for a three-course meal, excluding drinks, service, and 4% sales tax

$$$　✕　**Dining Room.** Reflecting the elegant country atmosphere of the Lodge at Kō'ele, the hotel's main restaurant has hefty wood beams, gleaming crystal, a roaring fireplace, and hand-painted stencils on the walls. Inventive island cuisine is created by a chef who works closely with local farmers and fishermen to keep the ingredients fresh. Try the marble of *'ahi* (yellowfin tuna) with radish, fennel, and mustard seed or the chilled roasted red banana and Kona coffee bisque with cinnamon croutons for an appetizer. Entrées include roasted axis deer marinated with *liliko'i* (passion fruit). ⊠ *Lodge at Kō'ele,* ☎ *808/565–7300. Reservations essential. Jacket required. AE, DC, MC, V. No lunch.*

$$$　✕　**'Ihilani.** The Mānele Bay Hotel's specialty dining room shimmers with crystal and silver and lace-trimmed tables. Executive chef Philippe Padovani uses fresh ingredients from the island to create a cuisine that he calls "Mediterranean French Gourmet." Menus change nightly and include such dishes as sautéed, fresh-caught prawns atop local greens, and fillet of sea bass in saffron sauce. There are 14 desserts, including concoctions made from Hawai'i-grown cocoa beans. ⊠ *Mānele Bay Hotel,* ☎ *808/565–7700. Reservations essential. AE, DC, MC, V. Closed Sun.–Mon. No lunch.*

$$ ✗ **Hotel Lānaʻi.** Don't overlook this charming spot where the locals go out to eat. Banana pancakes and specialty omelets are offered at breakfast, soups and sandwiches at lunch, and American cuisine at dinner (steaks, chops, chicken, and fish prepared simply). There's a pasta selection nightly, and on Wednesdays there's a Mexican buffet. The pretty dining room is just off the hotel's lānai and features large wooden tables, a fireplace at one end, and paintings and photographs by island artists. ✉ *828 Lānaʻi Ave.,* ☎ *808/565-7211. AE, MC, V.*

$ ✗ **Blue Ginger Cafe.** This small, no-frills eatery may look run-down, but the menu has enough diversity to appeal to the new breed of visitors on the island. There's even some art on the walls. At breakfast enjoy a three-egg omelet with rice or a big plate of French toast. As the only bakery in town, Blue Ginger also has fresh pastries each morning. Lunchtime brings more selections, including burgers, chef's salad, sandwiches, bento boxes, pizza, plate lunches, and *saimin* (Japanese noodles). Try the stir fry fish for dinner. There are no waiters here: You simply order at the counter and dine on Formica-top tables with mismatched silverware. ✉ *409 7th Ave.,* ☎ *808/565-6363. Reservations not accepted. No credit cards.*

$ ✗ **S-n-T Properties.** Occupying part of a general store, this place has an old-fashioned soda fountain with a counter and swivel stools. The food is classic local breakfast and lunch diner fare, like burgers, fries, saimin, sandwiches, and sundaes. ✉ *419 7th Ave.,* ☎ *808/565-6537. Reservations not accepted. No credit cards. 6:30 AM–12:30 PM and 4:30 PM–8:30 PM; closed Wed.*

LODGING

In years past the only accommodation on the island was the comfy old Hotel Lānaʻi in Lānaʻi City. Now two classy alternatives for the discriminating traveler are also available. Let your tastes and your budget determine which place you choose.

CATEGORY	COST*
$$$$	over $120
$$$	$90–$120
$$	$60–$90

All prices are for a standard double room, excluding 10% tax.

$$$$ 🏨 **Jasmine Garden.** The Hunters, who run the Dreams Come True B&B, also rent out a 3-bedroom house. Located in the older section of Lānaʻi City, it sleeps six, but up to 10 people can squeeze in. ✉ *547 12th St., Lānaʻi City 96763,* ☎ *808/565-6961,* FAX *808/565-7056.*

$$$$ 🏨 **Lodge at Kōʻele.** Open since 1990, the lodge resembles a luxurious ★ private mountain retreat. Sprawled over 21 acres, it sits on the edge of Lānaʻi City in the highlands, where the temperature is cool and the pine trees are plentiful. The two-story lodge features a reception building and a main hall with unusual furnishings and rare Pacific artifacts. The porch is a generous space in which guests may enjoy the view and take refreshments, and the interiors have high beam ceilings, natural stone fireplaces, and works by island artists. There are more than a mile and a half of pathways through orchid gardens, macadamia forests, and palm landscapes. Don't be surprised to see a flock of wild turkeys strolling across the back lawn. ✉ *Box 774, Lānaʻi City, 96763,* ☎ *808/565-7300 or 800/321-4666,* FAX *808/565-3868. 102 rooms and suites with bath. 2 restaurants, bar, lobby lounge, pool, 18-hole golf course, 3 tennis courts, croquet, horseback riding, shops. AE, DC, MC, V.*

$$$$ 🏨 **Mānele Bay Hotel.** This elaborate beachfront property has suites with views of Hulopo'e Bay, the coastline, and the island of Maui. Its design is reminiscent of traditional Hawaiian architecture, with lots of open-air lānai. Three two-story buildings overlook a courtyard, and a reception building houses the lobby and specialty boutiques. Ground- and second-level guest rooms feature private lānai and are surrounded by courtyards, waterfalls, ponds, and lawns landscaped with bromeliads, canopy trees, and other exotica. ⊠ *Box 774, Lāna'i City, 96763,* ☎ *808/565–7245 or 800/321–4666,* FAX *808/565–3868. 250 rooms and suites with bath. 3 restaurants, bar, pool, beauty salon, spa, 18-hole golf course, 6 tennis courts, exercise room, shops. AE, DC, MC, V.*

$$$$ 🏨 **Phyllis Cole.** Cole rents two homes in town, each fully furnished. While a house rental may cost more than a hotel room, in return you get a full kitchen, plenty of living space, and a taste of what it's like to live on Lāna'i. ⊠ *496 Akolu Pl., Lāna'i City 96763,* ☎ *808/565–6223.*

$$ 🏨 **Dreams Come True.** Michael and Susan Hunter's home in the heart of Lāna'i City has canopy beds, antique furnishings, and memorabilia from their 15 years in Asia and 10 on Lāna'i. Fresh fruit from their own trees enhances the big morning meal at this bed-and-breakfast. ⊠ *547 12th St., Lāna'i City 96763,* ☎ *808/565–6961,* FAX *808/565–7056. 3 bedrooms, 2 with private bath. Vehicle rental available.*

$$ 🏨 **Hotel Lāna'i.** Built in 1923 to house visiting plantation executives, this quaint 11-room inn was once the only accommodation on the island. Today, even though two luxury hotels may tempt you, you shouldn't overlook this Lāna'i institution. The old front porch with the big wicker chairs has long been a meeting place for residents and locals alike, who gather to read the paper, order a drink, and "talk story" (converse). The renovated rooms are simple, with single or twin beds, flowered wallpaper, and sometimes mismatched furniture, offering the feeling that you're in an eccentric great-aunt's country home. The grounds are well-maintained, with flower gardens and enormous Norfolk pines, and you can get three meals a day here (not included in the room fee). ⊠ *Box A119, Lāna'i City 96763,* ☎ *808/565–7211 or 800/624–8849,* FAX *808/565–4713. 11 rooms with bath. Restaurant. AE, MC, V.*

$$ 🏨 **Lāna'i Bed & Breakfast.** Lucille Graham, an elderly former nurse, runs a modest B&B service out of her three-bedroom home in Lāna'i City. A longtime island resident, she's an artist and collector of bottles, shells, and other curios. ⊠ *312 Mahana Pl., Lāna'i City 96763,* ☎ *808/565–6378. 2 bedrooms with shared bath.*

NIGHTLIFE AND THE ARTS

The locals entertain themselves by gathering on the front porch of the **Hotel Lāna'i** (☎ 808/565–7211) for drinks and talk-story sessions. There's loud live music on Friday nights.

The 153-seat **Lāna'i Theater and Playhouse** (☎ 808/565–7500) reopened in 1993 after a major renovation. Today this '30s landmark presents first-run movies, occasional plays, and special events.

The **Lodge at Kō'ele** (☎ 808/565–7300) features music in its Great Hall. Entertainment is offered by Lāna'i residents who share songs, dances, and chants of the island. In addition, the Music Room occasionally offers live entertainment.

OUTDOOR ACTIVITIES, BEACHES, AND SPORTS

Beaches

Only a few beaches on Lāna'i are worth seeking out, and only one of them has good swimming in protected waters. None has a phone number, so if you need more information, try **Destination Lāna'i** (⊠ Box 700, Lāna'i City 96763, ☎ 808/565–7600) or ask at your hotel desk. The beaches below are listed clockwise from the south.

Hulopo'e Beach. A sparkling crescent, this broad expanse is Lāna'i's only easily accessible white-sand beach. One of the best beaches in all of Hawai'i, it's an ideal spot for a picnic lunch, a dip in the water, and a nap under the trees. The waves are gentle enough for beginning bodysurfers, and the waters are full of fish that are easily visible to snorkelers, since it is a marine-life conservation area. The beach and its park facilities draw guests from the Mānele Bay Hotel as well as residents who enjoy spending the day here, cooking over the grills, swimming, and watching the sunset. Never fear; Hulopo'e is big enough to accommodate everyone. There are changing rooms, outdoor showers, picnic tables, and grills, but no lifeguards. Dolphins can often be spotted from the beach. ⊠ *On south shore of Lāna'i, 10 mi. south of Lāna'i City on Mānele Rd.*

Polihua Beach. Due to its more obscure location and frequent high winds, this beach is often deserted, except for the turtles which are known to nest here. That makes it all the more spectacular, with its long white-sand beach and glorious views of Moloka'i. Swimming is dangerous here due to strong currents. To find it, you need a four-wheel-drive. ⊠ *On northwest shore, 11 mi from Lāna'i City, past Garden of the Gods. Ask at your hotel desk for directions and a map.*

Shipwreck Beach. A nice beach for walking, but not swimming, Shipwreck is an 8-mile stretch of sand on the Kalohi Channel between Lāna'i and Moloka'i. Tricky winds have caused many boats to crash on the reef off the coast, and you can still see the remains of a World War II vessel offshore, not to mention sensational views of Moloka'i across the channel. The beach has no lifeguards, no changing rooms, and no outdoor showers. ⊠ *On north shore, 10 mi north of Lāna'i City at end of Keōmuku Hwy.*

Outdoor Activities and Sports

Golf

Experience at Kō'ele is an 18-hole championship course designed by Greg Norman, with Ted Robinson as architect, at the Lodge at Kō'ele (☎ 808/565–7300). Rates including carts are $99 for guests, $150 for nonguests. The lodge also has an 18-hole executive putting course, free for guests.

The **Challenge at Mānele** (☎ 808/565–7700), an 18-hole golf course with a Jack Nicklaus design, opened at the Mānele Bay Hotel in late 1993. Rates with carts are $99 for guests, $150 for nonguests.

The public **Cavendish Golf Course** presents nine holes in the pines. Although free to the public, the course requests visitors to leave a donation for upkeep. Call the Lodge at Kō'ele concierge (☎ 808/565–7300) for information.

Hiking

The most popular Lāna'i hike is the **Munro Trail,** a strenuous 8-mile trek that takes about eight hours. There is an elevation gain of 1,400

feet leading you to the lookout at Lāna'i's highest point, Lāna'ihale. No permission is necessary to hike this route.

Before taking off, fill a water bottle and arm yourself with provisions in case you get a little off the track. Also, look at Craig Chisholm's paperback, *Hawaiian Hiking Trails* (Touchstone Press, 1977), and Robert Smith's *Hawai'i's Best Hiking Trails* (Wilderness Press, 1987).

Horseback Riding
The **Stables at Kō'ele** (☎ 808/565–7300) takes you to scenic, high-country trails. They have a corral-full of well-groomed horses for riders of all ages and skill levels. Rides cost $35 for one hour, $65 for two hours, and $90 for one that includes lunch.

Scuba Diving
Trilogy Ocean Sports (☎ 808/565–6566 or 808/565–2097) offers introductory, one-tank, and two-tank dives. For novices, it runs a free diving session at the Mānele Bay Hotel pool. The intro dive is $115; one-tank dive $95; two-tank dive $124.

Cathedrals, a dive site off the south shore, gets its name from the numerous pinnacles that rise from depths of 60 feet to just below the water's surface, with spacious caverns creating a cathedral effect. Within these beautiful chambers live friendly spotted moray eels, lobsters, and ghost shrimp.

Sergeant Major Reef, on the south shore, is a dive site made up of three parallel lava ridges, a cave, and an archway, with rippled sand valleys between the ridges. Several large schools of sergeant major fish that live here give the site its name. Depths range from 15 to 50 feet. Other nearby sites include Lobster Rock; Menpachi Cave; Grand Canyon; Sharkfin Rock; and Monolith, home to Stretch, a 5-foot-long moray eel.

Snorkeling
Trilogy Ocean Sports (☎ 808/565–6566 or 808/565–2097) presents a daily 5-hour morning snorkel sail on a 51-foot sailing catamaran, for $85. Breakfast, lessons, equipment, and lunch are included. Trilogy's day-long circumnavigation of Lāna'i with stops for snorkeling and swimming is $125 per person.

Hulopo'e Beach is one of the most outstanding snorkeling destinations in all of Hawai'i. It attracts brilliantly colored fish to its protected cove, in which you can also marvel at underwater coral and lava formations. Ask at your hotel's activities desk about renting equipment.

Tennis
The **Lodge at Kō'ele** (☎ 808/565–7300) has three tennis courts, and **Mānele Bay Hotel** (☎ 808/565–7700) has six.

SHOPPING

Except for the specialty boutiques at the Lodge at Kō'ele and Mānele Bay Hotel, Lāna'i City is the only place on the island to buy what you need. Its main streets, 7th and 8th avenues, offer a small scattering of shops straight out of the 1920s. Each offers personal service and congenial charm.

Stores open their doors Monday through Saturday between 8 and 9 and close between 5 and 6. Some shops are closed on Sunday and between noon and 1:30 PM on weekdays.

General Stores

In the most literal sense, the main businesses in town are what you would call general stores. That means they try to carry whatever customers need, and no business has a specialty.

You can get everything from cosmetics to canned vegetables at **Pine Isle Market** (⊠ 356 8th Ave., ☎ 808/565–6488).

In 1946 Richard Tamashiro founded **Richard's Shopping Center** (⊠ 434 8th Ave., ☎ 808/565–6047), which is run today by his son Wallace. Among other things, the store has a fun selection of Lāna'i T-shirts, which make great souvenirs.

You may not find everything the name implies at **International Food and Clothing Center** (⊠ 833 'Ilima Ave., ☎ 808/565–6433). However, Joan de la Cruz, whose parents started the store in 1952, does carry a good supply of items for your everyday needs at this old-fashioned emporium.

Lāna'i City Service (⊠ 1036 Lāna'i Ave., ☎ 808/565–7227) is more than a gas station and car rental operation. It also sells microwave pizzas and burritos, sodas, sundries, paperbacks, T-shirts, and island crafts. The decor appeals to hunters, with trophy-style animals loaned by residents.

Specialty Stores

Crafts

Akamai Trading & Gifts (⊠ 408 8th Ave., ☎ 808/565–6587) sells Lāna'i crafts including pine-tree bowls and flower-dyed gourds alongside its Lāna'i posters, T-shirts, and tropical jellies and jams.

Lāna'i Art Studio (⊠ 339 7th Ave., ☎ 808/565–7503) is home of the Lāna'i Art Program, with art classes for residents and visitors. Its gift shop sells Lāna'i handcrafts, from painted silk scarves to beaded jewelry.

Hotel Shops

The **Lodge at Kō'ele** (☎ 08/565–7300) and **Mānele Bay Hotel** (☎ 808/565–7700) have sundry shops that are handy for guests who need to stock up on suntan lotion, aspirin, and other vacation necessities. They also carry classy logo wear, resort clothing, Hawai'i coffee-table books, and jewelry.

LĀNA'I A TO Z

Arriving and Departing

By Ferry

Expeditions (⊠ Box 10, Lahaina, 96767, ☎ 808/661–3756) offers passenger ferry service between Lahaina, Maui, and Manele Harbor, Lāna'i. The boat departs five times daily and reservations are recommended. Tickets can be purchased onboard; the one-way fare costs $25. The trip usually takes one hour unless the boat slows down for dolphins or whales.

By Plane

To meet the growing numbers of visitors to the island, in mid-1994 the state completed construction of a new passenger terminal at the **Lāna'i Airport** (☎ 808/565–6757), with a gift shop, food concession, and plenty of parking.

To reach Lāna'i from the mainland United States, you must first stop at O'ahu's Honolulu International Airport; from there, it takes about a half hour to fly to Lāna'i. **Hawaiian Airlines** (☎ 800/367–5320) offers one round-trip flight daily between Honolulu and Lāna'i. A round-trip on one of its DC-9 jets costs $156. **Island Air** (☎ 800/323–3345) has eight round-trip flights daily on its 18-passenger Twin Otters and its Dornier 228s, at a cost of $148.

BETWEEN THE AIRPORT AND HOTELS

Lāna'i's airport is a 10-minute drive from Lāna'i City. If you're staying at the Hotel Lāna'i, the Lodge at Kō'ele, or the Mānele Bay Hotel, you will be met by a complimentary shuttle that will take you to your accommodations. Don't expect to see any public buses at the airport; there are none on the island.

By Car. There is a distinct advantage to renting your own vehicle on Lāna'i, because public transportation is nonexistent and attractions are far apart. Make your car- or Jeep-rental reservation way in advance of your trip, because Lāna'i is small and its fleet of vehicles is limited. Contact **Lāna'i City Service** (⌧ Box N, Lāna'i City 96763, ☎ 808/565–7227), which is the Dollar Rent-a-Car affiliate on the island.

By Taxi. For taxi transfers between Lāna'i City and the airport, **Lāna'i City Service** (☎ 808/565–7227) covers the market. The one-way charge is $5 per person.

Getting Around

Some sort of private transportation is advised on Lāna'i, unless you plan to stay in one place during your entire visit. Avoid that urge, because the island has natural splendors from one end to the other.

By Bicycle

A mountain bike is a fun way to explore the pineapple fields and back roads of Lāna'i. The Lodge at Kō'ele provides them free to guests.

By Car

Driving around Lāna'i isn't as easy as on other islands, because most roads outside of Lāna'i City aren't marked. But renting a car can be fun, and a good way to really see the island (☞ Car Rentals, *below*). From town, the streets extend outward as paved roads with two-way traffic. Keōmuku Road runs north to Shipwreck Beach, while Highway 440 leads south down to Mānele Bay and Hulopo'e Beach and west to Kaumālapa'u Harbor. The rest of your driving takes place on bumpy and muddy dirt roads, which are best navigated by a four-wheel-drive Jeep or van.

The island has no traffic lights, and you'll never find yourself in a traffic jam. However, heed these words of caution: Before heading out on your explorations, ask at your hotel desk for a road and site map, and ask them to confirm that you're headed in the right direction. Some of the major attractions don't have signs, and it's easy to get lost.

By Taxi

It costs about $5 per person for a cab ride from Lāna'i City to almost any point on the paved roads of the island. Call **Lāna'i City Service** (☎ 808/565–7227).

Contacts and Resources

Car Rentals

Only one company on Lāna'i rents vehicles to visitors. Contact **Lāna'i City Service** (⌧ Box N, Lāna'i City 96763, ☎ 808/565–7227), which

is the Dollar Rent-a-Car affiliate on the island. You'll pay $60 a day for a compact car, $129 a day for a 7-passenger minivan, and from $119 to $129 a day for a four-wheel-drive Jeep Wrangler. The company offers complimentary airport pickup and drop-off for car renters.

Emergencies

Police, fire, or **ambulance** (☏ 911).

HOSPITALS

The **Lāna'i Community Hospital** (✉ 628 7th Ave., Lāna'i City, ☏ 808/565–6411) is the center of health care for the island. It offers 24-hour ambulance service and a pharmacy.

Guided Tours

HIKING

The **Nature Conservancy of Hawai'i** (☏ 808/537–4508) has trained docents (who are also Lāna'i residents) leading monthly hikes through Kānepu'u, a 590-acre preserve northwest of Lāna'i City, on the island's western plateau. Kānepu'u contains the state's largest remnant of native dryland forest, hosting 48 plant species unique to Hawai'i, such as *'iliahi* (sandalwood). Call for reservations.

OFF-ROAD

Many of the highlights of Lāna'i are accessible only from the unpaved back roads of the island. On a guided tour you can leave the navigation to a driver who knows what he's doing, while you simply hang on and enjoy the ride in a Geo Tracker. Along the way you will see petroglyphs, the Garden of the Gods, and the Munro Trail. Tours are at least two hours long and are limited to three people. **Lāna'i City Service** (☏ 808/565–7227) offers such tours three times a week for guests of the Lodge at Kō'ele.

PROPERTY

The **Lodge at Kō'ele** (☏ 808/565–7300) and **Mānele Bay Hotel** (☏ 808/565–7700) offer guests free one-hour tours of the hotels and the lush grounds. Tours depart daily; check with the concierge desk for tour times.

Visitor Information

The two major hotels—the Lodge at Kō'ele and the Mānele Bay Hotel—have information desks. In addition, you should write ahead of time to **Destination Lāna'i** (✉ Box 700, Lāna'i City 96763, ☏ 808/565–7600). The **Maui Visitors Bureau** (✉ Box 580, Wailuku, Maui 96793, ☏ 808/244–3530) offers information about Lāna'i as well as Maui.

9 Portraits of Maui

Heavenly Hana! Greener than Eden!

Watered and warmed by our God above!

What shall we grow here?

What shall we show here?

The trees of Truth, Faith, Hope and Love. *

*Second verse of the "Hanna Hymn," as translated from the Hawaiian

HAWAIIAN HISTORY AT A GLANCE: A CHRONOLOGY

ca. AD 500 The first human beings to set foot on Hawaiian shores are Polynesians, who travel 2,000 miles in 60- to 80-foot canoes to the islands they name *Havaiki* after their legendary homeland. Researchers today believe they were originally from Southeast Asia, and that they discovered the South Pacific Islands of Tahiti and the Marquesas before ending up in Hawai'i.

ca. 1758 Kamehameha, the Hawaiian chief who unified the Islands, is born.

1778 In January, British Captain James Cook, commander of the HMS *Resolution* and the consort vessel HMS *Discovery,* lands on the island of Kaua'i and "discovers" it for the Western world. He names the archipelago the Sandwich Islands after his patron, the Earl of Sandwich. In November, he returns to the Islands for the winter, anchoring at Kealakekua Bay on the Big Island.

1779 In February, Cook is killed in a battle with Hawai'i's indigenous people at Kealakekua.

1785 The isolation of the Islands ends as British, American, French, and Russian fur traders and New England whalers come to Hawai'i. Tales spread of thousands of acres of sugarcane growing wild, and farmers come in droves from the United States and Europe.

1790 Kamehameha begins his rise to power through a series of bloody battles to unify the Islands of Hawai'i.

1791 Kamehameha builds Pu'ukoholā *Heiau* (temple) and dedicates it by sacrificing a rival chief he has killed.

1795 Using Western arms, Kamehameha fights a decisive campaign on O'ahu to unite the Islands. Except for Kaui'a (which he tries to invade in 1796 and 1804) this completes his military conquest of the Islands.

1810 The chief of Kaua'i acknowledges Kamehameha's rule, giving him suzerainty over Kaua'i and Ni'ihau and uniting the Islands under one chief. Kamehameha becomes known as King Kamehameha I, and he rules the unified Kingdom of Hawai'i with an iron hand.

1819 Kamehameha I dies, and his eldest son, Liholiho, becomes Kamehameha II, beginning his short reign with Ka'ahumanu, Kamehameha I's favorite wife, as co-executive. Ka'ahumanu persuades the new king to abandon old religious taboos, including those that forbade women to eat with men or to hold positions of power. The first whaling ships land at Lahaina on Maui.

1820 By the time the first missionaries arrive from Boston, Hawai'i's social order is beginning to break down. First, Ka'ahumanu and then Kamehameha II defy *kapu* (taboo) after kapu without attracting divine retribution. Hawaiians, disillusioned with their own gods, are receptive to the ideas of Christianity. The influx of Western culture also introduces Hawai'i to Western disease, liquor, and what some view as moral decay.

1824 King Kamehameha II and his favorite wife die of measles during a visit to England. Honolulu missionaries gave both royals a Christian burial outside Kawaiaha'o Church, inspiring many Hawaiians to convert to the Protestant faith. His younger brother, Kau'ikea'ōuli, becomes King Kamehameha III, a wise and gentle sovereign who reigns for 30 years with Ka'ahumanu as regent.

1832 Ka'ahumanu is baptized and dies a few months later.

1840 The Wilkes Expedition, sponsored by the U.S. Coast and Geodetic Survey, pinpoints Pearl Harbor as a potential Naval Base.

1845 Kamehameha III and the legislature move Hawai'i's seat of government from Lahaina, on Maui, to Honolulu, on O'ahu.

1849 Kamehameha III turns Hawai'i into a constitutional monarchy and wins official recognition of Hawai'i as an independent country by the United States, France, and Great Britain.

1850 The Great Mahele, a land commission, reapportions land among crown, government, chiefs, and commoners, thus introducing for the first time the Western principle of private ownership. Commoners now were able to buy and sell land, but this great division becomes the great dispossession: By the end of the 19th century white men owned four acres for every one owned by a native. Even today, current land disputes originate from this division of property.

1852 As Western diseases depopulate the Islands, a labor shortage occurs in the sugarcane fields. For the next nine decades, a steady stream of foreign labor pours into Hawai'i, beginning with the Chinese. The Japanese begin arriving in 1868, followed by Filipinos, Koreans, Portuguese, and Puerto Ricans.

1872 Kamehameha V dies without heirs, ending the direct descendants of the first king. A power struggle ensues between the adherents of David Kalākaua and William Lunalilo.

1873 Lunalilo is elected Hawai'i's sixth king in January. The bachelor rules only 13 months before dying of tuberculosis.

1874 Kalākaua vies for the throne with the Dowager Queen Emma, half-Caucasian widow of Kamehameha IV. Kalākaua is elected by the Hawai'i Legislature, against protests by supporters of Queen Emma. American and British marines are called in to restore order, and Kalākaua begins his reign as the "Merrie Monarch."

1875 The United States and Hawai'i sign a treaty of reciprocity assuring Hawai'i a duty-free market for sugar in the United States.

1882 King Kalākaua builds 'Iolani Palace, an Italian Renaissance–style structure, on the site of the previous royal palace.

1887 The reciprocity treaty of 1875 is renewed, giving the United States the exclusive use of Pearl Harbor as a coaling station. Coincidentally, successful importation of Japanese laborers begins in earnest (after a false start in 1868).

1891 King Kalākaua dies and is succeeded by his sister, Queen Lili'uokalani, the last monarch of Hawai'i.

1893 After reigning only two years, Lili'uokalani is removed from the throne by American business interests led by Lorrin A. Thurston (grandson of missionary and newspaper founder Asa Thurston). Lili'uokalani is imprisoned in 'Iolani Palace for nearly eight months.

1894 The provisional government converts Hawai'i into a republic and proclaims Sanford Dole president.

1898 The outbreak of the Spanish-American War and Hawai'i's strategic military importance in the Pacific lead the next U.S. president, William McKinley, to move toward Hawai'i's annexation. On

August 12, Hawai'i is officially annexed by a joint resolution of Congress.

1901 Sanford Dole is appointed first governor of the territory of Hawai'i. The first major tourist hotel, the Moana (now called the Sheraton Moana Surfrider), is built on Waikīkī Beach.

1903 James Dole (a cousin of Sanford Dole) produces nearly 2,000 cases of pineapple, marking the beginning of Hawai'i's pineapple industry. Pineapple eventually surpasses sugar as Hawai'i's number-one crop.

1907 Fort Shafter Base, headquarters for the U.S. Army, becomes the first permanent military post in the Islands.

1908 Dredging of the channel at Pearl Harbor begins.

1919 Pearl Harbor is formally dedicated by the U.S. Navy. Prince Jonah Kūhiō Kalaniana'ole (the adopted son of Kalākaua's wife, Kapi'olani, and with his brother an heir designated by the childless Lili'uokalani to her throne), representing the Territory of Hawai'i in the U.S. House of Representatives, introduces the first bill proposing statehood for Hawai'i.

1927 Army Lieutenants Lester Maitland and Albert Hegenberger make the first successful nonstop flight from the mainland to the Islands. Hawai'i begins to increase efforts to promote tourism, the industry that eventually dominates development of the Islands. The Matson Navigation Company builds the Royal Hawaiian Hotel as a destination for its cruise ships.

1929 Hawai'i's commercial interisland air service begins.

1936 Pan American World Airways makes history as the first to start regular commercial passenger flights to Hawai'i from the mainland.

1941 Pearl Harbor becomes a tragic part of U.S. history when the U.S. Pacific Fleet is attacked by the Japanese, causing the U.S. to enter World War II. Nearly 4,000 casualties result from the surprise attack.

1942 James Jones, with thousands of others, trains at Schofield Barracks on O'ahu. He later writes about his experience in *From Here to Eternity*.

1959 Congress passes legislation granting Hawai'i statehood. In special elections the new state sends to the U.S. House of Representatives its first American of Japanese ancestry, Daniel Inouye, and to the U.S. Senate its first American of Chinese ancestry, Hiram Fong. Later in the year, the first Boeing 707 jets make the flight from San Francisco in a record five hours. By year's end 243,216 tourists visit Hawai'i, and tourism becomes Hawai'i's major industry. Today the Islands draw more than 6 million visitors a year.

1986 Hawai'i elects its first native Hawaiian governor, John Waihe'e.

1993 After Native Hawaiians commemorate the 100th anniversary of the overthrow of Queen Lili'uokalani with a call for sovereignty, Congress issues an apology to the Hawaiian people for the annexation of the Islands.

THE HOUSE OF THE SUN

THERE ARE HOSTS of people who journey like restless spirits round and about this earth in search of seascapes and landscapes and the wonders and beauties of nature. They overrun Europe in armies; they can be met in droves and herds in Florida and the West Indies, at the pyramids, and on the slopes and summits of the Canadian and American Rockies; but in the House of the Sun they are as rare as live and wriggling dinosaurs. Haleakala is the Hawaiian name for "the House of the Sun." It is a noble dwelling situated on the island of Maui; but so few tourists have ever peeped into it, much less entered it, that their number may be practically reckoned as zero. Yet I venture to state that for natural beauty and wonder the nature lover may see dissimilar things as great as Haleakala, but no greater, while he will never see elsewhere anything more beautiful or wonderful. Honolulu is six days' steaming from San Francisco; Maui is a night's run on the steamer from Honolulu, and six hours more, if he is in a hurry, can bring the traveler to Kolikoli, which is 10,032 feet above the sea and which stands hard by the entrance portal to the House of the Sun. Yet the tourist comes not, and Haleakala sleeps on in lonely and unseen grandeur.

Not being tourists, we of the *Snark* went to Haleakala. On the slopes of that monster mountain there is a cattle ranch of some 50,000 acres, where we spent the night at an altitude of 2,000 feet. The next morning it was boots and saddles, and with cowboys and pack horses we climbed to Ukulele, a mountain ranch house, the altitude of which, 5,500 feet, gives a severely temperate climate, compelling blankets at night and a roaring fireplace in the living room. Ukulele, by the way, is the Hawaiian for "jumping flea," as it is also the Hawaiian for a certain musical instrument that may be likened to a young guitar. It is my opinion that the mountain ranch house was named after the young guitar. We were not in a hurry, and we spent the day at Ukulele, learnedly discussing altitudes and barometers and shaking our particular barometer whenever anyone's argument stood in need of demonstration. Our barometer was the most graciously acquiescent instrument I have ever seen. Also, we gathered mountain raspberries, large as hen's eggs and larger, gazed up the pasture-covered lava slopes to the summit of Haleakala, 4,500 feet above us, and looked down upon a mighty battle of the clouds that was being fought beneath us, ourselves in the bright sunshine.

Every day and every day this unending battle goes on. Ukiukiu is the name of the trade wind that comes raging down out of the northeast and hurls itself upon Haleakala. Now Haleakala is so bulky and tall that it turns the northeast trade wind aside on either hand, so that in the lee of Haleakala no trade wind blows at all. On the contrary, the wind blows in the counter direction, in the teeth of the northeast trade. This wind is called Naulu. And day and night and always Ukiukiu and Naulu strive with each other, advancing, retreating, flanking, curving, curling, and turning and twisting, the conflict made visible by the cloud masses plucked from the heavens and hurled back and forth in squadrons, battalions, armies, and great mountain ranges. Once in a while, Ukiukiu, in mighty gusts, flings immense cloud masses clear over the summit of Haleakala; whereupon Naulu craftily captures them, lines them up in new battle formation, and with them smites back at his ancient and eternal antagonist. Then Ukiukiu sends a great cloud army around the eastern side of the mountain. It is a flanking movement, well executed. But Naulu, from his lair on the leeward side, gathers the flanking army in, pulling and twisting and dragging it, hammering it into shape, and sends it charging back against Ukiukiu around the western side of the mountain. And all the while,

---

Although it was written in the early 20th century, before Haleakalā became a popular tourist attraction, Jack London's account of camping among the crater's cinder cones is still fascinating to read today.

above and below the main battlefield, high up the slopes toward the sea, Ukiukiu and Naulu are continually sending out little wisps of cloud, in ragged skirmish line, that creep and crawl over the ground, among the trees and through the canyons, and that spring upon and capture one another in sudden ambuscades and sorties. And sometimes Ukiukiu or Naulu, abruptly sending out a heavy charging column, captures the ragged little skirmishers or drives them skyward, turning over and over, in vertical whirls, thousands of feet in the air.

BUT IT IS ON THE western slopes of Haleakala that the main battle goes on. Here Naulu masses his heaviest formation and wins his greatest victories. Ukiukiu grows weak toward late afternoon, which is the way of all trade winds, and is driven backward by Naulu. Naulu's generalship is excellent. All day he has been gathering and packing away immense reserves. As the afternoon draws on, he welds them into a solid column, sharp-pointed, miles in length, a mile in width, and hundreds of feet thick. This column he slowly thrusts forward into the broad battle front of Ukiukiu, and slowly and surely Ukiukiu, weakening fast, is split asunder. But it is not all bloodless. At times Ukiukiu struggles wildly, and with fresh accessions of strength from the limitless northeast smashes away half a mile at a time at Naulu's column and sweeps it off and away toward West Maui. Sometimes, when the two charging armies meet end-on, a tremendous perpendicular whirl results, the cloud masses, locked together, mounting thousands of feet into the air and turning over and over. A favorite device of Ukiukiu is to send a low, squat formation, densely packed, forward along the ground and under Naulu. When Ukiukiu is under, he proceeds to buck. Naulu's mighty middle gives to the blow and bends upward, but usually he turns the attacking column back upon itself and sets it milling. And all the while the ragged little skirmishers, stray and detached, sneak through the trees and canyons, crawl along and through the grass, and surprise one another with unexpected leaps and rushes; while above, far above, serene and lonely in the rays of the setting sun,

Haleakala looks down upon the conflict. And so, the night. But in the morning, after the fashion of trade winds, Ukiukiu gathers strength and sends the hosts of Naulu rolling back in confusion and rout. And one day is like another day in the battle of the clouds, where Ukiukiu and Naulu strive eternally on the slopes of Haleakala.

AGAIN IN THE MORNING, it was boots and saddles, cowboys and pack horses, and the climb to the top began. One pack horse carried 20 gallons of water, slung in five-gallon bags on either side; for water is precious and rare in the crater itself, in spite of the fact that several miles to the north and east of the crater rim more rain comes down than in any other place in the world. The way led upward across countless lava flows, without regard for trails, and never have I seen horses with such perfect footing as that of the 13 that composed our outfit. They climbed or dropped down perpendicular places with the sureness and coolness of mountain goats, and never a horse fell or balked.

There is a familiar and strange illusion experienced by all who climb isolated mountains. The higher one climbs, the more of the earth's surface becomes visible, and the effect of this is that the horizon seems uphill from the observer. This illusion is especially notable on Haleakala, for the old volcano rises directly from the sea, without buttresses or connecting ranges. In consequence, as fast as we climbed up the grim slope of Haleakala, still faster did Haleakala, ourselves, and all about us sink down into the center of what appeared a profound abyss. Everywhere, far above us, towered the horizon. The ocean sloped down from the horizon to us. The higher we climbed, the deeper did we seem to sink down, the farther above us shone the horizon, and the steeper pitched the grade up to that horizontal line where sky and ocean met. It was weird and unreal, and vagrant thoughts of Simm's Hole and of the volcano through which Jules Verne journeyed to the center of the earth flitted through one's mind.

And then, when at last we reached the summit of that monster mountain, which summit was like the bottom of an inverted

cone situated in the center of an awful cosmic pit, we found that we were at neither top nor bottom. Far above us was the heaven-towering horizon, and far beneath us, where the top of the mountain should have been, was a deeper deep, the great crater, the House of the Sun. Twenty-three miles around stretched the dizzy walls of the crater. We stood on the edge of the nearly vertical western wall, and the floor of the crater lay nearly half a mile beneath. This floor, broken by lava flows and cinder cones, was as red and fresh and uneroded as if it were but yesterday that the fires went out. The cinder cones, the smallest over 400 feet in height and the largest over 900, seemed no more than puny little sand hills, so mighty was the magnitude of the setting. Two gaps, thousands of feet deep, broke the rim of the crater, and through these Ukiukiu vainly strove to drive his fleecy herds of trade-wind clouds. As fast as they advanced through the gaps, the heat of the crater dissipated them into thin air, and though they advanced always, they got nowhere.

I T WAS A SCENE OF vast bleakness and desolation, stern, forbidding, fascinating. We gazed down upon a place of fire and earthquake. The tie-ribs of earth lay bare before us. It was a workshop of nature still cluttered with the raw beginnings of world-making. Here and there great dikes of primordial rock had thrust themselves up from the bowels of earth, straight through the molten surface ferment that had evidently cooled only the other day. It was all unreal and unbelievable. Looking upward, far above us (in reality beneath us) floated the cloud battle of Ukiukiu and Naulu. And higher up the slope of the seeming abyss, above the cloud battle, in the air and sky, hung the islands of Lanai and Molokai. Across the crater, to the southeast, still apparently looking upward, we saw ascending, first, the turquoise sea, then the white surf line of the shore of Hawaii; above that the belt of trade clouds, and next, 80 miles away, rearing their stupendous bulks out of the azure sky, tipped with snow, wreathed with cloud, trembling like a mirage, the peaks of Mauna Kea and Mauna Loa hung poised on the wall of heaven.

It is told that long ago, one Maui, the son of Hina, lived on what is now known as West Maui. His mother, Hina, employed her time in the making of kapas. She must have made them at night, for her days were occupied in trying to dry the kapas. Each morning, and all morning, she toiled at spreading them out in the sun. But no sooner were they out than she began taking them in, in order to have them all under shelter for the night. For know that the days were shorter then than now. Maui watched his mother's futile toil and felt sorry for her. He decided to do something—oh, no, not to help her hang out and take in the kapas. He was too clever for that. His idea was to make the sun go slower. Perhaps he was the first Hawaiian astronomer. At any rate, he took a series of observations of the sun from various parts of the island. His conclusion was that the sun's path was directly across Haleakala. Unlike Joshua, he stood in no need of divine assistance. He gathered a huge quantity of coconuts, from the fiber of which he braided a stout cord, and in one end of which he made a noose, even as the cowboys of Haleakala do to this day. Next he climbed into the House of the Sun and laid in wait. When the sun came tearing along the path, bent on completing its journey in the shortest time possible, the valiant youth threw his lariat around one of the sun's largest and strongest beams. He made the sun slow down some; also, he broke the beam short off. And he kept on roping and breaking off beams till the sun said it was willing to listen to reason. Maui set forth his terms of peace, which the sun accepted, agreeing to go more slowly thereafter. Wherefore Hina had ample time in which to dry her kapas, and the days are longer than they used to be, which last is quite in accord with the teachings of modern astronomy.

We had a lunch of jerked beef and hard poi in a stone corral, used of old time for the night impounding of cattle being driven across the island. Then we skirted the rim for half a mile and began the descent into the crater. Twenty-five hundred feet beneath lay the floor, and down a steep slope of loose volcanic cinders we dropped, the sure-footed horses slipping and sliding, but always keeping their feet. The black surface of the cinders, when broken by the horses' hoofs, turned to a yellow ocher dust, virulent in appearance and acid of

taste, that arose in clouds. There was a gallop across a level stretch to the mouth of a convenient blowhole, and then the descent continued in clouds of volcanic dust, winding in and out among cinder cones, brick-red, old rose, and purplish black of color. Above us, higher and higher, towered the crater walls, while we journeyed on across innumerable lava flows, turning and twisting a devious way among the adamantine billows of a petrified sea. Sawtoothed waves of lava vexed the surface of this weird ocean, while on either hand rose jagged crests and spiracles of fantastic shape. Our way led on past a bottomless pit and along and over the main stream of the latest lava flow for 7 miles.

AT THE LOWER END of the crater was our camping spot, in a small grove of olapa and kolea trees, tucked away in a corner of the crater at the base of walls that rose perpendicularly 1,500 feet. Here was pasturage for the horses, but no water, and first we turned aside and picked our way across a mile of lava to a known water hole in a crevice in the crater wall. The water hole was empty. But on climbing 50 feet up the crevice, a pool was found containing half a dozen barrels of water. A pail was carried up, and soon a steady stream of the precious liquid was running down the rock and filling the lower pool, while the cowboys below were busy fighting the horses back, for there was room for one only to drink at a time. Then it was on to camp at the foot of the wall, up which herds of wild goats scrambled and blatted, while the tent rose to the sound of rifle firing. Jerked beef, hard poi, and broiled kid was the menu. Over the crest of the crater, just above our heads, rolled a sea of clouds, driven on by Ukiukiu. Though this sea rolled over the crest unceasingly, it never blotted out nor dimmed the moon, for the heat of the crater dissolved the clouds as fast as they rolled in. Through the moonlight, attracted by the camp fire, came the crater cattle to peer and challenge. They were rolling fat, though they rarely drank water, the morning dew on the grass taking its place. It was because of this dew that the tent made a welcome bedchamber, and we fell asleep to the chanting of hulas by the unwearied Hawaiian cowboys, in whose veins, no doubt, ran the blood of Maui, their valiant forebear.

The camera cannot do justice to the House of the Sun. The sublimated chemistry of photography may not lie, but it certainly does not tell all the truth. The Koolau Gap [may be] faithfully reproduced, just as it impinged on the retina of the camera, yet in the resulting picture the gigantic scale of things is missing. Those walls that seem several hundred feet in height are almost as many thousand; that entering wedge of cloud is a mile and a half wide in the gap itself, while beyond the gap it is a veritable ocean; and that foreground of cinder cone and volcanic ash, mushy and colorless in appearance, is in truth gorgeous-hued in brick-red, terra cotta, rose, yellow, ocher, and purplish black. Also, words are a vain thing and drive to despair. To say that a crater wall is 2,000 feet high is to say just precisely that it is 2,000 feet high; but there is a vast deal more to that crater wall than a mere statistic. The sun is 93 million miles distant, but to mortal conception the adjoining county is farther away. This frailty of the human brain is hard on the sun. It is likewise hard on the House of the Sun. Haleakala has a message of beauty and wonder for the human soul that cannot be delivered by proxy. Kolikoli is six hours from Kahului; Kahului is a night's run from Honolulu; Honolulu is six days from San Francisco; and there you are.

WE CLIMBED THE CRATER walls, put the horses over impossible places, rolled stones, and shot wild goats. I did not get any goats. I was too busy rolling stones. One spot in particular I remember, where we started a stone the size of a horse. It began the descent easy enough, rolling over, wobbling, and threatening to stop; but in a few minutes it was soaring through the air 200 feet at a jump. It grew rapidly smaller until it struck a slight slope of volcanic sand, over which it darted like a startled jack rabbit, kicking up behind it a tiny trail of yellow dust. Stone and dust diminished in size, until some of the party said the stone had stopped. That was because they could not see it any longer. It had vanished into the distance beyond their ken. Others saw it rolling farther on—I know I did;

and it is my firm conviction that that stone is still rolling.

Our last day in the crater, Ukiukiu gave us a taste of his strength. He smashed Naulu back all along the line, filled the House of the Sun to overflowing with clouds, and drowned us out. Our rain gauge was a pint cup under a tiny hole in the tent. That last night of storm and rain filled the cup, and there was no way of measuring the water that spilled over into the blankets. With the rain gauge out of business there was no longer any reason for remaining; so we broke camp in the wet-gray of dawn and plunged eastward across the lava to the Kaupo Gap. East Maui is nothing more or less than the vast lava stream that flowed long ago through the Kaupo Gap; and down this stream we picked our way from an altitude of 6,500 feet to the sea. This was a day's work in itself for the horses; but never were there such horses. Safe in the bad places, never rushing, never losing their heads, as soon as they found a trail wide and smooth enough to run on, they ran. There was no stopping them until the trail became bad again, and then they stopped of themselves. Continuously, for days, they had performed the hardest kind of work, and fed most of the time on grass foraged by themselves at night while we slept, and yet that day they covered 28 leg-breaking miles and galloped into Hana like a bunch of colts. Also, there were several of them, reared in the dry region on the leeward side of Haleakala, that had never worn shoes in all their lives. Day after day, and all day long, unshod, they had traveled over the sharp lava, with the extra weight of a man on their backs, and their hoofs were in better condition than those of the shod horses.

THE SCENERY BETWEEN Vieiras's (where the Kaupo Gap empties into the sea) and Hana, which we covered in half a day, is well worth a week or a month; but, wildly beautiful as it is, it becomes pale and small in comparison with the wonderland that lies beyond the rubber plantations between Hana and the Honomanu Gulch. Two days were required to cover this marvelous stretch, which lies on the windward side of Haleakala. The people who dwell there call it "the ditch country," an unprepossessing name, but it has no other.

Nobody else ever comes there. Nobody else knows anything about it. With the exception of a handful of men, whom business has brought there, nobody has heard of the ditch country of Maui. Now a ditch is a ditch, assumably muddy, and usually traversing uninteresting and monotonous landscapes. But the Nahiku Ditch is not an ordinary ditch. The windward side of Haleakala is serried by a thousand precipitous gorges, down which rush as many torrents, each torrent of which achieves a score of cascades and waterfalls before it reaches the sea. More rain comes down here than in any other region in the world. In 1904 the year's downpour was 420 inches. Water means sugar, and sugar is the backbone of the territory of Hawaii, wherefore the Nahiku Ditch, which is not a ditch, but a chain of tunnels. The water travels underground, appearing only at intervals to leap a gorge, traveling high in the air on a giddy flume and plunging into and through the opposing mountain. This magnificent waterway is called a "ditch," and with equal appropriateness can Cleopatra's barge be called a boxcar.

There are no carriage roads through the ditch country, and before the ditch was built, or bored, rather, there was no horse trail. Hundreds of inches of rain annually, on fertile soil, under a tropic sun, means a steaming jungle of vegetation. A man, on foot, cutting his way through, might advance a mile a day, but at the end of a week he would be a wreck, and he would have to crawl hastily back if he wanted to get out before the vegetation overran the passageway he had cut. O'Shaughnessy was the daring engineer who conquered the jungle and the gorges, ran the ditch, and made the horse trail. He built enduringly, in concrete and masonry, and made one of the most remarkable water farms in the world. Every little runlet and dribble is harvested and conveyed by subterranean channels to the main ditch. But so heavily does it rain at times that countless spillways let the surplus escape to the sea.

The horse trail is not very wide. Like the engineer who built it, it dares anything. Where the ditch plunges through the mountain, it climbs over; and where the ditch leaps a gorge on a flume, the horse trail takes advantage of the ditch and crosses on top of the flume. That careless trail thinks nothing of traveling up or down the faces of precipices. It gouges its

narrow way out of the wall, dodging around waterfalls or passing under them where they thunder down in white fury; while straight overhead the wall rises hundreds of feet, and straight beneath it sinks a thousand. And those marvelous mountain horses are as unconcerned as the trail. They fox-trot along it as a matter of course, though the footing is slippery with rain, and they will gallop with their hind feet slipping over the edge if you let them. I advise only those with steady nerves and cool heads to tackle the Nahiku Ditch trail. One of our cowboys was noted as the strongest and bravest on the big ranch. He had ridden mountain horses all his life on the rugged western slopes of Haleakala. He was first in the horse breaking; and when the others hung back, as a matter of course, he would go in to meet a wild bull in the cattle pen. He had a reputation. But he had never ridden over the Nahiku Ditch. It was there he lost his reputation. When he faced the first flume, spanning a hair-raising gorge, narrow, without railings, with a bellowing waterfall above, another below, and directly beneath a wild cascade, the air filled with driving spray and rocking to the clamor and rush of sound and motion—well, that cowboy dismounted from his horse, explained briefly that he had a wife and two children, and crossed over on foot, leading the horse behind him.

The only relief from the flumes was the precipices; and the only relief from the precipices was the flumes, except where the ditch was far underground, in which case we crossed one horse and rider at a time, on primitive log bridges that swayed and teetered and threatened to carry away. I confess that at first I rode such places with my feet loose in the stirrups, and that on the sheer walls I saw to it, by a definite, conscious act of will, that the foot in the outside stirrup, overhanging the thousand feet of fall, was exceedingly loose. I say "at first"; for, as in the crater itself we quickly lost our conception of magnitude, so, on the Nahiku Ditch, we quickly lost our apprehension of depth. The ceaseless iteration of height and depth produced a state of consciousness in which height and depth were accepted as the ordinary conditions of existence; and from the horse's back to look sheer down 400 or 500 feet became quite commonplace and nonproductive of thrills. And as carelessly as the

trail and the horses, we swung along the dizzy heights and ducked around or through the waterfalls.

AND SUCH A RIDE! Falling water was everywhere. We rode above the clouds, under the clouds, and through the clouds! and every now and then a shaft of sunshine penetrated like a searchlight to the depths yawning beneath us, or flashed upon some pinnacle of the crater rim thousands of feet above. At every turn of the trail a waterfall or a dozen waterfalls, leaping hundreds of feet through the air, burst upon our vision. At our first night's camp, in the Keanae Gulch, we counted 32 waterfalls from a single viewpoint. The vegetation ran riot over that wild land. There were forests of koa and kolea trees, and candlenut trees; and then there were the trees called ohia-ai, which bore red mountain apples, mellow and juicy and most excellent to eat. Wild bananas grew everywhere, clinging to the sides of the gorges, and, overborne by their great bunches of ripe fruit, falling across the trail and blocking the way. And over the forest surged a sea of green life, the climbers of a thousand varieties, some that floated airily, in lacelike filaments, from the tallest branches; others that coiled and wound about the trees like huge serpents; and one, the ie-ie, that was for all the world like a climbing palm, swinging on a thick stem from branch to branch and tree to tree and throttling the supports whereby it climbed. Through the sea of green, lofty tree ferns thrust their great delicate fronds, and the lehua flaunted its scarlet blossoms. Underneath the climbers, in no less profusion, grew the warm-colored, strangely marked plants that in the United States one is accustomed to seeing preciously conserved in hothouses. In fact, the ditch country of Maui is nothing more nor less than a huge conservatory. Every familiar variety of fern flourishes, and more varieties that are unfamiliar, from the tiniest maidenhair to the gross and voracious staghorn, the latter the terror of the woodsmen, interlacing with itself in tangled masses five or six feet deep and covering acres.

Never was there such a ride. For two days it lasted, when we emerged into rolling

country, and, along an actual wagon road, came home to the ranch at a gallop. I know it was cruel to gallop the horses after such a long, hard journey; but we blistered our hands in a vain effort to hold them in. That's the sort of horses they grow on Haleakala. At the ranch there was a great festival of cattle driving, branding, and horse breaking. Overhead Ukiukiu and Naulu battled valiantly, and far above, in the sunshine, towered the mighty summit of Haleakala.

— Jack London

HEAVENLY HANA

HYMNS SUNG IN Hawaiian filter from two nearby churches through fragrant butter-yellow and magenta plumeria blossoms. I slump in the slanting morning sunlight on my lanai at the Hotel Hana-Maui, dissipating my morning torpor with a cup of Kona's finest, made moments ago in my plantation-posh room. Silent thanks are offered to the management for supplying whole coffee beans, a machine to grind them and another to brew them. Such welcome surprises in such a removed, ethereal place.

It is odd but fascinating to hear familiar hymns transmuted into Polynesian dialect, and I actually heave myself up in curiosity and stumble with cup in hand across the hotel's broad central lawn to squint through an archway at the 150-year-old Wananalua Congregational Church. The singing swells dramatically through the old church's open doors and then fades into the rustle of palm fronds and the faint slapping of swells against a rocky shoreline. Not even the shrill cry of an annoyed mynah can break the reflective spell.

As the hymn ends I head back to my lanai, mostly awake but lost in the kind of dreamy contemplation that Hana often induces. I had read that the church's walls, 2½ feet thick at the base, were constructed in 1842 by local volunteers directed by a Yankee *kahu* (shepherd or pastor), the Rev. Daniel Conde. The walls were built of volcanic stone, much of it scavenged from the ruins of the many ancient and highly sacred *heiaus* (shrines or temples) dotting this once heavily populated coastline. The mortar was made from coral brought up from depths of two or three fathoms by pure-blooded Hawaiians diving from ancestral canoes.

The church, like everything else along this storied eastern coast, is interwoven with the legends, history, and people of the remote, rainy area. The way things interconnect here is frequently so eerie that the strains of the *Twilight Zone* theme begin playing unbidden in the back of your mind. A heightened sense of the physical

and the spiritual binds the inhabitants of this extraordinary place into a dedicated community of protectors of its legend, superstition, and beauty.

Even the Hotel Hana-Maui, first opened in 1946 (and ever since the sophisticated centerpiece of this otherwise rural area) is inexorably intertwined with the community. Along with the surrounding 4,500-acre Hana Ranch, it was rescued from decrepitude in 1984 by Texas oil heiress Caroline Rose Hunt's Rosewood Corporation. It is certainly one of the most casually luxurious—and expensive—hotels in Hawaii.

The small hotel alone received a $24 million renovation in 1987 that added rooms, rebuilt most others, completely remodeled the lobby, library, dining room, and bar. What had been a slowly moldering pile was transformed into a showcase of tasteful design, quiet luxury, and innovative menus thoroughly unexpected in such a bucolic environment. Spaces that before were dim and enclosed are now open and airy. Granite flagstones, bleached wood, skylights, and masses of cut flowers add to the air of costly ease.

NEWER GUESTS have been surprised that the hotel is set in the midst of the modest town of Hana rather than plunked on some pristine beach, as its cachet and price might suggest. Traffic from the one main road chugs by just feet from many of the rooms, and the most expensive accommodations in the new Sea Ranch Cottages are a considerable stroll away, across another well-used public road. The community tennis courts and ball field lie adjacent, a lob away between Hana Bay and the hotel. This is no remote hideaway, at least not in the Robinson Crusoe sense.

Visitors to Hana have little choice, for example, but to join the estimated 1,500 sightseers who come daily in rental cars or on van tours to rubberneck through town, pause for lunch, lurch out to see the

Seven Pools of Oheo Gulch, perhaps search futilely for Lindbergh's grave in Kipahulu and then turn around for the long drive back. If they want to stay overnight, alternatives to the Hotel Hana-Maui are the decidedly funky little Heavenly Hana Inn, the nice but few condo units of the Hana Kai-Maui Resort, or one of the private houses that can be booked through Hana Bay Vacation Rentals. Added together, there are only about 100 rooms for rent at Hana.

It rains a lot here: in the average year, 70 to 100 inches, and more than that just up the slope of 2-mile-high Haleakala, whose largely unseen bulk looms over the rugged coastline its eruptions created. All of Hawaii's islands have a wet and a dry side, created by the convergence of steady trade winds and high mountains. On Maui, resort areas like Kaanapali Beach are on the arid leeward coasts, which have better beaches and a reliably sunny climate. Not so with lush, green Hana. The rain comes year-round, though much of it falls at night and in the early morning, and the most popular months of December and January, along with November, February, and March, are the rainiest of all. Then it comes at any time and in frequent downpours, causing visitors to seek indoor entertainment that largely does not exist here. Scenic drives, beach barbecues, horseback rides, hiking, jogging, bicycling and the other normally wonderful outdoor diversions popular at Hana do not tend to be successful in wet weather. And the limited undercover activities, such as a visit to the Hana Cultural Center, seem to use up minutes instead of hours. The Hotel Hana-Maui has a well-stocked library but no television or radio in the rooms.

BUT, OF COURSE, unending activity and utter comfort are not the things that have made Hana so alluring for so long to so many different people. Ex-Beatle George Harrison, Jim Nabors, and other celebrities chose to live part-time in the Hana area because of the seclusion and the deep sense of physical and spiritual wonder. At Henry Kahula's Chevron station the windows are signed in grease pencil by entertainers like Kris Kristofferson and Steve Forrest.

The real Hana takes a while to work its peculiar magic on visitors. It is in the air all around, in this place where cultures gracefully glance off one another and legends mix as freely with facts as the broad-faced Hawaiians intermingle with the town's anachronistic contingent of backwoods hippies. One moment you will see two Hawaiians peacefully lounging in a pickup truck parked at the end of the old sugarcane-loading wharf that juts into Hana Bay quietly smoking *pakalolo* (marijuana), and the next, there is a placid blond, barefoot haole padding happily along Hana Highway as calves packed against a fence moo and eye her curiously. It is the sort of place where the Bank of Hawaii—the only bank—opens for 1½ hours every weekday except Friday (clearly the big day of the week), when it's open for three hours.

Sitting in the hotel's airy dining room eating banana waffles with ginger syrup—a breakfast as trendily correct as it is jarring and unlikely in such a determinedly retro place—my gaze rises from the torch ginger in the gardens to the modest mound of Kauiki Hill standing at one arm of Hana Bay. Clouds brush over the low ironwood-covered cinder cone, stirring up stories from the past.

In legend, it was here that the lovers Kauiki and Noenoe were forever united by the demigod Maui, who changed them into a hill and the mist that clings to it. In reality, it was the birthplace in 1768 of Queen Kaahumanu, Kamehameha the Great's favorite wife and later the regent, who turned Hawaii away from the past by fostering the breaking of the old *kapus* (taboos) and converting to Christianity. And it was around this ancient natural fortress that bloody battles raged for control of the coveted region.

Hana has always been cherished and important. Before the arrival of the first European ships offshore in the mid-1700s, Hana's rich agricultural lowland and forested upper reaches supported an estimated 45,000 to 75,000 people. The population had dropped to about 11,000 by 1831, and despite the importation of contract labor from China, Japan, and other countries during the sugarcane boom that started in 1864, it's dwindled steadily ever since. In the 1930s, when the plantations began to close and various

agricultural experiments failed, people began leaving at an even greater rate. A stabilized population of about a thousand people occupies the district today, many of predominantly Hawaiian blood, others bliss-seeking haole or the descendants of Chinese, Japanese, and Portuguese workers.

In Hana, the issues of growth and tourism are as hotly debated and uses of the land are as fiercely contested as when armies fought over it in past centuries. Isolation and attitude discourage development and, sometimes, even curiosity here. Residents are fiercely protective of the land, chary of change. They will not hear of plans to expand the tiny airport so it can accommodate jets.

IN THIS PLACE of almost-mesmerizing tranquillity, the most peaceful, serene spot touched by man must be Palapala Hoomau Congregational Church, a place I find purely by instinct and have visited four times without encountering another human being. You drive out past Hana about 10 miles on a road far worse and more tortuous than the serpentine highway to the town, past the place called Seven Pools that is the terminus of most day tours, past the scattered ramshackle and grand houses of Kipahulu, past tiny St. Paul's Church and, on the right, the nearly hidden massive chimney of a ruined sugar mill.

Just past the mill, on the left side of the road, is a pasture and then a galvanized-steel gate swung permanently open on a rutted track that heads toward the sea. The road goes to the Palapala Hoomau Congregational Church, a few hundred yards away, mostly hidden behind thick vegetation. There is no sign on the road and nothing at all to indicate that anything lies down this country lane, but unlike the other gates in the area this one has no "kapu," or "keep out," sign. Founded in 1857 and built in 1864, the simple one-room church sits on a bluff over the sea, with a small graveyard on the ocean side.

It is a place of such healing aura and calming silence that the temptation is overwhelming to linger, to sit in the quiet, musty church reading the program from the last service—the call to worship, doxology, and three hymns in Hawaiian—and then to stroll around the grounds. It is small wonder that Charles A. Lindbergh loved it so that he wanted his grave here. There it is, dated 1974, with three tiny American flags planted in the soil. Almost no one ever finds it.

At dusk on the way back to Hana, just after passing a grinning Hawaiian with his handsome small son, and driving cautiously along the bad road, I glanced up to see a small snow-white owl perched on a wire, gazing down at me. It was a *pueokea*, the rarely seen and endangered Hawaiian owl, a sighting some locals later told me was fraught with good fortune, for it is a blessing promising a safe journey. Minutes later I saw a second, also curiously watching me. This, I was told, was almost unprecedented. I was regarded with new respect in Hana. I might be home.

— *Richard J. Pietschmann*

Freelance writer Richard J. Pietschmann contributes regularly to many national publications, including Travel Holiday *and* Outside *magazines. A Los Angeles resident, he is also the West Coast editor of* Departures *magazine.*

HIGHWAY TO HANA

THE ROAD TO HANA is paved, I was told, with rude inventions. For starters, its 44 spine-tingling miles were said to contain 56 one-lane bridges—guaranteed to elevate adrenaline to levels associated with such activities as gladiatorial combat—along with precisely 617 whirligig curves, several stretches of one-way traffic, innumerable potholes, much evidence of recent washouts, a few crumbled cliffsides, and significant numbers of pinprick-pupiled tourists whose fingers would have to be removed surgically from the steering wheels of their rental cars.

This run of fabled highway along Maui's wild, windward, sparsely populated, and stunningly scenic northeast coast seemed to have been the scene of countless cases of cracked nerves and hair-raising mishaps, dreadful weather, and backed-up traffic. "I just *hate* that drive," said the waitress at Mama's Fish House outside Paia (usually cited as the beginning point for the journey) as she cleaned up the remains of my *ahi* sandwich just before I hit the road. "Something *always* happens."

I knew better. During three previous trips on the Hana Highway nothing particularly untoward had occurred, except a bit of hesitant traffic and some light rain, along with plenty of gorgeous scenery. And travel time was well below the 2½-hour minimum quoted to timid tourists. On the last run, in fact, I had established a personal best of less than 1½ hours from Hana to Paia—in an open Jeep, to boot. Sure, occasional mists descended to dampen my baseball cap, tires sometimes squealed around some of the more serious switchbacks, and a backseat passenger emerged at the end dazed and hobbling but grinning happily.

The mostly two-lane road—ancient footpaths widened by convict gangs in 1926, paved in 1962 and upgraded into passable shape for normal traffic only in 1982—is in fairly good shape. But all that weather and those winter washouts tend to age the road quickly in its more vulnerable spots, so don't expect smooth sailing for the entire length. The two slowest stretches have many places where 10 mph is the norm, and careful drivers inch around the hairpins much more slowly than that.

But what a small price to pay for such a spectacular journey—through rain forest and jungle, past streams and waterfalls, with postcard vistas of windswept peninsulas, deep bays, and green valleys. Tiny villages, each centered by a steepled church, pop up unexpectedly in the midst of all this natural grandeur. The sprinkling of people, most with a high percentage of Polynesian blood, live simply, farming taro, bananas, and other crops. It's not hard to see why this part of Maui is called the true Hawaii, away from any sign of tourism or commerce.

Easily distracted from missions of most sorts, I made it only a couple of miles past Mama's to Hookipa Beach Park, situated on a windy bluff overlooking the most famous wind-surfing waters in the world. Usually, one quick look at the scores of boards with brightly colored sails skipping through and flipping over the churning waves is fortifying enough to make the most harrowing drive seem dull and uneventful. Not today, though. It was so rough and windy that even the notoriously devil-may-care windsurfers had furled their sails and slunk back to the saloons of Paia. No matter. Hana, ho.

The drive was actually fun as well as beautiful, and the one-way bridges over steep gullies were welcome opportunities to slow and even pause to gaze at the rain forest and stream-fed waterfalls. The wonder of Hawaii's renowned microclimates becomes gradually evident as the drive unfolds from rolling pastureland to jungled cliffs sliced by narrow valleys and then level tropical upland.

THE MODEST TONGUE of flatland that is the Keanae Peninsula materializes suddenly, its simple weathered church and taro patches a shock after miles of rain forest. Just beyond, spread far below the road, is the

community of Wailua, its white-steeple church boldly visible from the great distance. Then the jungle closes in to swallow a road that once more plunges in cramped surrender. During previous drives I had been fascinated by a tree whose spade-shape leaves shimmered so filmily from above that the jungle below appeared like a sea of glistening white. I stopped to follow a stream a short distance until I found one of those trees and picked a leaf. A gardener at the Hotel Hana-Maui later identified it as from the Kukui tree—one of the few native trees able to compete with such imported varieties as guava, mango, eucalyptus, and bamboo that now dominate the forest. Even the wild white and torch ginger that bloom along the roadside are imports.

Toward the end, just a few miles outside Hana and giddy with the pleasant vertigo of it all, I began drifting into some other road-warrior dimension. Here as the highway begins to untwist, drivers are lulled into thinking they can relax, but another series of one-lane bridges appears. By then I was making up stories for each bridge, at one noting mynah birds standing guard "like tiny Horatios." Ninety minutes after stopping at Hookipa to look for windsurfers, the drive was over.

I thought that was *hauling* until Clyde Min, who manages the Hotel Hana-Maui, casually mentioned that his best-ever time was at night after dinner at Mama's. No traffic. No sightseeing. And all in 50 minutes flat. He swears.

— *Richard J. Pietschmann*

BOOKS AND VIDEOS

Before your trip, pick up a copy of James Michener's *Hawaii,* one of the best novels set in the Hawaiian Islands. Other excellent novels with a Hawaiian setting include James Jones's *From Here to Eternity* and John Dominis Holt's *Waimea Summer,* based on the author's experiences growing up in Hawai'i.

Hawaii: An Uncommon History, by Edward Joesting, gives a behind-the-scenes look at the factual side of some of the same events in the Michener novel. *A Voyage to the Pacific Ocean,* by Captain James Cook, ranks as one of the first guidebooks to the Islands and still contains many valid insights. Gavan Daws's definitive *Shoal of Time* will take you from Captain Cook's landing until statehood in 1959.

Maui, How It Came to Be, by Will Kyselka, will tell you more about Maui's origins. *Maui, Mischievous Hero,* by Barbara Lyons, illuminates the legends of the Valley Isle. Mary Kawena Pukui's *Place Names of Hawai'i* can tell you how some of the interesting names in the state originated.

Rita Ariyoshi's *Maui on My Mind* is a beautiful collection of photographs in a coffee-table-book format, as is *A Day in the Life of Hawaii. Hawaiian Hiking Trails,* by Craig Chisholm, gives a good idea of the best paths to take around Maui. John R. K. Clark's *The Beaches of Maui County* offers a good overview of the island's surf and sand. *Surfing: The Ultimate Pleasure,* by Leonard Lueras, covers everything about the sport from its early history to the music and films of its later subculture. Those interested in the physical attractions of the Islands may want to read *A Guide to Tropical and Semitropical Flora,* by Loraine Kuck and Richard Tongg. The *Handbook of Hawaiian Fishes,* by W. A. Gosline and Vernon Brock, is a must for snorkelers; *Hawaii's Birds,* by the Hawai'i Audubon Society, is perfect for the bird-watchers.

Movie buffs will enjoy *Made in Paradise: Hollywood's Films of Hawaii and the South Seas* by Luis Reyes; it points out movie locations and pokes gentle fun at some of the misinformation popularized by Tinseltown's version of island life. Albert J. Schütz's little souvenir-worthy paperback, *All About Hawaiian* discusses the history, spelling, and pronunciation of Hawaiian words, as well as recent efforts to preserve the Islands' language. *Pidgin to Da Max,* by Douglas Simonson, explains the humorous creole language—known as Pidgin—which you'll no doubt hear all over the Hawaiian Islands.

If you want to prepare your palate for an upcoming Maui visit, or have returned from the Islands in love with haute Hawaiian cuisine, get *The New Cuisine of Hawaii,* by Janice Wald Henderson, published by Villard Books, Random House. This beautifully designed and photographed book features recipes from the 12 chefs who are credited with defining Hawai'i regional cuisine. If your interests run to the everyday, not-so-haute local diet of dishes inspired by Hawai'i's unique ethnic mix, try *The Foods of Paradise* by Rachel Laudan.

At Kahului Airport you'll find racks of free weekly visitor guides, including *Maui Gold, This Week Maui,* and *Maui Beach Press,* full of coupons, discount offers, and suggestions for what to see and do on the Valley Isle.

Hawaiian Glossary and Menu Guide

HAWAIIAN GLOSSARY

ALTHOUGH AN UNDERSTANDING of Hawaiian is by no means required on a trip to the Aloha State, a *malihini,* or newcomer, will find plenty of opportunities to pick up a few of the local words and phrases. Visitors are likely to read or hear at least a few words each day of their stay.

Hawaiian had no phonetic alphabet until the missionaries came in the early 1800s. There is a strong movement here to preserve Hawaiian language, as an important part of Hawaiian culture. Traditional names and expressions are widely used in the Islands, thanks in part to legislation enacted in the early 1990s to encourage the use of authentically spelled Hawaiian language. The diacriticals, which are an aid to pronunciation, are appearing on more and more public signage, so you may notice authentic spelling more now than in the past.

With a basic understanding and some uninhibited practice, anyone can have enough command of the local tongue to ask for directions and to order off a restaurant menu. One recent visitor announced she would not leave until she could pronounce *humuhumunukunukuāpua'a,* the Hawaiian name of the reef triggerfish, the state fish. Luckily, she had scheduled a nine-day stay.

Simplifying the learning process is the fact that the Hawaiian language contains only eight consonants—H, K, L, M, N, P, W, and the silent *'okina* or glottal stop, written '—plus the five vowels. All syllables, and therefore all words, end in a vowel. Each vowel, with the exception of a few diphthongized double vowels such as *au* (pronounced ow) or *ai* (pronounced eye), is pronounced separately. Thus *'Iolani* is four syllables (ee-oh-la-nee), not three (yo-la-nee). Although some Hawaiian words have only vowels, most also contain some consonants, but consonants are never doubled.

Pronunciation is simple. Pronounce *A* "ah" as father; *E* "ay" as in weigh; *I* "ee" as in marine; *O* "oh" as in no; *U* "oo" as in true. Consonants mirror their English equivalents, with the exception of *W.* When the letter begins any syllable other than the first one in a word, it is usually pronounced as a V. *'Awa,* the Polynesian drink, is pronounced "ava"; *'Ewa* is pronounced "Eva."

Nearly all long Hawaiian words are combinations of shorter words; they are not difficult to pronounce if you segment them into shorter words. *Kalaniana'ole,* the highway running east from Honolulu, is easily understood as *Kalani ana 'ole.* Apply the standard pronunciation guidance—the stress falls on the next-to-last syllable of most two- or three-syllable Hawaiian words—and Kalaniana'ole Highway is as easy to say as Adam Clayton Powell Boulevard.

Now about that fish. Try *humu-humu nuku-nuku āpu a'a.*

The other unusual element in Hawaiian language is the *kahakō* or macron, written as a short line (ˉ) placed over a vowel. Like the accent (´) in Spanish, the kahakō puts emphasis on a syllable that would normally not be stressed. The most familiar example is probably *Waikīkī.* With no macrons, the stress would fall on the middle syllable; with only one macron on the last syllable, the stress would fall on the first and last syllables. Some words become plural with the addition of a macron, often on a syllable that would have been stressed anyway. No Hawai-

ian word becomes plural with the addition of an *S* since that letter does not exist in *'ōlelo Hawai'i* (which is Hawaiian for "Hawaiian language").

What follows is a glossary of some of the most commonly used Hawaiian words. Don't be afraid to give them a try. Hawaiian residents appreciate visitors who at least try to pick up the local language.

'a'ā: rough, crumbling lava, contrasting with *pāhoehoe,* which is smooth.

'ae: yes.

akamai: smart, clever, possessing savoir-faire.

ala: a road, path, or trail.

ali'i: a Hawaiian chief, a member of the chiefly class.

aloha: love, affection, kindness. Also a salutation meaning both greetings and farewell.

'a'ole: no.

'auwai: a ditch.

auwē: alas, woe is me!

'ehu: a red-haired Hawaiian.

'ewa: in the direction of 'Ewa plantation, west of Honolulu.

hala: the pandanus tree, whose leaves (*lau hala*) are used to make baskets and plaited mats.

hale: a house.

hana: to work.

haole: originally a stranger or foreigner. Since the first foreigners were Caucasian, *haole* now means a Caucasian person.

hapa: a part, sometimes a half; often used as a short form of *hapa haole,* to mean a person who is part-Caucasian; thus, the name of a popular local band, whose members represent a variety of ethnicities.

hau'oli: to rejoice. *Hau'oli Makahiki Hou* means Happy New Year. *Hau'oli lā hānau* means Happy Birthday.

heiau: an ancient Hawaiian place of worship.

holo: to run.

holoholo: to go for a walk, ride, or sail.

holokū: a long Hawaiian dress, somewhat fitted, with a yoke and a train. Influenced by European fashion, it was worn at court, and at least one local translates the word as "expensive muumuu."

holomū: a post–World War II cross between a *holokū* and a muumuu, less fitted than the former but less voluminous than the latter, and having no train.

honi: to kiss, a kiss. A phrase that some tourists may find useful, quoted from a popular *hula,* is *Honi Ka'ua Wikiwiki:* Kiss me quick!

ho'omalimali: flattery, a deceptive "line," bunk, baloney, hooey.

huhū: angry.

hui: a group, club, or assembly. A church may refer to its congregation as a *hui* and a social club may be called a *hui.*

hukilau: a seine; a communal fishing party in which everyone helps to drive the fish into a huge net, pull it in, and divide the catch.

hula: the dance of Hawai'i.

iki: little.

ipo: sweetheart.

ka: the. This is the definite article for most singular words; for plural nouns, the definite article is usually *nā.* Since there is no S in Hawaiian, the article may be your only clue that a noun is plural.

kahuna: a priest, doctor, or other trained person of old Hawai'i, endowed with special professional skills that often included the gift of prophecy or other supernatural powers; plural: *kāhuna.*

kai: the sea, salt water.

kalo: the taro plant from whose root poi is made.

kama'āina: literally, a child of the soil, it refers to people who were born in the Islands or have lived there for a long time.

kanaka: originally a man or humanity in general, it is now used to denote a male Hawaiian or part-Hawaiian, but is occasionally taken as a slur when used by non-Hawaiians. *Kanaka maoli,* originally a full-blooded Hawaiian person, is used by some native Hawaiian rights activists to embrace part-Hawaiians as well.

kāne: a man, a husband. If you see this word on a door, it's the men's room. If you see *kane* on a door, it's probably a misspelling; that is the Hawaiian name for the skin fungus, Tinea.

kapa: also called by its Tahitian name, *tapa,* a cloth made of beaten bark and usually dyed and stamped with a repeat design.

kapakahi: crooked, cockeyed, uneven. You've got your hat on *kapakahi.*

kapu: keep out, prohibited. This is the Hawaiian version of the more widely known Tongan word *tabu* (taboo).

keiki: a child; *keikikāne* is a boy, *keikiwahine* a girl.

kona: the leeward side of the Islands, the direction (south) from which the *kona* wind and *kona* rain come.

kuleana: a homestead or small plot of ground on which a family has been installed for some generations without necessarily owning it. By extension, *kuleana* is used to denote any area or department in which one has a special interest or prerogative. You'll hear it used this way: If you want to hire a surfboard, see Moki; that's his *kuleana.* And conversely: I can't help you with that; that's not my *kuleana.*

lamalama: to fish with a torch.

lānai: a porch, a balcony, an outdoor living room. Almost every house in Hawai'i has one. Don't confuse this two-syllable word with the three-syllable name of the island, Lāna'i.

lani: heaven, the sky.

lau hala: the leaf of the *hala* or pandanus tree, widely used in Hawaiian handcrafts.

lei: a garland of flowers.

luna: a plantation overseer or foreman.

mahalo: thank you.

makai: toward the ocean.

malihini: a newcomer to the Islands.

mana: the spiritual power that the Hawaiian believed inhabited all things and creatures.

manuwahi: free, gratis.

mauka: toward the mountains.

mauna: mountain.

mele: a Hawaiian song or chant, often of epic proportions.

Mele Kalikimaka: Merry Christmas (a transliteration from the English phrase).

Menehune: a Hawaiian pixie. The *Menehune* were a legendary race of little people who accomplished prodigious work, such as building fish ponds and temples in the course of a single night.

moana: the ocean.

muumuu: the voluminous dress in which the missionaries enveloped Hawaiian women. Now made in bright printed cottons and silks, it is an indispensable garment in a Hawaiian woman's wardrobe. Culturally sensitive locals have embraced the Hawaiian spelling, but often shorten the spoken word to "mu'u." Most English dictionaries include the spelling *muumuu,* and that version is a part of many apparel companies' names.

nani: beautiful.

nui: big.

Pākē: Chinese. This *Pākē* carver makes beautiful things.

palapala: document, printed matter.

pali: a cliff, precipice.

pānini: prickly pear cactus.

paniolo: a Hawaiian cowboy, a rough transliteration of *español,* the language of the Islands' earliest cowboys.

pau: finished, done.

pilikia: trouble. The Hawaiian word is much more widely used here than its English equivalent.

puka: a hole.

pupule: crazy, like the celebrated Princess Pupule. This word has replaced its English equivalent in local usage.

wahine: a female, a woman, a wife, and a sign on the ladies' room door; plural: *wāhine.*

wai: fresh water, as opposed to salt water, which is *kai.*

wikiwiki: to hurry, hurry up. (Since this is a reduplication of *wiki,* quick, neither *W* is pronounced as a V.)

Pidgin is the unofficial language of Hawai'i. It is a creole language, with its own grammar, evolved from the mixture of English, Hawaiian, Japanese, Portuguese, and other languages spoken in 19th-century Hawai'i, and it is heard everywhere: on ranches, in warehouses, on beaches, and in the hallowed halls (and occasionally in the classrooms) of the University of Hawai'i. It's not much tougher to follow than Brooklynese; it just takes a little getting used to.

MENU GUIDE

Much of the Hawaiian language encountered during a stay in the Islands will appear on restaurant menus and lists of luau fare. Often these menus will also include terms from Japanese, Chinese, and other cultures. Here's a quick primer.

'ahi: locally caught tuna.

aku: skipjack, bonito tuna.

'ama'ama: mullet; it's hard to get, but tasty.

bento: a box lunch.

chicken lū'au: a stew made from chicken, taro leaves, and coconut milk.

dim sum: Chinese dumplings.

guava: This tasty fruit is most often used in juice and in jellies. As a juice, it's pink and quenches a thirst like nothing else.

haupia: a light, gelatinlike dessert made from coconut.

imu: the underground ovens in which pigs are roasted for luaus.

kālua: to bake underground. A *kālua* pig is the pièce de résistance of a Hawaiian feast.

kaukau: food. The word's derivation is Chinese, but it is widely used in the Islands.

kim chee: pickled Chinese cabbage made with garlic and hot peppers.

Kona coffee: coffee grown in the Kona district of the Big Island; prized for its rich flavor.

laulau: literally, a bundle. In everyday usage, *laulau* are morsels of pork, butterfish, or other ingredients wrapped along with young taro shoots in ti leaves for steaming.

liliko'i: passion fruit; a tart, seedy yellow fruit that makes delicious desserts, jellies, and sherbet.

lomilomi: to rub or massage; also a massage. Lomilomi salmon is fish that has been rubbed with onions and herbs, commonly served with minced onions and tomatoes.

lū'au: a Hawaiian feast, also the leaf of the taro plant used in preparing such a feast.

lū'au leaves: cooked taro tops with a taste similar to spinach.

macadamia nuts: These little round, buttery-tasting nuts are mostly grown on the Big Island, but are available throughout the Islands.

mahimahi: mild-flavored dolphin fish, not to be confused with the marine mammal.

mai tai: fruit punch with rum, from the Tahitian word for "good."

malasada: a Portuguese deep-fried doughnut without a hole, dipped in sugar.

manapua: dough wrapped around diced pork.

mango: a juicy sweet fruit, with a yellowish-red smooth skin and a yellow pulpy interior.

manō: shark.

niu: coconut.

'ōkolehao: a liqueur distilled from the ti root.

onaga: pink or red snapper.

ono (n.)—a long, slender mackerel-like fish; also called a wahoo.

'ono (adj.)—delicious; also hungry.

'ōpakapaka: blue snapper.

'opihi: a tiny shellfish, or mollusk, found on rocks; also called limpets.

papaya: This green or yellow melonlike fruit will grow on you; it's high in vitamin C and is most often eaten at breakfast with a squeeze of lemon or lime.

pāpio: a young ulua or jack fish.

pohā: Cape gooseberry. Tasting a bit like honey, the poha berry is often used in jams and desserts.

poi: a paste made from pounded taro root, a staple of the Hawaiian diet.

poke: chopped pickled raw fish and seafood, tossed with herbs and seasonings.

pūpū: Hawaiian hors d'oeuvre.

saimin: long thin noodles and vegetables in a thin broth, often garnished with small pieces of fishcake, scrambled egg, luncheon meat, and green onion.

sashimi: raw fish sliced thin, usually eaten with soy sauce.

sushi: a variety of raw fish, served with vinegared rice and Japanese horseradish.

uku: deep-sea snapper.

ulua: crevalle, or jack fish; the giant trevally.

Index

X = *restaurant,* 🏨 = *hotel*

What's hot, where it's hot!

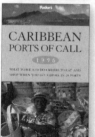

NOTES

NOTES

NOTES

NOTES

NOTES

NOTES

Fodor's Travel Publications

Available at bookstores everywhere, or call 1–800–533–6478, 24 hours a day.

Gold Guides

U.S.

Alaska

Arizona

Boston

California

Cape Cod, Martha's Vineyard, Nantucket

The Carolinas & the Georgia Coast

Chicago

Colorado

Florida

Hawai'i

Las Vegas, Reno, Tahoe

Los Angeles

Maine, Vermont, New Hampshire

Maui & Lāna'i

Miami & the Keys

New England

New Orleans

New York City

Pacific North Coast

Philadelphia & the Pennsylvania Dutch Country

The Rockies

San Diego

San Francisco

Santa Fe, Taos, Albuquerque

Seattle & Vancouver

The South

U.S. & British Virgin Islands

USA

Virginia & Maryland

Washington, D.C.

Foreign

Australia

Austria

The Bahamas

Belize & Guatemala

Bermuda

Canada

Cancún, Cozumel, Yucatán Peninsula

Caribbean

China

Costa Rica

Cuba

The Czech Republic & Slovakia

Eastern & Central Europe

Europe

Florence, Tuscany & Umbria

France

Germany

Great Britain

Greece

Hong Kong

India

Ireland

Israel

Italy

Japan

London

Madrid & Barcelona

Mexico

Montréal & Québec City

Moscow, St. Petersburg, Kiev

The Netherlands, Belgium & Luxembourg

New Zealand

Norway

Nova Scotia, New Brunswick, Prince Edward Island

Paris

Portugal

Provence & the Riviera

Scandinavia

Scotland

Singapore

South Africa

South America

Southeast Asia

Spain

Sweden

Switzerland

Thailand

Tokyo

Toronto

Turkey

Vienna & the Danube

Fodor's Special-Interest Guides

Caribbean Ports of Call

The Complete Guide to America's National Parks

Family Adventures

Gay Guide to the USA

Halliday's New England Food Explorer

Halliday's New Orleans Food Explorer

Healthy Escapes

Kodak Guide to Shooting Great Travel Pictures

Net Travel

Nights to Imagine

Rock & Roll Traveler USA

Sunday in New York

Sunday in San Francisco

Walt Disney World, Universal Studios and Orlando

Walt Disney World for Adults

Where Should We Take the Kids? California

Where Should We Take the Kids? Northeast

Worldwide Cruises and Ports of Call

Fodor's
Special Series

Affordables

Caribbean

Europe

Florida

France

Germany

Great Britain

Italy

London

Paris

Fodor's Bed & Breakfasts and Country Inns

America

California

The Mid-Atlantic

New England

The Pacific Northwest

The South

The Southwest

The Upper Great Lakes

The Berkeley Guides

California

Central America

Eastern Europe

Europe

France

Germany & Austria

Great Britain & Ireland

Italy

London

Mexico

New York City

Pacific Northwest & Alaska

Paris

San Francisco

Compass American Guides

Arizona

Canada

Chicago

Colorado

Hawaii

Idaho

Hollywood

Las Vegas

Maine

Manhattan

Montana

New Mexico

New Orleans

Oregon

San Francisco

Santa Fe

South Carolina

South Dakota

Southwest

Texas

Utah

Virginia

Washington

Wine Country

Wisconsin

Wyoming

Fodor's Citypacks

Atlanta

Hong Kong

London

New York City

Paris

Rome

San Francisco

Washington, D.C.

Fodor's Español

California

Caribe Occidental

Caribe Oriental

Gran Bretaña

Londres

Mexico

Nueva York

Paris

Fodor's Exploring Guides

Australia

Boston & New England

Britain

California

Caribbean

China

Egypt

Florence & Tuscany

Florida

France

Germany

Ireland

Israel

Italy

Japan

London

Mexico

Moscow & St. Petersburg

New York City

Paris

Prague

Provence

Rome

San Francisco

Scotland

Singapore & Malaysia

Spain

Thailand

Turkey

Venice

Fodor's Flashmaps

Boston

New York

San Francisco

Washington, D.C.

Fodor's Pocket Guides

Acapulco

Atlanta

Barbados

Jamaica

London

New York City

Paris

Prague

Puerto Rico

Rome

San Francisco

Washington, D.C.

Mobil Travel Guides

America's Best Hotels & Restaurants

California & the West

Frequent Traveler's Guide to Major Cities

Great Lakes

Mid-Atlantic

Northeast

Northwest & Great Plains

Southeast

Southwest & South Central

Rivages Guides

Bed and Breakfasts of Character and Charm in France

Hotels and Country Inns of Character and Charm in France

Hotels and Country Inns of Character and Charm in Italy

Hotels and Country Inns of Character and Charm in Paris

Hotels and Country Inns of Character and Charm in Portugal

Hotels and Country Inns of Character and Charm in Spain

Short Escapes

Britain

France

New England

Near New York City

Fodor's Sports

Golf Digest's Best Places to Play

Skiing USA

USA Today The Complete Four Sport Stadium Guide

Fodor's Vacation Planners

Great American Learning Vacations

Great American Sports & Adventure Vacations

Great American Vacations

Great American Vacations for Travelers with Disabilities

National Parks and Seashores of the East

National Parks of the West

WHEREVER YOU TRAVEL, *H*ELP IS NEVER FAR AWAY.

From planning your trip to providing travel assistance along the way, American Express® Travel Service Offices are always there to help.

Maui

OAHU
American Express Travel Service
Honolulu
808/536-3377

Hilton Hawaiian Village
Honolulu
808/947-2607

Hyatt Regency Waikiki
Honolulu
808/926-5441

American Express Travel Service
Honolulu
808/946-7741

KAUAI
Hyatt Regency Kauai
Koloa
808/742-2323

BIG ISLAND OF HAWAII
Hilton Waikoloa Village
Kamuela
808/885-7958

The Ritz Carlton Hotel
Kohala Coast
808/885-6600

MAUI
Westin Maui Hotel, Shop #101
Lahaina
808/661-7155

Ritz Carlton Kapalua
Lahaina
808/669-6018

Grand Hyatt Wailea
Wailea
808/875-4526

Travel

http://www.americanexpress.com/travel

In case you want to be welcomed there.

We're here to see that you're always welcomed at establishments everywhere. That's why millions of people carry the American Express® Card – for peace of mind, confidence, and security, around the world or just around the corner.

do more

Cards

And just in case.

We're here with American Express® Travelers Cheques and Cheques *for Two*.® They're the safest way to carry money on your vacation and the surest way to get a refund, practically anywhere, anytime.
Another way we help you...

do more ®

Travelers Cheques

In case you're running low.

We're here to help with more than 118,000 Express Cash locations around the world. In order to enroll, just call American Express before you start your vacation.

do more

Express Cash